Overcoming Obstacles and Finding Success

This valuable book identifies common obstacles in any endeavor that can impact on success and offers highly accessible exercises to help readers overcome them. Featuring expertise from dozens of high-level performers regarding their journey to the top of their domain, it offers practical advice on how to separate yourself from your competition and stand out from the crowd.

All performers, whether beginners or world class, in sports, business, the arts, and beyond, have encountered obstacles in their careers. Acknowledging that every successful person must work hard, this book offers a blueprint for those wanting to map out their own success based on over twenty years of research into performance, and the authors' experiences of guiding career development among their mentees and teaching courses on the topic. Each chapter includes a case study that exemplifies one of the most common obstacles individuals face in their efforts to be successful, including topics like impostor syndrome, artificial ceilings, facing rejection, and not allowing for rest or recovery. Following this, the chapter goes on to provide a series of engaging exercises for readers to reflect on their own performance and techniques, and enables them to strategize ways they can modify their performance to achieve better results. Throughout, the book is underpinned by theoretical frameworks from performance psychology, clear actionable steps for achieving success, and suggested readings for further study.

Written with career development in mind, the applications of this book are far-reaching, with relevance for all those looking to excel in their chosen fields.

Kevin R. Harris is the associate chair and a professor in the Department of Psychological Science and Counseling at Austin Peay State University, USA. He has spent the past quarter century studying performers at the highest level.

Emily Pica is an associate professor in the Department of Psychological Science and Counseling at Austin Peay State University, USA. Her current research interests involve investigating ways in which we can improve eyewitness identification accuracy as it is one of the leading causes of wrongful convictions.

Overcoming Obstacles and Finding Success

The Power of Performance Psychology

KEVIN R. HARRIS AND EMILY PICA

Routledge
Taylor & Francis Group

NEW YORK AND LONDON

Cover Image: t_kimura via Getty Images

First published 2025
by Routledge
605 Third Avenue, New York, NY 10158

and by Routledge
4 Park Square, Milton Park, Abingdon, Oxon, OX14 4RN

Routledge is an imprint of the Taylor & Francis Group, an informa business

ISBN: 978-1-032-45555-6 (hbk)
ISBN: 978-1-032-45551-8 (pbk)
ISBN: 978-1-003-37754-2 (ebk)

DOI: 10.4324/9781003377542

Typeset in Dante and Avenir
by Newgen Publishing UK

Contents

About the Authors   vii

Acknowledgments   viii

1 Historical vs. Recent Views of Success   1

2 Satisficing: This is Good Enough!   19

3 Impostor Syndrome: Feeling Like a Fraud   33

4 Artificial Ceilings: This is Where I Top Out   52

5 Giving Up: I Should Just Quit   72

6 Limiting Your Scope: Think Like a Kid   95

7 Facing Rejection: Taking "No" as a Cue to
   Stop Grinding   110

8 Aiming for Perfection: Identify Your Threshold and
   Dive In   127

9 Being Vague: Evaluate Your Own Path/Needs   143

10 Sugarcoating: Acknowledge What You Aren't
Doing Well   155

11 Not Allowing for Rest/Recovery: Make Rest a PRIORITY   168

12 Staying Off the Rails: Forgive Yourself and Regroup   182

13 Not Standing Out: Be Blueberry Yogurt   194

14 Tough Crowd: Seek Out Feedback/Criticism   210

15 Not Selling Your Accomplishments: It's Not Bragging   229

16 Advice for the Aspirational   246

   Index   258

About the Authors

Kevin R. Harris is the associate chair and a professor in the Department of Psychological Science and Counseling at Austin Peay State University, USA. He has spent the past quarter century studying performers at the highest level, and co-created *The Path Distilled* podcast to facilitate discussions on this topic. Dr. Harris had the opportunity to study at the Center for Expert Performance Research with heavyweights of the field, such as K. Anders Ericsson, A. Mark Williams, Paul Ward, and David W. Eccles. He fell in love with studying expert performance and recognized how the concepts were applicable to not only his own background, but to the students he was encountering daily. This book was conceptualized with a goal of sharing these views on maximizing the potential to be successful as widely as possible.

Emily Pica is an associate professor in the Department of Psychological Science and Counseling at Austin Peay State University, USA. Her current research interests involve investigating ways in which we can improve eyewitness identification accuracy as it is one of the leading causes of wrongful convictions. Additionally, she examines which factors may be more (or less) influential in jurors' decision making. She is a first-generation college student who overcame most of the obstacles presented in this book, ultimately finding success in academia, and enjoys giving back to her students through her own experiences.

Acknowledgments

The authors wish to acknowledge and thank some of the individuals who helped make this book a reality.

First, our interviewees. The advice and wisdom each of you shared was priceless. The book was exponentially better because of your willingness to speak with us.

We also want to thank James Dylan Brown and Bristia Hartley for assisting us with organizing the content of the interviews. We appreciate your help.

A huge thanks to Connie Harris for editing the seemingly never-ending drafts of the manuscript and serving as a general sounding board. Your skills and experience were invaluable.

Finally, we wish thank Zoe Thomson-Kemp at Taylor & Francis for the patience and support.

Historical vs. Recent Views of Success

1

And they lived happily ever after. These are the closing lines of your first novel – what a relief! Six hundred and thirty pages and more hours than you wish to count. You almost tear up recalling your internal daily struggle – the difficulty of keeping everything in your head while extracting what was needed to complete the next line. It would have been much easier to give up on it long ago. But, you finally did it.

Now delete it and start over.

This counterintuitive approach is advocated in actual practice both literally and figuratively. Author Joyce Carol Oates took this approach literally as a college student. Oates "would write a novel longhand, then turn the pages over, writing another novel on the flipside. Both novels would then be tossed in the trash" (Kellogg, 2006, p. 397).

Oates often modeled these "practice" novels after the works of famous authors. She obviously intended to improve the quality of her writing by adopting this process. More importantly, she believed that she *could* improve and knew how to go about improving it. These types of intensive, often grueling activities have not always been observed by us mere mortals. The traditional view, heavily influenced by the writings of Sir Francis Galton (discussed more extensively in Chapter 4), was that each person was allotted (at birth) a given amount of ability in a particular domain, and there would be limits to how

DOI: 10.4324/9781003377542-1

much we could improve based upon this "ceiling" we were born with. Consequently, only a select few have been aware of how to go about significantly improving their performance, and even fewer have engaged in activities designed to do so. This approach has been predominant for generations.

You might be thinking that Joyce Carol Oates is the exception. Surely this level of involvement is not common practice. Well, it is and it is not. The best performers in the world operate this way, but your neighbor, Trevor, likely does not.

Consider the wise words of accomplished screenwriter and producer, Jonathan Goyer: "Your first five scripts will probably suck. And I do mean five. *Blade* was my eighth script. Everything before that, I'm embarrassed about" (Donnelly, 2005, p. 56).

Think about that for a moment. These are not the words of your server at the coffee shop declaring that their first seven scripts were embarrassing. These are the words of someone who is the writer, cowriter, and/or producer of an impressive number of blockbuster films, television series and video games – including *Batman Begins* (Nolan, 2005), *Terminator: Dark Fate* (Miller, 2019), and a *Call of Duty* video game series (Treyarch 2010a; 2010b; 2012). Obviously, Goyer's advice, embedded in that quote, is to keep writing until you get considerably better.

Now, we have mentioned two examples of scribes from different genres who believe that one must put in their time with their craft – writing in their cases – to get really good at it. You already might be wondering about pursuits beyond creative writing and if this level of dedication is applicable.

The answer is a definitive, "yes!" Consider Stephen Curry who is known to get in 1,000 shots before practice even begins (Fleming, 2015). Michael Jordan captured this sentiment well with one of his better-known quotes, "I'm not out there sweating for three hours every day just to find out what it feels like to sweat." Similarly, Usain Bolt stated, "I trained four years to run nine seconds, and people give up when they don't see results in two months."

There are limitless examples across any domain, for pursuits that are mentally and/or physically draining. Implicitly, and sometimes explicitly, the message in these examples and from these performers is threefold.

First, one must put in their time to get really good at something. Even if your cousin was pretty impressive and way better than you at bowling after two weeks on the lanes, she has a long way to go before she will be competing with professionals. Additionally, she likely will never reach that level of world class performer (more on this point later). This sentiment is applicable to any other skilled pursuit you can imagine – playing guitar, playing chess, learning to be an accountant, and so on.

The second message is that one must believe at some level that they can improve by putting in their time. This might sound obvious, but there is anecdotal evidence illustrating that we do not believe it. You might not have taken a difficult class because, "I'm just not good at that," or not taken an art class because you do not consider yourself artistic. Stanford University's Carol Dweck spent decades studying how the beliefs one holds about their own abilities – she labeled it "mindset" – impacts what one eventually accomplishes by influencing every step of their journey (Dweck, 2006). We will spend considerable time on what her research tells us in a subsection below and her work on mindset will be repeated throughout the book.

The third message is that *how* one practices is important, and knowing the techniques that others used is beneficial for improvement. These three messages will be revisited often throughout the book as we do our best to unpack the issues related to understanding the best performers and what we can learn from them. Because these themes arise so frequently, we now provide brief overviews of each of these messages in the sections below.

Putting in the Time

My (Kevin speaking) home is located in a heavily wooded, rural area. There is a significant amount of upkeep with regard to the trees and land in the form of mowing and trimming, and the typical needs of a rural property. While trimming the perimeter of the property near the woods-line I noticed a seedling of an oak tree emerging among the blades of grass. Since we did not want a tree growing in that particular spot, I used the trimmer to easily remove it. This act left me thinking about how easy it was to remove the seedling that had the potential to become a mighty oak tree. Then it hit me – this is a great analogy for the importance of putting in the time. In the beginning, the oak tree is as easy to take down as a blade of grass. However, it grows into one of the hardiest trees in the forest when given the time and necessary cultivation.

The development of a performer also takes time. Nobel Laureate Herbert Simon and his colleague, William Chase, systematically investigated the best chess players in the world to identify what made them better players than others (Chase & Simon, 1973; Simon & Chase, 1973). Though we will revisit their work throughout the book, the specifics of what they did and found is beyond the scope of our present focus. For now, we mention them because they were one of the first, if not the first, to propose that an expert requires roughly ten years or 10,000 hours of intense and specific training to reach world-class status.

Roughly two decades later, Simon's former post-doctoral mentee, K. Anders Ericsson, coined the term "deliberate practice" to describe the activities in which performers reaching the highest levels had engaged to reach their current levels (Ericsson, Krampe, & Tesch-Römer, 1993). Moreover, Ericsson and his colleagues' study of world-class musicians led them also to conclude that around ten years or 10,000 hours of intense training was needed to reach world-class status. Critically, Ericsson and his colleagues also discovered that the most elite musicians had engaged in a greater amount of deliberate practice than the next closest group of musicians, the near-elite musicians, who had engaged in a greater amount of deliberate practice than the lesser-skilled musicians. The implication of the findings was that there is a direct relationship between the amount of time someone had dedicated to engaging in intense practice and their ultimate performance level.

These early discoveries – Simon and colleagues in the late 1960s and Ericsson and colleagues in the early 1990s – led to what was eventually dubbed the ten-year rule. Malcolm Gladwell's *New York Times* bestseller, *Outliers*, can be credited with introducing the ten-year rule to the mainstream (2008). The so called ten-year rule ultimately generated a healthy amount of debate, some of which was surprisingly heated. Since the popularization of the term, we have known that the 10,000-hour benchmark was a starting point for reflecting the idea of the need for putting in time with specialized training to reach the top performance levels for most domains. Some domains might require longer periods of investment to reach world-class status than others. Traditional times to reach world-class status might also be shortened as new techniques are developed and/or effective techniques are shared. Again, the intent was never to specify immutable time requirements but to reflect the requirements for a specific domain by exploring the best performers operating within it. Thus, akin to the mighty oak tree, fragile beginnings can turn into an impressive being.

Just as the seedling transitions to a sapling, and ultimately a full-grown tree, so too do performers engaging in deliberate practice activities transform. We begin unpacking the idea of transformations resulting from prolonged engagement in activities designed to improve performance by considering a relatively straightforward, and uncontroversial, example. Let us assume that you have the financial means, required time to allot, and social connections to secure a physical fitness trainer whose clients have included some of the fittest celebrities in Hollywood. It would be a safe bet to assume that if someone, even you or we, followed their proposed training regimen and incorporated their feedback, they would become physically fit within the expected timeframe. Underweight individuals would gain needed weight, and overweight individuals would lose weight. More importantly, everyone sticking with the trainer and their award-winning regimen would ultimately reach their fitness goals. This transformation is not difficult to imagine. We have seen it play out in real life with Chris Pratt and Kumail Nanjiani transforming their physiques for *Guardians of the Galaxy* (Gunn, 2014) and *The Eternals* (Zhao, 2021) respectively.

Because we have observed actors and athletes physically transform their bodies, and possibly have personally experienced our own transformations, these types of changes are readily accepted. However, changes that are visually apparent are not the only types of transformations experienced by the best performers following prolonged training. There also are changes to the way the brains of high performers function and how they process information when they dedicate time and effort to appropriate training.

Consider the case of licensed London taxi drivers. London taxi drivers must be tested in order to be licensed. One of the requirements is that the entirety of the street layout of London be *memorized*. Keep in mind that London's street layout is considered one of the most complex in the world, so memorization is a difficult task, to put it mildly. An interesting research finding is that the posterior hippocampi, an area of the brain associated with memory formation, of London taxi drivers is significantly larger than that of an average person (Maguire et al., 2000). Such findings suggest that engaging in rigorous mental activity – in this case, memorizing the archaic street layout of London – led to a change in the size of the taxi drivers' hippocampi. In a similar example, a different group of researchers found that the cerebellum, an area of the brain responsible for coordinating movement, was significantly larger in elite mountain climbers than in non-climbers (Di Paola, Caltagirone, & Petrosini, 2013). Presumably, the larger cerebellum was the end result of the volume of frequent climbs over time in which the elite mountain climbers had engaged.

A skeptical reader might suggest that the findings from the London taxi drivers and elite mountain climbers could have been due to something different altogether. A skeptic might explain the findings as individuals with good memorization skills having a greater likelihood of becoming a London taxi driver and someone with excellent motor skills having a greater likelihood of becoming a mountain climber. While this is possible, other studies have provided evidence that more strongly supports domain engagement as being the causal factor for changes to brain anatomy and functioning. A bonus to this line of research is that the findings are applicable to each and every one of the readers of this book, and anyone else who has learned to read.

Researchers designed a clever fMRI study and determined that learning to read led to anatomical changes to the brain, as well as changes in brain activity, in readers compared to non-readers. A key finding was that these changes occurred for adults who learned to read as adults but not for illiterate adults (Dehaene et al., 2011). Such findings suggest that it is engaging in the activities to improve performance that leads to changes in the brain as progress is made. In this particular example, the brain functioning associated with learning to read did not occur until after someone had learned to read, even if it did not occur until adulthood.

Prolonged engagement also can lead to changes in cognition that will benefit the performer. At the most basic level, the performer becomes more comfortable as they gain experience and has a better understanding of the performance requirements for a particular domain. As engagement in the appropriate training activities continues, and/or other engagement such as formal competitions or carrying out occupational responsibilities, the way that the performer processes information related to task performance also can be enhanced. These changes can include an elevated ability to keep situation-relevant information easily accessible in long-term memory to be pulled rapidly into short-term memory as needed. This enhanced retrieval ability was named long-term working memory and can be thought of as a specialized filing system within our brains for relevant information (Ericsson & Kintsch, 1995). The high-level performer has task/domain related information organized very precisely in their long-term memory, and, as a result, has the ability to place information that is relevant at a given time, or potentially could be, into the existing structure – a type of efficient mental filing cabinet.

In contrast, a novice would miss many of the relevant environmental/task cues and would need to search long-term memory in a traditional way without the aid of having acquired the long-term working memory abilities. You might have experienced a version of this as you progressed through your academic major. Early on, reading textbook or research materials might have seemed overwhelming, but you eventually began to see the connections and interrelatedness as you gained experience. Once you were seeing these connections, each new reading was processed differently than before as you were then able to mentally, often subconsciously, file the new information as "similar to study on X," or "counter to the work on Y." Hopefully, this simplified example illustrates the premise of long-term working memory.

Typically, high performers also will have developed enhanced domain-relevant anticipatory and pattern recognition skills as they progress. There are numerous examples related to enhanced anticipatory and pattern recognition skills – too many to consider each one in full. However, we will briefly consider a number of examples for which this enhancement is considered one of the key components of the high-performers' advantage. The enhanced ability to anticipate what will happen next is considered to be a tremendous advantage for high-level tennis players, especially for their ability to return a high-speed serve (Williams et al., 2002). High-level tennis players are better able to predict than most of us where the served ball will travel based on cues provided by the server's body positioning during the serve itself. This information derived before the tennis ball is even struck is then used by high-level players to better plan their return. Similarly, better batters in baseball are able to identify how to successfully hit the ball sooner in the pitch via anticipation based on their reading of the pitchers' body position and movement (Fadde, 2016). Presumably, this advantage of anticipatory ability is applicable to any performer in a sport for which an object must be struck with a hand-held object while airborne.

In potentially life-threatening domains, such as firefighting, medicine, and the military, enhanced anticipation is aided in part by the superior pattern recognition of the high performer. For example, as an experienced firefighter enters a burning building, they might store multiple environmental cues in memory as described above – how the smoke is behaving and appears, the color of the fire, the direction and intensity of the flames, and other relevant cues. The firefighter might then anticipate a potentially catastrophic event, such as a collapsed roof, based on their reading of the combination of cues (Klein, Calderwood, & Clinton-Cirocco, 2010). Making these connections also is enhanced by the long-term working memory functionality described above.

While it is important to put in the time to become a high performer, we also must have the belief that we can improve in a given domain.

Believing That One Can Improve

I jokingly told a friend several years ago that one of my fitness goals was to have six-pack abs. The friend's priceless response was, "That will be quite the undertaking." In reality, though it would be nice, having six-pack abs is not one of my fitness goals. One of the biggest reasons is that there does not seem to be enough time in a day that I would be willing to dedicate to attempting to get there (and there also is a level of personal doubt that it would be possible for me to have six-pack abs at all).

This example illustrates that we all have areas of our lives for which we think our goals are reachable, and other areas for which they seem impossible. In other words, do not beat yourself up if you find yourself battling self-doubt or imposter syndrome (which is covered extensively in Chapter 3) with some pursuits. However, it is important to realize that you can accomplish way more than you probably realize, and one of the mechanisms for doing so is putting in the time with a focus on the proper activities. If you do not believe that improvement is possible then the likelihood is that you will not be putting in the amount of work required – it would be analogous to me not taking any steps to obtain the six-pack abs or giving up on it pretty quickly.

Returning to Carol Dweck's work at Stanford, she spent much of her career investigating the views one might hold about their own abilities. Among other contributions from this line of research, she ended up coining the terms "fixed mindset" and "growth mindset." The bare bones idea behind these are that someone with a fixed mindset believes that they have been given the capability to perform at a maximum level and/or possess a certain amount of given ability, which they cannot move beyond – academically, athletically, and/or musically. This view very much mirrors Galton's arguments which have been consistently perpetuated over generations. In contrast, someone with a growth mindset believes that there are no arbitrary limits on performance beyond natural human limitations (e.g., we never will be able to outrun a car), and performance can be enhanced over time.

It is important to remember that you generally can have a growth mindset, but there will be areas you believe to not be *your* area, a *selective* fixed mindset, to add to Dweck's terminology. In reality, you probably recognize that you could excel in that same area if a list of stipulations could be met, such as unlimited time to train, study, or practice, along with access to excellent resources. In other words, my goal of six-pack abs would be more likely to happen if a movie studio gave me one year to get in shape with no other responsibilities and provided me with the best personal trainer on their roster. The important point is that having these areas of selective fixed mindsets does not diminish an overall growth mindset for most, as long as the ratio of selective fixed mindsets to the overall growth mindset remains relatively low – you believe that improvement is possible for most things. However, you must also know what to do to get better at something or achieve your goal.

Knowing the Techniques

A multicolored puzzle was all the rage when I was a youngster. The Rubik's Cube had just made its USA debut, and demand was palpable.

Eight-year-old me was very excited when my father took me to the store to purchase one of my very own. The memory of sitting in the passenger side of my father's car as we pulled into the driveway with my newest possession is one of the more vivid ones from my childhood. As my father was placing the car's gearshift into "Park," I was eagerly shuffling the pieces around as quickly as possible. My father was in no hurry at the time and paused to watch my activity from the driver's seat. After a minute or so of eager shuffling, I turned to my father and earnestly asked, "Do you think that's enough or do you think it will it be too easy?"

The cube was never fully solved. It never had more than roughly one side solved at any given time. This occurred not long after the invention of the Rubik's Cube, and unlike today, the algorithms for solving the cube were not widely known. My unsuccessful approach was that of trial-and-error, and I eventually gave up because of my lack of success. It was decades later before I learned that the key to solving the Rubik's Cube was in algorithms that one should follow, choosing the appropriate one depending on the starting point of the cube. If someone wants to learn to solve the puzzle these days, there is a great deal of information on how to go about doing so using these algorithms. It will still take putting in the time to learn to solve it easily, and the best at solving them are impressive to watch.

My experience with the Rubik's Cube mirrors the experiences of many others in their own pursuits. Potentially unaware of what to do, the uninformed aspiring performer might also give up on their pursuits because they do not experience the progress that they are expecting. Critically, they might have found an impressive level of success had they been aware of techniques used by performers who were already successful. It is impossible to know how much more successful my Rubik's Cube pursuits would have been had I known the techniques used by the best Rubik's Cube solvers, but one can assume that they would have been greater with the additional knowledge.

Let us now consider some examples of when knowledge of the appropriate techniques led to improved outcomes, which can, in some cases, transform altogether how the best performers in a domain go about training. One of our favorite examples for illustrating this concept comes from the area of minesweeping. The minesweeping example also illustrates the hierarchical nature of knowledge of appropriate techniques; it is not uncommon to discover as one advances within an area that the "best of the best" have a seemingly secret toolkit of ways to improve.

At some point, everyone has likely had the experience of learning a new job or task and later being told by someone experienced in that activity, "Yeah, that's not what we really do." The gap in how you were doing it and what is really done can vary, ranging from inconsequential to potentially deadly – as in the minesweeping domain. Unfortunately, soldiers typically are not initially very good at detecting mines, even when they have received training on the techniques for detecting them. Because minesweeping is a skill like any other – for which a notable amount of time must be invested to get good at it – anything that might accelerate performance improvement is a good thing. This is an example of a situation in which researchers who study expertise can, and did, make a difference.

Expertise researchers James Staszewski and Alan Davison reasoned that a minesweeper with over 30 years of experience had demonstrated a level of excellence, just by nature of their decades of survival in the job, worthy of attempting to uncover their techniques for mine detecting (2000). Staszewski carefully studied how the expert mine-sweeper went about detecting mines and realized that the technique being used was notably different from the minesweeping technique officially taught in the military. Compellingly, when minesweepers who recently completed training that emphasized traditional methods were then provided additional training incorporating the experts' techniques, their performance increased to a shocking degree, improving mine detection performance on some types of mines up to nine times (!!) compared to a group not using the expert techniques. A nine-fold improvement in performance would be remarkable in any field. It is especially remarkable for a task for which there could be deadly consequences.

The domain of chess provides a similar example in which learning additional training techniques led to a shift in the way training was viewed. During the days of the former Soviet Union, the Soviets produced a considerable number of competitive chess players. The common view was that the people of the former Soviet Union had a natural proclivity for chess. However, following the fall of the Soviet Union – the so-called Iron Curtain – it was discovered that the Soviets operated chess-training academies (Shadrick & Lussier, 2004). It was the training activities in these academies that was responsible, at least in part, for the high number of chess players emerging from the Soviet Union. Further strengthening this assumption is the notable progress made by aspiring chess masters upon adopting the same, or similar, training techniques.

This approach of identifying the best performers in a particular domain, pinpointing the parts of their performance responsible for the observed performance differences, tracing their paths and developmental progress, and translating what is learned into training for performers in various phases of development has been increasing in recent years (see Harris & Eccles, 2021 for a review). Variations of this approach have been named Expert Performance Based Training (ExPerT; Ward, Suss, & Basevitch, 2009) and expertise-based training XBT (Fadde, 2009), depending on which researchers' camp is being discussed. This approach and/or the related components also has been used informally, without the title, by an even greater number of expertise researchers. The main consideration is that the knowledge of the appropriate techniques needed to improve performance is very important and can often be shared.

Chapter Summary

In this chapter, we briefly reviewed the traditional view of what is responsible for high levels of performance. We also proposed a more recent explanation of expertise and high performers for which some basic considerations typically occur. The first is that one must put in their time in order to get really good at something. It need not be the misunderstood 10 years/10,000 hours, but it will require an extended stretch of putting in the work. Our second element was that someone must believe that what they are doing will lead to improvements or be working with someone who does. The third element was that the *appropriate* type of practice is crucial. We will revisit these themes throughout the book as they can be considered an underpinning of the approach.

Do not get too caught up in the terminology here. In simplified terms, you typically must work hard at the right things for some time in order to get really good at something. It also is important to understand that the "right things" part of the equation is of the utmost importance. It has been repeatedly noted that one will minimally benefit from simply repeating a task without a strategy in place, such as simply returning tennis balls from a machine for an hour per day. A second consideration is that you should think of this approach with a wide lens. In other words, while perfecting a tennis serve can be accomplished using this approach, so can almost any other aspiration. The remaining chapters will fill in some of the potential gaps in relation to how to go about applying this to your own life. More importantly, it will do so in a manageable way regardless of your current performance level.

That's a Lot of Work!

Chapter 1: *Historical vs. Recent Views of Success*

This multi-part exercise will help you to realize how much work some of your favorite performers have put into their craft, and to reflect on something that you have spent time trying to improve. In the **first part** of the exercise, you will be asked to choose two well-known performers whom you admire and identify some of the activities they credit for their success. These should be quantifiable when possible. In the **second part**, you will be asked to identify something for which you attempted to improve, unpack what you did, and assess how well it worked.

1. Choose two performers and identify some of the activities they have said contributed to their success.
Performer 1:
Performer 1's Activities:

Performer 2:
Performer 2's Activities:

2. Answer the following questions.
What is something that you have attempted to improve?

What specifically did you do when you attempted to improve? What is your assessment of your plan? Please discuss which parts worked well and which parts were least successful.

References

Chase, W.G., & Simon, H.A. (1973). The mind's eye in chess. In W.G. Chase (Ed.), *Visual Information Processing* (pp. 215–281). Academic Press.

Dehaene, S., Pegado, F., Braga, L.W., Ventura, P., Nunes Filho, G., Jobert, A., ... & Cohen, L. (2010). How learning to read changes the cortical networks for vision and language. *Science, 330*(6009), 1359–1364. https://doi.org/10.1126/science.1194140.

Di Paola, M., Caltagirone, C., & Petrosini, L. (2013). Prolonged rock climbing activity induces structural changes in cerebellum and parietal lobe. *Human Brain Mapping, 34*(10), 2707–2714. https://doi.org/10.1002/hbm.22095.

Donnelly, S. (2005, June). How to: Write a screenplay. *Maxim, 90, 56.*

Dweck, C.S. (2006). *Mindset.* Random House.

Ericsson, K.A., & Kintsch, W. (1995). Long-term working memory. *Psychological Review, 102*(2), 211–245. https://doi.org/10.1037/0033-295X.102.2.211.

Ericsson, K.A., Krampe, R.T., & Tesch-Römer, C. (1993). The role of deliberate practice in the acquisition of expert performance. *Psychological Review, 100, 363–406.* DOI:10.1037/0033-295X.100.3.363

Fadde, P. J. (2009). Expertise-based training: Getting more learners over the bar in less time. *Technology, Instruction, Cognition and Learning, 7, 171–197.*

Fadde, P.J. (2016). Instructional design for accelerated macrocognitive expertise in the baseball workplace. *Frontiers in Psychology, 7.* DOI: 10.3389/fpsyg.2016.00292.

Fleming, D. (2015, April). Stephen Curry, the full circle. *ESPN the Magazine.* Retrieved from http://www.espn.com/espn/feature/story/_/id/12728744/how-golden-stat.

Gladwell, M. (2008). *Outliers: The Story of Success.* Little, Brown.

Gunn, J. (Director). (2014). *Guardians of the Galaxy* [Film]. Marvel Studios.

Harris, K.R., & Eccles, D.W. (2021). Training derived from expert performers: The extractable components of deliberate practice and the expert performance approach. *Journal of Expertise, 4*(2), 208–219. https://www.journalofexpertise.org/articles/volume4_issue2/JoE_4_2_Harris_Eccles.pdf.

Kellogg, R.T. (2006). Professional writing expertise. In K.A. Ericsson, N. Charness, P.J. Feltovich, & R.R. Hoffman (Eds.), *The Cambridge Handbook of Expertise and Expert Performance* (pp. 389–402). Cambridge University Press.

Klein, G., Calderwood, R., & Clinton-Cirocco, A. (2010). Rapid decision making on the fire ground: The original study plus a postscript. *Journal of Cognitive Engineering and Decision Making, 4*(3), 186–209.

Maguire, E.A., Gadian, D.G., Johnsrude, I.S., Good, C.D., Ashburner, J., Frackowiak, R.S., & Frith, C.D. (2000). Navigation-related structural change in the hippocampi of taxi drivers. *Proceedings of the National Academy of Sciences, 97*(8), 4398–4403. https://doi.org/10.1073/pnas.070039597.

Miller, T. (Director). (2019). *Terminator: Dark Fate* [Film]. 20th Century Fox.

Nolan, C. (Director). (2005). *Batman Begins* [Film]. Warner Brothers Pictures.

Shadrick, S.B., & Lussier, J.W. (2004). *Assessment of the Think Like a Commander Training Program.* (ARI Research Report 1824). US Army Research Institute for the Behavior and Social Sciences.

Simon, H.A., & Chase, W.G. (1973) Skill in chess. *American Scientist, 61*, 394–403.

Staszewski, J., & Davison, A. (2000). Mine detection training based on expert skill. In A.C. Dubey, J.F. Harvey, J.T. Broach, & R.E. Dugan (Eds.), Detection and remediation technologies for mines and mine-like targets V. *Proceedings of Society of Photo-Optical Instrumentation Engineers 14th Annual Meeting, SPIE, 4038*, 90–101.

Treyarch. *Call of Duty: Black Ops* [Microsoft Windows, Play Station 3, Wii, and Xbox 360]. (2010a). Activision.

Treyarch. *Call of Duty: Cold War* [Windows, Play Station 4, Play Station 5, Xbox One]. (2010b). Activision.

Treyarch. *Call of Duty: Black Ops II* [Microsoft Windows, Play Station 3, Wii U, and Xbox 360]. (2012). Activision.

Ward, P., Suss, J., & Basevitch, I. (2009). Expertise and expert performance-based training (ExPerT) in complex domains. *Technology, Instruction, Cognition and Learning, 7*, 121–146.

Williams, A.M., Ward, P., Knowles, J.M., & Smeeton, N.J. (2002). Anticipation skill in a real-world task: Measurement, training, and transfer in tennis. *Journal of Experimental Psychology: Applied, 8*, 259–270.

Zhao, C. (Director). (2021). *Eternals* [Film]. Marvel Studios.

Satisfi cing

2

This is Good Enough!

I make enough money for me. I don't want a raise; don't want a promo-tion. I just want to get my work done and then do stuff I want to do.
— Anonymous

Invariably, no matter what your genetic makeup is, I think you need to have a real passion of interest in what it is that you want to do. Finding something that you have that passion and interest in, I think, is very, very important. And then, after that, of course, then it is a long, long road.
— A. Mark Williams, world-renowned expertise researcher

Gerald was the epitome of stagnation and mediocrity. He avoided diffi-cult courses as much as possible during the entirety of his academic life. He currently works as a salesperson for an auto dealership and is con-sistently near the bottom of the monthly sales rankings. Gerald likes to play tennis and bowl with friends, but has not improved much over the past decade. As jarring as this sounds, Gerald's current circumstances and lack of identifiable progress is not atypical. It is not uncommon for us to reach a level of performance that allows us to get by on a daily basis and stay there – enough to keep our jobs, pay our bills, or play a competitive sport recreationally with friends.

Nobel Laureate Herbert Simon (introduced in Chapter 1) labeled this phenomenon "satisficing" while studying decision-making

DOI: 10.4324/9781003377542-2

limitations when one is provided a given amount of information on the issue (e.g., Simon, 1972). Essentially, Simon found that we typically do not make the optimal decision when given the opportunity. Rather, we commonly satisfy some level of need and then settle – the satisficing part. For example, we might choose the first car we encounter that seems to work for our needs when looking to buy a new one – one that is within our price range, seems to drive okay, and has four doors. This type of satisficing stands in contrast to an attempt at maximizing the purchase by exhaustively researching fuel consumption, safety ratings, longevity, and other related factors to make the absolute best purchase possible. We will return to these differences momentarily; however, it should be obvious that while there are some people who will make attempts to maximize at all costs, most will choose the route of satisficing for at least some of the decisions that must be made. This sentiment can extend beyond the original laboratory decision-making studies to include stagnation or mediocrity in someone's life, to explain how one might adopt this approach – intentionally or unintentionally. In other words, if we consider all of our life choices within this framework – whether to take a certain class or ask for a raise, or how to set up a workout regimen – *every aspect of our lives* can be viewed through the lens of satisficing.

It actually can be very reasonable for one to engage in satisficing. This is particularly true when the stakes are low and one has reached a level of comfort with how things stand. For example, Tristan might decide that making just enough sales to keep his job and pay his bills is preferable to making as many sales as possible. If Tristan and others in his life are good with how he is managing his career, then Tristan's satisficing seems appropriate. However, satisficing will not be considered a wise choice when there are areas in which someone wants to improve. Despite being okay with staying where he is with his sales at work, Tristan might be interested in improving in other areas of his life – his tennis game or painting skills. Let's now consider why there is a level of comfort in satisficing, and later we will consider reasons it can persist even when you want to move to the next level.

There certainly is a level of comfort in satisficing and "good enough" thinking. It would be very taxing to attempt, and unlikely to succeed, if we insisted upon maximizing everything in our lives. Trying to maximize every single thing in our lives, as opposed to satisficing some of the time, would slow us down both mentally and physically. Think of how much it would slow down your grocery shopping if you did all you could to get the *absolute* lowest price per ounce for every single item of food that you purchased. This might require a comparison of all sizes of mustard available for a particular style, and doing the calculations for each brand to identify the lowest price per ounce. While feasible, it becomes apparent that this can become quite time consuming with a fairly large list of items to purchase. While there are undoubtedly shoppers who already engage in this practice in order to have the lowest possible grocery bill, it does not seem to be a widely adopted practice. The other extreme would be shoppers who paid no attention to the cost of the items. Presumably, most shoppers will engage in satisficing and make a judgment as to whether an item is reasonable to purchase given their individual needs and preferences.

While such a maximizing approach as the one described above might result in some savings, it likely would not be worth it for all shoppers. Some might decide that the time and energy directed at obtaining the savings could be better spent elsewhere, such as making additional sales at work, resulting in a greater payoff monetarily. Additionally, there are motivational differences to consider, with some individuals possessing high levels of motivation and others having little, or no, motivation. For the latter, the "good enough" of satisficing might be all that is ever needed. There also are those who find deserved comfort in having reached a level of stability, and derive contentment from being able to engage in satisficing for some areas while maximizing others. In the example above, Tristan might appreciate the work-life balance of his current job situation and use it as an opportunity to maximize the time he is able to spend with loved ones. Without knowledge of such considerations, it is difficult to compare one person's satisficing to another's.

In Chapter 9, we discuss the need for one to analyze their own needs and goals. This individualization is critical and the picture is incomplete without it. We mention this because the discussion about satisficing thus far should not be viewed as a judgment call – the pieces of the puzzle comprising the picture of your life are unique. One need not seek out a trophy, position, or other specific aspiration to find contentment. Some will aspire to a Nobel Prize, a world record, or to become a C-suite member, and many will not. Both approaches are equally reasonable. A goal to have six-pack abs in no way diminishes someone else's goal to be physically fit, or just healthy, overall. To summarize, engaging in satisficing is to be expected, is normal, and can provide a certain level of satisfaction.

However, many of you have what is often described as a "burning desire" or longing for certain things in life. This longing could be for almost anything, including the variety of domains we cover in this book – a particular hobby, career, sport, or similar pursuit. For many satisficing is not an option when it comes to something for which they have experienced this longing. You might have had this type of longing experience yourself when you have attempted to discontinue a pursuit but found yourself unable to give it up. This longing to get better was a common theme in our interviews with top performers, and among top performers across the board – let us now consider a few examples.

Comedian Henry Cho described it as a "never-ending pursuit" and that he is still working every day to get better after decades of performing. Music executive Randall Foster noted:

> "I think we get to a point in our roles where we do feel like we've mastered the role. I think, at that moment, we have the ability to operate at a high caliber doing that role. But I just know my personal curiosity, my yearning for growth in a consistent way, definitely needs to be fed. So, when I get to those points, it's when I kind of start looking over the bush and I look over the hedge."

A second theme from the interviews with top performers was a commitment to going all in with what you are pursuing. Major League Baseball pitcher Alec Mills shared his thoughts on this, "I wanted to commit to something 100 percent versus commit to two things at 60 percent or 75 percent. I thought it was only fair to myself, and honestly fair to my teammates, that I commit to something 100 percent, all in." Committing to "something 100 percent, all in" certainly paid off for Alec. This decision was one of the factors that propelled him from a walk-on collegiate pitcher to a major leaguer with a rare no-hitter to his credit. We dedicate entire chapters to not giving up (Chapter 5) and facing rejection along your path (Chapter 7); but it is this longing to both be around and to succeed within a domain that is one of the foundations of the desire to move beyond your current level of performance and give it 100 percent by going "all in."

In a particularly memorable example, Tony Hawk was describing a fall he experienced attempting to perfect a skateboarding move in the documentary film *Bones Brigade* (Peralta, 2012). This fall was particularly gruesome, resulting in a trip to the hospital, broken bones, and the loss of several teeth. Counterintuitively, Tony recalled that this was the moment he knew that he would never give up skateboarding. He knew that skateboarding was something he would be unable to live without, regardless of the dangers he was experiencing.

My life is littered with similar occurrences in which a novel pursuit was ended abruptly – from my failed first aerial bicycle trick to crossing the foul line on a bowling lane and falling in front of the other youth players on the first day. Both incidents ended my pursuit of those goals; for me, the risk was not worth continuing. There were other pursuits for which my persistence lasted longer than an initial botched attempt and for which a relative degree of skill was obtained. However, it is unlikely that my interest would have survived a tumble similar to the one Tony Hawk experienced. Ultimately, it can come down to that longing one experiences for a pursuit and the degree to which it tips the scales towards doing what is required to not only find some level of success within the domain but to withstand the demands required of you.

Scholars have explored this concept extensively, referring to it as "passion" in their work. The research suggests that passion was a key predictor of performance and ultimate achievement. This makes sense when considering the time commitment necessary to reach the highest levels of performance discussed in Chapter 1. In particular, passion was as important as perseverance in determining the ultimate level of success. True passion combined with perseverance was likely to lead to immersion in a domain (the going "100 percent all in" or really close to 100 percent), and this immersion could lead to significant gains in performance (Jachimowicz et al., 2018). It is also important to acknowledge that it is unlikely, if not impossible, to reach world-class status without immersion. This is because immersion will include prolonged engagement in a domain, if not engagement in deliberate practice specifically.

Thus, satisficing, as considered here, is a very different concept to immersion. Arguably one could immerse themselves in a domain and only satisfice, but this seems unlikely given the driving role of passion in leading to immersion. In other words, it seems contradictory that someone would exhibit passion at a level that compels them to immerse themselves in an area, but settle for "good enough" once there. Consider a hobby such as baseball card collecting – it would be difficult to imagine someone considering themselves immersed in the area of collectibles by learning a "smidge" about baseball cards and owning only a few. Rather, someone with a passion for collecting baseball cards, or similar collectibles, likely will know a great deal about them and possess a large number of them.

As previously mentioned, satisficing often is a choice and can be a very reasonable option for someone. There also are considerations beyond our control that may impact whether one engages in satisficing. The first three considerations were mentioned in Chapter 1, (a) that putting in the time is required to become a high-level performer; (b) belief that one can improve, i.e., mindset; and (c) degree of awareness of the appropriate techniques. We also present a fourth consideration related to the concept of satisficing, (d) access to, and lack of, resources.

To consider each of these in relation to satisficing, we must consider why one would choose to satisfice – essentially choosing to settle at their current level – and satisficing out of necessity because of a lack of resources or similar. Moreover, it seems unlikely that satisficing by choice will persist once someone is able to get past an initial stage of involvement and into immersion. The immersion likely will lead to performance gains (e.g., Jachimowicz et al., 2018) and knowledge that will render the satisficing-by-choice considerations moot.

Putting in the Time

Typically, there were only three to five of my fellow undergraduate students who earned A grades in one of my classes – one large enough to meet in an auditorium. Mysteriously, one of my fellow students identified me as one of the "A students." He approached me to learn the secrets of my success in the course and asked if we could study together for the next exam. In our study session, I unpacked my approach to studying step-by-step (the *knowing the techniques* part discussed below). Within 30 seconds of my spiel, my "study partner" declared, "That seems like a lot of work," and abruptly ended the study session. This experience illustrates that not everyone is willing to commit the time required to obtain the results they are seeking.

Thus, when it comes to putting in the time in the context of satisficing, the choice is pretty straightforward: choose to invest time and effort, or choose not to. This can apply to a range of decisions, from whether to study for an exam to whether to attempt to qualify for the Olympics. It is certainly reasonable to be aware that world-class performers invest a tremendous amount of time and effort, and make a deliberate decision not to pursue a similar path. Potential reasons for such a decision were discussed earlier in the chapter, such as finding a "sweet spot" that works within life circumstances (e.g., preferring a better work-life balance or deciding to pursue another endeavor instead). We now consider a different factor in relation to satisficing, the impact of believing or not believing that one can improve their performance.

Believing That One Can Improve – The Impact of Mindset

The position that there was no way to prepare for the Graduate Record Exam (GRE; a test often required for master's or doctoral program admission) was common advice during my undergraduate years. We commonly heard that scores were rarely impacted by studying for the standardized exam and that any gains would be inconsequential. Thankfully, I disregarded this advice and formed a GRE study group, resulting in significant improvements in the scores for everyone in the group. We almost certainly would not have formed the study group had we bought into the idea that such preparation would not lead to noteworthy improvements in our actual scores. This simple example illustrates the idea that one generally must believe that one can improve at a given pursuit, or an effort will not be made.

This stance makes intuitive sense. I would not have prepped for the GRE if I did not believe that prepping would help me when taking the actual exam. Likewise, we generally would not study for an exam, exercise, or do anything else if we did not expect a resulting payoff. It is unlikely that someone believing that improvement is impossible will "double down" whenever things get difficult or after experiencing early failures. Most likely, they will either choose to satisfice from that point onward, or leave the domain altogether if that is an option.

The impact of the type of mindset one holds about abilities and how one goes about preparing seems straightforward, at least as described in the paragraph above. However, considerable debate has emerged on the topic of mindset. The concept of mindset has been studied frequently by scholars since its introduction, and it eventually made it into the mainstream.

As awareness of the proposed impact of mindset grew, mindset interventions became very popular. The best way to go about conducting mindset interventions, including what to emphasize, is currently still being sorted by researchers. However, what is important for us here is that the crux of the idea is that you must believe that you can improve before you will begin, or continue, attempting to improve in a given area. Thus, we are using growth mindset (Dweck, 2006) as a belief that one can improve in a given area. In Chapter 4, we discuss the idea that once you believe that improvement is possible, you can proceed with everything else. However, what happens if you believe you can improve but do not have access to the resources?

Lack of Resources

The late Neil Peart was a legendary drummer for the successful progressive rock band *Rush*. Widely considered one of the best of all time, Peart's name has come up in many conversations of drumming greats during my lifetime. In particular, he was known for his technical prowess and innovative style; any other drummer is considered to have advanced skills if they were able to play almost any one of the *Rush* songs. Yet, when I came across Deden Noy, an Indonesian drummer, playing a *Rush* classic almost perfectly, I was surprised by what I saw. Why the surprise? Deden was playing on a hodge-podge set created with homemade pieces – metal tubes with material stretched over them, used fast-food buckets, and homemade circular metal pieces. To complete the tableau, Deden was seated on two stacked green plastic chairs that you would be seated on to eat your bologna sandwich by the swimming pool. Digging a little deeper, he also was nailing a selection of other legendary rock songs.

There are countless pursuits that require resources. Sometimes the needed resources are minimal or can be easily mimicked. A bag stuffed with whatever was available and taped shut has been used as the ball for many football (soccer) matches. A stick and your choice from the variety of other objects lying around can easily be the basis of a game that resembles baseball to varied degrees. However, the cost can be prohibitive to participate in a domain in many other cases. These costs can include equipment needs, membership fees, and specialized training. This prohibitive access is not limited to sporting domains. For example, schools located in affluent areas typically have an abundance of resources as a function of greater tax revenues and general financial support. Similarly, there are opportunities and connections made in costly preparatory schools and exclusive country clubs that will be unavailable to many of us.

This assessment of restricted resources can be discouraging on the surface, and someone might decide that a pursuit is not worth it, given the limited resources available to them. To counter this view, there are many cases of successes by people who carried on despite dealing with limited resources. Instead of giving up, someone might decide that they will do their best with what is available. We could devise an effective fitness routine using an old car axle, blocks of wood, buckets filled with dirt, and a hill to sprint up and down. There is no reason to assume that someone could not achieve the same level of physical performance and exertion using a low-tech environment as one could using multimillion-dollar facilities. Granted, some domains likely would still be out of reach without the appropriate resources. For example, horse-jumping, motorsports, or fencing would all require significant financial investments. We now discuss a fourth consideration of whether someone might choose to satisfice.

Lack of Awareness of Techniques

It felt like time had slowed to a crawl. I was not even sure how long it had been. Looking around the room, there were no obvious clues on what to do get out of there. Finally, I heard someone else coming. A welcome relief. They had been sent in to check on me. The gentleman asked me what I was doing, just sitting there, and began manipulating items in the room. Around the eighth thing he did was pick up a bowling bowl and roll it down a guide into a hole in a box – an action that opened an exit door. A great sense of relief overcame me, and I stepped out into the sunlight. My relieved father asked why I stayed in there for so long. I was a 6-year-old who had been trapped in a puzzle room (a precursor of an escape room) at the local fair. I was oblivious to what the room was and that I was supposed to solve the puzzles to get out. In other words, I was unaware of the necessary techniques. Casting aside the question of why a 6-year-old was sent into the room alone without explanation, this example illustrates the importance of knowing appropriate techniques.

Access to equipment or resources will not magically endow you with the ability to maximize, or even use, the resources. The highest-end flight simulator would be a mix of buttons and knobs that would likely have little meaning. Similarly, a simulated patient would not transform you into a skilled nurse by simply existing. Both of these examples require an awareness of techniques that you would learn through training. Such training could occur in multiple ways, including computer/AI systems set up to provide training or through a skilled human trainer (at least more skilled than your current level).

Other examples of the importance of techniques are plentiful. Examples could include a variety of things, such as knowledge of the proper form when executing an athletic move, how to produce music/film, how to diagnose medical conditions, and many more. The appropriate techniques can sometimes be discerned by sticking with a domain.

I became a pretty decent tennis player with no official lessons while learning with an antiquated wooden racquet that had been handed down by my brother-in-law. A good friend and I would hit the courts almost daily just for fun. Full disclosure – I had modeled my tennis strokes after the poster displayed near the water fountain in the park where we played. Imagine my surprise when I discovered that my technique was actually pretty accurate upon taking my first official tennis class in college. It was also quite a shock to discover that I was able to beat every former high-school player (though not the current scholarship collegiate players) in the advanced tennis class a few semesters later. This example shows that, while there are some cases in which one can become relatively skilled without extensive resources, it would not have been unusual if I had given up the pursuit of tennis given the lack of resources available.

Chapter Summary

In this chapter we discussed the concept of satisficing, or the idea of settling where one currently is. We revisited the three primary considerations introduced in Chapter 1; (a) putting in the time is required to become a high-level performer, (b) belief that one can improve, i.e., mindset, and (c) degree of awareness of the appropriate techniques. We have now presented a fourth consideration related to the concept of satisficing, (d) access to, and lack of, resources. Each of these were considered in relation to how they might lead one to decide to satisfice – resolving that where they are is good enough. In a nutshell, you could see this option as the best for you if you did not want to work hard, did not think that working toward something would make you better, lacked access to the required resources, or were unaware of how to go about your desired pursuit. This chapter was dedicated to the influence such considerations might have on whether you decide to embark on a pursuit. In Chapter 4 we unpack the influence these same considerations can have on the artificial limits you might place on yourself *after* deciding to begin the pursuit of your goals.

Meh, I'm Good

Chapter 2: *Satisficing: This is Good Enough!*

This exercise is intended to help you become familiar with the concept of satisficing. In the **first part** of the exercise, you will be asked to write-down at least one example of a time you stopped a pursuit when you knew that you could have accomplished more. The **second part** will ask you to reflect on the reasoning for this stalling.

1. Please provide at least one example of a time you stopped pursuing something despite thinking you could have gone further.

2. What are some reasons behind why you stopped pursuing the example(s) you noted above?

References

Dweck, C.S. (2006). *Mindset*. Random House.

Jachimowicz, J.M., Wihler, A., Bailey, E.R., & Galinsky, A.D. (2018). Why grit requires perseverance and passion to positively predict performance. *Proceedings of the National Academy of Sciences, 115*(40), 9980–9985.

Peralta, S. (2012). *Bones Brigade: An Autobiography* [Film]. Power Peralta company.

Simon, H.A. (1972). Theories of bounded rationality. *Decision and Organization, 1*, 161–176.

Impostor Syndrome

3

Feeling Like a Fraud

When you take on new things that maybe push the envelope on your core competencies, I think that there is a tendency to question and doubt yourself. And I also think that we are our very own worst critics.
– Randall Foster, Chief Creative Officer and General Manager of the National Operation for Symphonic Distribution

I feel, from what I've learned in my experience, and in talking with other artists and animators, [impostor syndrome]'s something that never goes away. I still deal with that. I've been in working professionally since 1997, and I still struggle with that.
– Thomas Estrada, feature film and videogame illustrator

Marcus was in his fourth year of undergraduate studies, getting ready to submit his application for graduation when thoughts of self-doubt started plaguing his mind. He questioned his own knowledge of his major and second guessed his abilities as a student. Marcus was feeling overwhelmed with his responsibilities and class work when he heard other students mention that their coursework was easy, and they were breezing through their classes. Granted, his was the more advanced coursework of the program. Nevertheless, he felt as though there was no way he would accomplish anything after he graduated. He felt like an impostor.

Soon after these feelings crept in, he was watching the news and learned Lady Gaga had experienced something similar. When she was younger and aspiring to be a singer, classmates said she would never

DOI: 10.4324/9781003377542-3

make it, and even resorted to attacking her character and looks. Marcus thought to himself that, despite the naysayers, and Lady Gaga's similar feelings of being an impostor, she went on to become a successful – even famous – singer and actress. He regained the motivation he needed, ultimately completed his undergraduate training, went on to graduate school, and became a university professor.

We have likely all felt the same way as Marcus at one point in our lives. This feeling that we are somehow masquerading as being able to do something is a phenomenon known as Impostor Syndrome. The term itself was first coined in 1978 when two Georgia State University researchers and psychotherapists, Pauline Rose Clance and Suzanne Imes, found that a number of high-achieving women were unable to attribute their accomplishments to their abilities. According to Clance and Imes, the women in their study "do not experience an internal sense of success" (p. 1). These successful women felt as if they had fooled everyone despite earning advanced degrees and praise from their colleagues, as well as other objective measures of success. The researchers concluded, at the time, that the women had self-doubts which contributed to difficulty taking ownership of their accomplishments, and furthermore, impostor syndrome was less likely to be observed in men and more likely to appear in women who worked in male-dominated professions.

Since the original study introducing the concept, it has become clear that impostor syndrome is much more common than originally thought – chances are that you have felt it yourself. Scholars studying imposter syndrome estimate that a large percentage of us – 70 percent – will experience it at least once (Sakulku & Alexander, 2011). While this number is remarkable on the surface, the scope becomes even more apparent when applying the percentage to theoretical populations with large numbers. For example, at an event with an attendance of 10,000, there would be 7,000 people who would report that they have experienced imposter syndrome. When considering 500,000 people, the number of us reporting imposter syndrome would be 350,000. Our suspicion is that the percentage could be even higher and is either not recognized or the person chose not to share the information.

While it is good to know that we are not alone in our feelings, when we as individuals experience impostor syndrome, we convince our-selves that we are the *only* one in our circle who feels like a fraud.

From Co-author Emily:

> During my dissertation defense, I was asked the simple question, "What is a theory?" I couldn't think of an answer on the spot. It was at the point that I thought there was no way I got to this point in school because of my competency. Rather, it was sheer luck I made it that far. Who doesn't know what a theory is? I felt like a fraud – like an impostor. I wasn't alone (remember the 70% of us we discussed), although at the time I sure felt like I was.

In this chapter, we will discuss the common characteristics of impostor syndrome, how common it is, and some possible ways to overcome these feelings when they arise.

What Do They See in Me? Common Characteristics of Impostor Syndrome

There are common characteristics of those who are facing impostor syndrome, and if we think hard enough, we might even see that we are displaying some of these characteristics without realizing it. Jaruwan Sakulku and James Alexander are two international scholars who do an excellent job discussing the six characteristics of impostor syndrome reported through Clance's (1985) research:

(1) The impostor cycle
(2) The need to be special or to be the very best
(3) Superman/superwoman aspects
(4) The fear of failure
(5) The denial of competence and discounting praise
(6) Fear and guilt about success.

As we explore these six characteristics further, note that they essentially boil down to one common theme: individuals feel that others have overestimated their abilities, attribute their success to external factors, and are fearful that their limitations will be revealed.

For those experiencing it, the vicious cycle of impostor syndrome restarts with every opportunity we encounter. Think about the last time you faced a consequential task – closing a game-changing account with a prestigious client, playing a guitar solo in front of thousands, or completing an important class assignment. As we will discuss in Chapter 8, it is very common to feel nervous when facing these opportunities, even when we are excited about the task at hand. However, someone experiencing impostor syndrome might experience a level of anxiety that exceeds that of the proverbial butterflies. In such cases, this anxiety might lead the person experiencing impostor syndrome to take one of two extreme approaches – overpreparing or procrastinating with a later rush to be prepared (Sakulku & Alexander, 2011).

Critically, the self-perceived impostors who overprepared attributed their success to the amount of work they put in, rather than recognize that they were not impostors or frauds (Sakulku & Alexander, 2011). The procrastinators attributed their success to luck. In both cases, the impostor cycle was perpetuated because the individuals did not allow themselves to be credited for the outcome – at least for their capabilities. Additionally, regardless of which route the perceived impostor took, they also tended to discount positive feedback, and focus instead on negative feedback, even considering what most of us would label to be constructive criticism as a sign of how much of an impostor they really are. This inability to accept positive feedback or accept due credit for their accomplishments feeds self-doubt, which then increases the feelings of being a fraud. This vicious impostor cycle then starts all over again (Clance, 1985; Sakulku & Alexander, 2011).

Let us return to the story of Marcus from the beginning of the chapter. Even though there were self-doubts about his abilities while submitting his graduate school applications, he was accepted, restoring his confidence. With relief, he realized he was among the very best of his cohort in his studies and assumed it would be the same when he began graduate study. He could not have been more wrong. The very first graduate school paper Marcus got back with feedback had a huge "D" handwritten on the title page. He felt a horrible sinking feeling, and his belief that he was a fraud returned. Marcus's experience – earning a "D" on his first graduate school paper – highlights the interrelated second and third characteristics of impostor syndrome: the need to be the best and superwoman/superman aspects (Clance, 1985; Sakulku & Alexander, 2011).

The need to be the best is a pretty straightforward consideration – someone wants to be the best at something. They might even have a history of being the best in a variety of situations. However, increased level of competition can prevent them from being the best – potentially triggering the feeling of being an impostor. The superwoman/superman aspect of impostor syndrome is exemplified when self-perceived impostors strive to perform as flawlessly as possible. When they do not, they take it as evidence that they are an impostor (Clance, 1985; Sakulki & Alexander, 2011). Marcus was not an impostor; he simply had not acclimated to the increased demands and differences between an undergraduate and graduate education. Additionally, while Marcus wanted to be perfect in everything he did, that does not happen in reality (see Chapter 8 for more on perfectionism).

Pass or fail. Passing or failing are the two options introduced to most of us in elementary school and stick with us until we are finished with formal education. Of course, there are variations of these options. The passing option typically has several gradients. The pass/fail concept is engrained in us from an early age as an objective measure of performance, and the failure component looms large. (We discuss failure throughout the book; see Chapters 4 and 8 for more on how we think about failure). Some of us may even develop a fear of failure – the fourth characteristic of impostor syndrome (Clance, 1985; Sakulki & Alexander, 2011). Because failure can be viewed by a self-perceived impostor as proof of their assessment, they tend to overwork themselves in an attempt to avoid failure. For example, Marcus (from the opening vignette of the chapter) might spend triple the time needed on his second paper to avoid another grade of "D." While this may seem to be a relatively rational response to the first bad grade, the tendency to overwork can be common among self-perceived impostors. They might spend an inordinate, and often unnecessary, amount of time on task as a consequence of their fear of failure.

Another common characteristic of impostor syndrome reviewed by Sakulki and Alexander (Clance, 1985; Sakulki & Alexander, 2011) is the denial of competence and discounting praise. Self-perceived impostors have a mental barrier to acknowledging their success for what it is. Consider Lauren, a very accomplished female STEM researcher with many publications and a multi-year, multi-million-dollar grant. She experiences impostor syndrome and does not give herself the credit she deserves for her accomplishments. Instead, she credits her success to being part of a good team and even finds ways to discount her undeniable individual contributions. Relatedly, the self-perceived impostor discounts praise or dismisses it altogether.

From Co-author Emily:

> I passed my dissertation defense, even after I could not explain the definition of a theory. While my committee heaped praise upon me for how well I performed in the defense, I was unable to accept the praise in that moment, still stuck on the fact that I couldn't answer such a simple question.

For self-perceived impostors this can be the norm – they tend to dismiss the positive feedback/praise, even when it is plentiful and from trusted sources. Moreover, the tendency is to focus on any available evidence to support the idea that they are an impostor. Emily's example illustrates this concept. She couldn't move beyond her inability to provide an explanation of what a theory is.

Lastly, those with impostor syndrome share guilt about, and maybe moreso, a fear of, success. While self-perceived impostors do not want to feel like frauds, they also do not want their hard work to come with the consequences of *more* work. The risk of higher demands precipitates a fear that they will be eventually exposed as the fraud they perceive themselves to be. It is important to note that those experiencing impostor syndrome typically, indeed, have the competence to perform the task at hand; however, they attribute their success to external forces rather than their own skills and knowledge (Kastelic & Ogilvie, 2022).

We All Experience Impostor Syndrome?

Dr. Tim Hunt won a Nobel prize in Physiology and Medicine. When interviewed, it was clear he also faced impostor syndrome – in disbelief that it had really happened:

> Well, the news sinks in slowly, and you feel uncomfortable because you worry that other people might think that you are not really worthy of it: that's what I thought. Interestingly, about a couple of weeks after the announcement, I ran into Paul [Nobel prize co-awardee] and he said, 'Oh Tim, I've just had most

ghastly weekend because I felt so unworthy.' I was not alone, then! Winning a Nobel certainly leads to a lot of soul searching and you end up thinking, 'Why me?' You reflect back upon your career. If you read the autobiographies of previous Laureates, you will see that this reaction is common (Cerejo, 2015; see also Grossman, 2023).

This description of a Nobel Laureate feeling unworthy of the prize was quite an eye-opener. We tend to think of anyone performing at that level to be immune from such feelings of self-doubt. While impostor syndrome was initially examined among females in a male-dominated career, researchers have found that impostor syndrome can affect anyone. And, impostor syndrome can emerge with anything, where any level of performance is required – compared to me, you are a better bowler, antiques buyer, speller, writer, parent, professor, and so on. This makes sense as there is no reason to assume that feelings of self-doubt would not exist in such areas. Having said that, it is unlikely that there is much research or conversation about how the car buyer at the auto dealership secretly felt that they were winging it, did not really know what they were doing, and would be found to be an impostor any day now. This is in part because it is unlikely that anyone has even asked, and it is unlikely that they would proactively bring it up. However, we will now explore some of the research into those who experience impostor syndrome and highlight additional examples – some may come as a surprise.

We now know that all of us are susceptible to feeling like an impostor, even Nobel Laureates. It is also not limited to any specific domains – we may feel like a fraud in anything we pursue. Recall the estimate that 70 percent of us have experienced or will experience impostor syndrome. Not surprisingly, impostor syndrome is evident among many students pursuing a college degree. Researchers have found that physician assistant, psychology, nurse practitioner, medical residency, and molecular biology were among the top academic programs where students experienced impostor syndrome (Joshi & Mangette, 2018). This is likely due to the competitive nature of the fields. If the winner of the Nobel prize in Physiology and Medicine can experience self-doubt about his accomplishment, then college sophomore Katrina is likely also prone to questioning whether she belongs.

Impostor syndrome may be especially present for those just starting out in their careers. For example, physicians who are in the early stages of their careers may make mistakes and experience moments of self-doubt when they believe their medical skills and knowledge are not as good as others thought (LaDonna et al. 2017). They might start to question themselves and ask, "what am I doing here?" Academic scholars may compare themselves to others at the same level by comparing the number of publications or length of their CVs to those of others, which can increase self-doubt if they do not measure up. We consider such comparisons and some of the potential roots of impostor syndrome later in this chapter.

Even the best-known performers, such as celebrities and professional athletes have discussed their feelings of impostor syndrome. For example, Kate Winslet, known for her role in *Titanic* (Cameron, 1997), stated "I'd wake up in the morning before going off to a shoot and think, I can't do this; I'm a fraud" (Warrell, 2014; see also Grossman, 2023). Maya Angelou also described her experiences, "I have written 11 books, but each time I think, 'uh oh, they're going to find out now. I've run a game on everybody and they're going to find me out'" (Warrell, 2014; see also Grossman, 2023). Thus, achieved success at the level mentioned in these examples is often not enough to douse these feelings of self-doubt. A recent documentary produced by ABC underscores this point. Country-rapper Jelly Roll, who is experiencing tremendous success for his music and is now a household name, discussed having impostor syndrome and battling it every day (Pearlman & Roll, 2023).

Our own interviews with high performers led to stories of their experiences with impostor syndrome. Comedian Henry Cho said:

> I still [experience impostor syndrome]. I walk off going, 'Wow! I can't believe I got away with another one!' It's still one of those things. I can't believe I get to do this. I wouldn't say I feel like a fraud, but I'm getting away with it.

On a similar note, actor Talon Beeson shared the frequency with which he experiences impostor syndrome:

> I still every day wake up and think, 'Today's the day they figure out I'm a fraud. I have no idea what I'm doing.' But, you know,

I don't think any of us really know what we're doing. It doesn't change the fact that I know I'm not alone in this, that we all wake up and think, 'Well, I don't really understand how this works. It's just kind of working, and today's the day.

Alec Mills, a professional baseball pitcher, shared with us his experience with impostor syndrome:

I think that [impostor syndrome] happens a lot in baseball. I think it happens in any career, or anything anybody wants to do, but baseball, especially. It can really kick you while you're down. My first outing ever in professional ball was in Idaho Falls. I got drafted in '12, and it was some time after that … and my first appearance. First batter I ever faced was a double off the wall that I'm not sure got any higher than 15 feet. It was hit so hard. And then the next guy had a homer, and I think, *you hit it right on the head*. It was definitely like, 'Okay, do I belong here? Did I miss? Did I mess up?' And, all these thoughts creep in your head, and I'm on the mound. I remember several times, you know, kind of being in the shower after a game, and just like leaning my head against the wall like, 'Man, this is not for the faint of heart. This is not easy. This is not something that I guess I thought it was going to be.

It is helpful knowing that we are not alone and that even people we look up to in various contexts experience the same feelings of impostor syndrome that we do. These examples show us that anyone can experience impostor syndrome, not just those in an academic setting. These feelings of being a fraud are becoming more and more talked about in the public domain which makes it easier for others to relate and develop skills to help overcome their self-doubt and feelings of being an impostor.

Why Are We Prone to Experiencing Impostor Syndrome?

Monica and John were discussing their feelings of impostor syndrome over lunch one day, and they were trying to determine the reasons for their feelings. While they were deep in conversation,

Monica realized that she had always been very critical of herself while growing up. This self-criticism became engrained as a personality trait, and because of its persistence, her feelings of being an impostor intensified. John realized during the conversation that he always compared himself to everyone else. In particular, John realized he was comparing himself to graduate students who were further along than him, and he felt like a fraud because he did not have as many publications as they did.

While the *feeling* of impostor syndrome is the same across the two examples above, we can distinguish the cause of the development of impostor syndrome between the individuals. Sanne Feenstra and a group of international colleagues identified the underlying causes of impostor syndrome as clinical-psychological, as with Monica, and social-psychological, as with John (Feenstra et al., 2020). The clinical-psychological perspective attributes impostor syndrome at the individual level and likens it to a personality trait. Early researchers suggest that the experience of impostor syndrome is due to a negative, critical self-concept (Clance & Imes, 1978). This is the proposed root of Monica's impostor syndrome. She developed a recurring tendency of self-criticism that perpetuated itself in an ongoing cycle of increasing self-criticism leading to further self-doubt, which magnified the self-criticism.

Feenstra and colleagues did not feel that the clinical-psychological approach adequately explained how everyone could be prone to impostor syndrome and proposed the social-psychological perspective. The social-psychological perspective considers an individual's social context and how it influences our susceptibility to impostor syndrome (Feenstra et al., 2020). This approach considers possible root causes from three perspectives: societal level, institutional level, and interpersonal level. Starting with the societal level, comparing ourselves to others is human nature, and this is one of the reasons we may experience impostor syndrome. Like John, we often compare ourselves to others to see where we stand in a social/performance hierarchy (see Chapter 6 for more on such comparisons).

A problem can occur when we compare with the wrong person or group. This could be an undergraduate student comparing themselves to a graduate student (inherently more advanced in the field) or a medical resident comparing themselves to an attending (who would have years more experience with hands-on care). These comparisons often make us feel as though we are falling short, exacerbating the feeling of impostor syndrome. We are functionally comparing our weaknesses with others' strengths (Warrell, 2014). This can occur even when comparing to others at the same level by not taking contextual or historical factors into account. For example, a newly enrolled piano student may compare themselves to another who began classes on the same day. However, they did not know that the other student was the child of a professional piano player, with the opportunity to observe their parent's performance from a very young age and thus have the advantage of previous, though informal, training. Taking this information into account, we are essentially comparing apples to oranges.

The societal-level explanation of impostor syndrome illustrates that the groups we belong to, and the portrayal of these groups in society, can impact how we view ourselves and our accomplishments (Feenstra et al., 2020). This reflects the themes we discussed in Chapters 1 and 2 related to how society has conditioned us to see our potential as limited. Someone buying into the traditional view of set performance ceilings can certainly fall into the impostor cycle by not believing in their true potential. The second consideration of the societal level is that getting really good at something takes time. This is true for everyone. However, the intensity of what it takes during training or practice often happens behind the scenes. Because of this, unless we are privy to that improvement process for others, we may expect our own progress to happen much more quickly than is reasonable. When getting better takes more time than initially expected, we might then blame ourselves and see it is as evidence of performance ceilings. We come to believe we are not able to achieve a higher level of success. These views lead to self-doubt and increase the likelihood that we give up altogether.

Conversely, we are often surprised at what we end up accomplishing when such thoughts do not get the best of us, and we stick with something. Doctoral student Tyler Tims shared his experience when we asked if he had ever faced impostor syndrome. "I feel impostor syndrome almost every day," he said. "But, now I'm starting to experience moments of developing my professional identity and feeling like I am finally coming into it." This underscores the need to keep plugging at something until you begin to feel comfortable.

The next consideration of the social-psychological causes of impostor syndrome is classified as the institutional level – the idea that we determine our worth by observing who is performing what and for whom at the institution. When we do not see anyone else similar to us or with similar backgrounds, we may conclude that we do not belong – that we are impostors. This is very much in alignment with the original studies that observed impostor syndrome at pervasive levels in women in STEM fields, when men, generally, were not believed to experience it at the same levels.

Lastly, when examining impostor syndrome through the interpersonal-level lens, Feenstra and colleagues (2020) suggest that there are social evaluative cues guiding our appraisals of self-worth and how we perceive whether we deserve our place in our careers. In other words, we are keenly aware of how others are treating us. If it seems we are being treated poorly, then we could internalize those feelings and conclude that we might not actually belong – we feel we are an impostor.

While everyone is at risk, certain groups might be more likely to experience impostor syndrome than others. Similar to women in STEM fields observed to have high levels of impostor syndrome – who likely saw very few other women in the ranks and may have been treated poorly, other groups who are underrepresented in their institutions often experience self-doubt. For example, first-generation college students, individuals from lower socio-economic backgrounds, members of ethnic minorities, and women in other male-dominated fields or institutions are all susceptible to impostor syndrome.

Researchers have found that, as a group, incidents of impostor syndrome are higher for students in minority populations. Cokely and colleagues (2013), examined impostor syndrome among African American, Asian American, and Latinx students, and found that the presence of impostor syndrome was a strong predictor of psychological stress, leading to a negative effect on their overall well-being. In fact, high-achieving members of underrepresented groups appear to face increased test anxiety, negative psychological effects, and reduced confidence in their own intelligence as a result of impostor syndrome (Cokely et al., 2013; Kumar & Jagacinski, 2006; McGregor, Gee, & Posey, 2008).

First-generation college students also have this predisposition. They are constantly navigating labyrinths of offices, terminology, and expectations unlike anything they have ever experienced. Making matters worse, college is the first taste of true freedom for many, making it essential to be diligent in following the correct processes at the right times, as well to learn from mistakes. It can be quite embarrassing to discover you are on the proverbial "wrong page." Clint Smith wrote an article in *The Atlantic* describing how difficult it can be for someone not fortunate enough to be from a prestigious background to navigate the world of an elite college (2019). In particular, he notes how something seemingly minor to some, such as "TR" on a class schedule referring to both Tuesday *and* Thursday, can cause inordinately negative consequences to someone unfamiliar with the abbreviation. This may be evident to anyone with more than a semester of college experience, but someone new to the notation may begin to have doubts that this environment – or college in general – is even for them. While this particular issue may not occur for everyone, it is an example of how simple issues can perpetuate the negative thinking that you do not belong because you are a fraud.

How Will I Know if It Is Impostor Syndrome?

Well-known author on impostor syndrome, Dr. Lisa Orbe-Austin, discusses identifiable signs of impostor syndrome, which can be helpful if we are unsure that we are experiencing impostor syndrome (2020, p. 4). They include:

(1) You are a high achiever
(2) You engage in the impostor cycle
(3) You want to be the best
(4) You attribute success to luck or mistake
(5) You discount praise
(6) You fear being discovered as a fraud
(7) You do not feel intelligent
(8) You have self-esteem issues
(9) You struggle with perfectionism
(10) You overestimate others and underestimate yourself
(11) You do not experience an internal feeling of success
(12) You overwork or self-sabotage.

Think of this as a checklist. Do these sound familiar? If so, you may be experiencing impostor syndrome without realizing it.

Further complicating the issue, impostor syndrome can present in multiple ways. Dr. Valerie Young unpacks some of these considerations in her book, *The Secret Thoughts of Successful Women and Men: Why Capable People Suffer from Impostor Syndrome and How to Thrive in Spite of It* (2011). For example, she describes the perfectionist who creates unattainable goals and feels like an impostor when they are not met; the expert who feels inadequate believing they do not have sufficient knowledge of the topic, leading to feelings of being a fraud; the super-person who takes on too much work to handle just to feel respected by peers; and the genius who experiences shame when they have to put in effort to develop a skill. Do any of these resonate with you? Sound like someone you know? We certainly see these behaviors quite frequently and probably engage in some of them ourselves. Any us of can demonstrate these behaviors without even realizing we are doing so or understanding the detrimental effects on our performance.

What Can I Do About It? Working Through Impostor Syndrome

The first step in working through impostor syndrome is recognizing that you have it (Arleo et al., 2021). Dr. Mardie Warrell, the author of several books to help you improve your performance provides advice on overcoming impostor syndrome (Warrell, 2014). She proposes that self-acceptance is critical to the process. We also must be intentional in owning our successes and training ourselves to think that we did not "get lucky" – that our achievements are products of our work and accomplishments. It seems easy enough to just say, "I am not an impostor; I got here because of my skills!" But, it is a lot easier said than done. Once we notice the feelings or characteristics of impostor syndrome, we can begin to mitigate those by making a list of our qualifications to help us own our accomplishments and manifest our success. A similar tactic, arising from other research focusing on a variety of academics led by Lisa Jaremka, is to focus on past successes to help refute the feeling of being an impostor (Jaremka et al. 2020).

Another theme that emerged from Jaremka's work is that we often subscribe to messages that we should "be" a certain way. For example, there is the stereotypical portrayal of how a professor should look, act, or sound. While we should recognize that these types of pre-conceptions are myths, we often internalize these messages. Working through impostor syndrome is not something that will happen over-night; rather, it is a series of skills developed over our lifetimes – impostor syndrome is something that does not fully go away.

Because awareness of the frequency of impostor syndrome is critical, a trusted network of your peers, colleagues, and friends from across different domains who suffer from impostor syndrome can create a space to discuss your struggles openly. Such communication allows for opportunities to learn from one another and provide support.

Chapter Summary

We have discussed how anyone can be susceptible to impostor syndrome – students, faculty, celebrities, professional athletes, and even the highest achievers – people we would not think would ever doubt themselves.

Additionally, impostor syndrome can actually cause psychological distress (Kumar & Jagacinksi, 2006; McGregor et al., 2008). Those experiencing impostor syndrome may actually push themselves to work harder so that their "secret" is never discovered, which can lead to burn out, overworking, and self-sabotage (Orbe-Austin, 2020). Furthermore, the relationship between perfectionism and impostor syndrome is reciprocal, meaning many battling impostor syndrome are likely also battling perfectionism (more on perfectionism in Chapter 8). Additionally, culture and environment can prevent these individuals from asking for help because of a fear of appearing inad-equate or being perceived as a failure, further confirming their feelings of inadequacy. This also can negatively impact professional develop-ment and create barriers to promotion, salary, and other advancement opportunities because they feel they are not good enough. A network of trusted individuals who have experienced impostor syndrome can help maintain a healthy perspective by openly discussing these feelings and learning from one another.

You belong here!

Chapter 3: *Impostor Syndrome: Feeling Like a Fraud*

This exercise is intended to help you realize how commonplace impostor syndrome is, and how to recognize and counteract it in your own life. In the **first part** of the exercise, you will be asked to identify three (or more) people who have stated they have experienced impostor syndrome. In the **second part**, you will be asked to list times you have personally felt impostor syndrome. In the **third part**, you will be asked to reflect on what this means for your own levels of respectability.

1. **Others:** Identify at least three people who have stated they have experienced impostor syndrome and/or did not have what it took. The three examples could be well-known performers or personal acquaintances.

2. **You:** Think about times when you have experienced impostor syndrome. List as many as you can recall.

3. **Reflection:** You have now identified multiple individuals who have stated they have experienced impostor syndrome. Most likely, these folks are widely respected. What is the implication for how others view you when such well-respected individuals have also experienced impostor syndrome?

References

Arleo, E.K., Wagner-Schuman, M., McGinty, G., Salazar, G., & Mayr, N.A. (2021). Tackling impostor syndrome: A multidisciplinary approach. *Clinical imaging, 74*, 170–172. https://doi.org/10.1016/j.clinimag.2020.12.035.

Cameron, J. (1997). *Titanic* [Film]. Paramount Pictures.

Cerejo, C. (2015). *Nobel Laureate Tim Hunt on What It's Like to Win a Nobel Prize.* https://doi.org/10.34193/EI-IV-5765. Accessed November 11, 2023.

Clance, P.R. (1985). *The Imposter Phenomenon: Overcoming the Fear that Haunts Your Success.* Peachtree Publishers.

Clance, P.R., & Imes, S.A. (1978). The impostor phenomenon in high achieving women: Dynamics and therapeutic intervention. *Psychotherapy: Theory, Research, and Practice, 15*, 241–247. https://doi.org/10.1037/h0086006.

Cokley, K., McClain, S., Enciso, A., & Martinez, M. (2013). An examination of the impact of minority status stress and impostor feelings on the mental health of diverse ethnic minority students. *Journal of Multicultural Counseling and Development, 41*(4), 82–95.

Feenstra, S., Bageny, C., Ryan, M., Rink, F., Stoker, J., & Jordan, J. (2020) Contextualizing the impostor "syndrome". *Frontiers in Psychology, 11*, 1–6. https://doi.org/10.3389/fpsyg.2020.575024.

Grossman, V.A. (2023). Impostor syndrome: Destructive self-doubt among nursing professionals. *Journal of Radiology Nursing, 41*, 242–246. https://doi.org/10.1016/j.jradnu.2022.08.002.

Jaremka, L., Ackerman, J., Gawronski, B., Rule, N., Sweeny, K., Tropp, L., … Vick, B. (2020). Common academic experiences no one talks about: Repeated rejection, impostor syndrome, and burnout. *Perspectives on Psychological Science, 15*. https://doi.org/10.1177/1745691619898848.

Joshi, A., & Mangette, H. (2018). Unmasking of impostor syndrome. *Journal of Research, Assessment, and Practice in Higher Education, 3*(1), 3. https://ecommons.udayton.edu/jraphe/vol3/iss1/3/.

Kastelic, J., & Ogilvie, T. (2022). Is the "impostor syndrome" affecting you and limiting your achievements? *The Canadian Veterinary Journal, 63*, 347–348.

Kumar, S., & Jagacinski, C.M. (2006). Imposters have goals too: The imposter phenomenon and its relationship to achievement goal theory. *Personality and Individual Differences, 40*(1), 147–157.

LaDonna, K.A., Ginsburg, S., & Watling, C. (2018). "Rising to the level of your incompetence": What physicians' self-assessment of their performance reveals about the imposter syndrome in medicine. *Academic Medicine, 93*(5), 763–768. https://doi.org/10.1097/ACM.0000000000002046.

McGregor, L., Gee, D., & Posey, K. (2008). I feel like a fraud and it depresses me: The relation between the imposter phenomenon and depression. *Social Behavior & Personality: An International Journal, 36,* 43–48.

Orbe-Austin, L. (2020). *Own Your Greatness: Overcome Impostor Syndrome, Beat Self-doubt, and Succeed in Life.* Ulysses Press.

Pearlman, B. (Director), & Roll, J. (Writer) (2023). *Jelly Roll. Save Me.* [documentary]. Hulu. https://www.hulu.com/welcome.

Sakulku, J., & Alexander, J. (2011). The impostor phenomenon. *The Journal of Behavioral Science, 6*(1), 75–97.

Smith, C. (2019). Elite colleges constantly tell low-income students that they do not belong. *The Atlantic.* https://www.theatlantic.com/education/archive/2019/03/privileged-poor-navigating-elite-university-life/585100/. Accessed November 10, 2023.

Warrell, M. (2014). Afraid of being 'found out?' How to overcome imposter syndrome. *Forbes.* https://www.forbes.com/sites/margiewarrell/2014/04/03/impostor-syndrome/?sh=7dd6012648a9. Accessed December 13, 2023.

Young, V. (2011). *The Secret Thoughts of Successful Women and Men: Why Capable People Suffer from Impostor Syndrome and How to Thrive in Spite of It.* Crown Currency.

Artificial Ceilings   **4**

This is Where I Top Out

I'll never feel complacent. I've always been a person that likes being uncomfortable. I feel like if I'm uncomfortable, that means it's something for me to aspire to. I guess that's how I've gotten into all these different avenues. Always being ready to learn something new and figure it out – okay, how can I do this? Or it's been somebody reached out to me. Why don't you try it?

– Justin Causey, artist and artist management

Always push to the next level. I wish I could say it has a lot to do with the entertainment industry, but it has a lot to do, I think, with any industry. If you sit on your laurels, you just kind of stagnate, specifically in the entertainment industry.

– Talon Beeson, actor and director

Stacey wanted to learn to use a leading video editing software system but was intimidated by the program's power. A similar, but freely available, software on her laptop seemed less complex and appeared to have some overlap with the higher-end version. Her plan was to get familiar with the free software's functionality first and then see what translated to the professional version that currently intimidated her. She opened both programs to get a first-hand look and to review any obvious shared functionality. Satisfied that she was at least tentatively comfortable with the two programs, she decided to dive in and practice. An hour

DOI: 10.4324/9781003377542-4

into her session, Stacey was impressed with her progress and decided to move on to the professional version. The catch is, she was already working in the professional program's interface. She had enlarged the wrong window at the start and never noticed the difference. Because Stacey had mistakenly started working in the more complex program, she was not bound by the artificial performance ceiling that she would have placed on herself. This allowed her to work without the anxiety that she would have encountered by knowingly trying to work through the higher-end professional version.

That is impossible! Chances are you have contemplated a project or goal and concluded that it was out of reach – a running time, GPA, dream job, or other aspiration. Collectively, humankind always has been aspirational. We harnessed fire, achieved flight, explored space, and so many more accomplishments. In some instances, progress is made only when an individual or a select few see things others have yet to see. Oftentimes, what was once deemed impossible becomes commonplace. Consider the painstaking process endured by Orville and Wilbur Wright, known commonly as the Wright brothers, to achieve flight in their rudimentary aircraft. They persisted despite an unrelenting barrage of doubt and ridicule aimed directly at them. Moreover, it is obvious to almost anyone that air travel is a ubiquitous component of modern life, and it would be difficult to find a single individual still proclaiming that the feat of air travel is impossible (though I am sure one might exist).

A message that can be gleaned from the Wright brothers' example is that it is not unusual for *certain achievements to be considered impossible until they are not.* However, these same achievements often become commonplace once they have been attained. In fact, we take many "impossible" achievements for granted on a daily basis, including electricity and the internet. The four-minute mile was once considered the Holy Grail for mid-distance runners but is now a very achievable, and common, running time (e.g., Krüger, 2006).

A more recent, fascinating example is when a change in *fabric* led to a mental recalibration of what was considered within the realm of human possibility. A new swimsuit – the "supersuit," made of a new fabric – was introduced for use by competitive swimmers for the 2008–2009 season. The athletes who wore the new suit were very successful.

Very successful. As in setting-43-world-records successful. As with most good things, the run of the swimsuit came to an end – it was banned by 2010. However, something fascinating occurred: overall swimming performance increased in the years that followed the introduction and banning of the "supersuit" (Robinson, 2022). The critical lesson is that it was not the fabric itself that led to improved performance; it was the removal of the mental barrier to reaching that level of performance. This example epitomizes the idea of an artificial ceiling. In the swimsuit example, it was a collectively agreed upon artificial ceiling among competitive swimmers and coaches, but an artificial ceiling nonetheless.

The swimming and four-minute mile examples reminded us of a practice used by the US motorsports organization NASCAR. The organization requires the use of restrictor plates on the racecars to control the speed at which the racecars can travel. This enhances the fan experience by increasing the likelihood of a close race, and it increases the need for strategy / skill by the drivers. This struck us as an excellent, and literal, parallel for the role of the artificial ceilings that we tend to place on ourselves. As mentioned, the root of these ceilings can be from a collective view, as in the banned swimsuit example, or from the individual themselves. However, removing these metaphorical restrictor plates allows you to move forward at "full speed."

More broadly, we often do not realize how much we are capable of accomplishing when the proper circumstances are cultivated. Granted, many of our life circumstances are beyond our control. However, as we hope to convey throughout this book, we have a greater degree of control than is often recognized. This chapter will focus on the artificial ceilings that we place on ourselves individually, along with the role that collective societal views can have on what we deem achievable. We will present some of the factors that potentially shaped how the general populace views impossible achievements, particularly with a lens toward the potential impact on individual performance, and discuss how all of this influences our own, individual, artificial limits. Finally, we unpack the lessons and themes gleaned from our discussions with some very successful performers and provide insights into how you can reduce the tendency toward artificial ceilings on your own capabilities.

The Impact of Default Societal Beliefs

As noted in Chapter 1, Sir Francis Galton's view of predetermined, individual ceilings on performance influenced the cultural lens through which performance was viewed for well over a century. In a nutshell, Galton proposed that each individual possesses a natural limit on performance that is impossible to exceed. According to this view, if Johnny has reached his ceiling in mathematical abilities, no amount of training or practice would allow him to move to a performance level beyond this proposed "ceiling." We presented the counterargument in Chapter 1 that continual improvements are possible through prolonged engagement in activities designed to improve performance along with iterative adaptations to training as needed. Several decades of research back up this view (e.g., Miller et al., 2020), and prolonged engagement is deemed a necessary component of improving performance (e.g., Campitelli & Gobet, 2011)

Despite this evidence, Galton's viewpoint of performance ceilings had a tremendous impact on how society collectively has viewed high performance – one that lingers today. It is common to hear the best performers be described as "gifted" or "naturals." Because this lens through which high performance is viewed is so engrained in society, it has taken tremendous efforts to convey widely that one can enhance their level of performance to a greater extent than they might have been aware. Rather than recognize the evidence of the impact of controllable factors in elite performance, many of us seem to have engaged in a type of collective confirmation bias related to natural abilities. For example, the athlete with an extensive training history is lauded for their natural abilities following an impressive game performance. Because many were looking for evidence that the player was in possession of disproportionate natural abilities, the work put in by the player was overshadowed by the belief that their natural abilities that had been "confirmed" – the confirmation bias. Legendary National Basketball Association player Michael Jordan was famously bothered when his hard work was dismissed and it was suggested that his success was primarily due to a special gift of some kind. He shared, "I'm not out there sweating for three hours every day just to find out what it feels like to sweat."

Thus, Galton's academic work contributed to the idea of artificial performance limits at the societal level. When observing amazing performances, there was a collective tendency to deem the performer a "natural talent." There is nothing inherently problematic with attributing the source of someone's performance to natural abilities. The problem arises when the label leads to overlooking the tremendous amount of preparation of most, if not all, top performers. In some instances, the performer reveals the degree of their preparation. Stephen Curry shared that he had adopted the very specific training regimen of a player deemed a great shooter by Curry's coach (Davis, 2015). This new training technique elevated him to the league leader in three-point shooting shortly thereafter. Unfortunately, but understandably, not all performers are as open to sharing their training processes with the masses. But why? In the particular example of Stephen Curry, adopting the training techniques of a fellow player performing at the highest level, the training techniques were relatively well known around the league and nowhere close to being secret training techniques. However, there are obvious competitive advantages to keeping proven techniques close to the vest for a variety of reasons.

The Advantages of Not Sharing Training Techniques

In a perfect world we all would encourage one another, celebrate each other's accomplishments, and openly share our path to achievement. Obviously, we do not live in a perfect world, and the main advantage of not sharing the techniques to reach a higher-level performance is pretty straightforward. Withholding such information provides a competitive advantage to the possessor, which in turn empowers them. Thus, sharing the source of a competitive advantage is a step too far for some performers under many circumstances, and for other performers under *any* circumstances. Although someone might not be willing to go as far as to sabotage a competitor, even the most generous person is unlikely to hand over the playbook in competitive situations. Such situations could span the spectrum from maintaining a lead as the best salesperson at an organization to actual competitive sports.

An interesting point here is that researchers have, in some instances, attempted to identify scientifically the factors that distinguish one level of performer from the other. Once identified, the path taken by the performer can be unpacked by having the performer share their training techniques to reach various benchmarks of development – maybe the training drills in which they initially engaged or how they overcame a plateau. A related approach for the researchers involves working to pinpoint the specific component(s) of performance responsible for their advantage and then develop training based on that information that accelerates the development of less-skilled performers.

For example, Peter Fadde, a researcher who does a great deal of work on baseball performance, and his colleagues, identified the best collegiate baseball hitters on their teams based on batting averages across actual game performances (2016). This meant that the batting performance level of each player was well-tested, having been accumulated over multiple games, and was not a judgment based on informal observations or hunches. This is an important point as it lends credibility to what the researchers discovered next. With a technique called visual occlusion, they were able to identify when the advantage of the best batters occurred – the points at which the players' predictions of how the pitch would behave were accurate for only the best batters. Once identified, the batters with lesser batting averages were then trained to develop the ability to better predict the behavior of the pitch at the points identified in the original phase. Did it work? Turns out that the team ended up leading the league in batting averages that season. As mentioned in Chapter 2, this approach has been codified under the names Expert Performance Based Training (ExPerT; Ward, Suss, & Basevitch, 2009) and XBT (Fadde, 2009).

Another advantage of not sharing the steps to reach a high level of success is a psychological one. It can provide a feeling of superiority. Many lucrative pursuits have what can only be described as "gatekeepers" – the entertainment industry, athletics, or competitive universities. Gaining access to these realms can provide a level of prestige and allow the grantees to feel as if they have been admitted to an exclusive club. Existing members of these exclusive groups might withhold guidance for reasons ranging from wanting others to "pay their dues" to a sense that they are among the chosen ones, essentially a feeling of superiority. Everyone presumably has experienced the desire to be granted access to something off-limits. It is understandably invigorating once access has been granted via landing a coveted acting gig, signing a contract to play professional sports, or securing a spot in a prestigious law school.

It should be noted that not everyone will perform at the level required to be successful in competitive domains and some degree of gatekeeping is a necessity. However, a greater number of performers would potentially make the cut if the information on how it can be accomplished were more widely available. Unlike gatekeepers of the past, such gatekeeping in the modern era often takes the form of collective judgment via likes or similar engagement on social media. Moreover, while the degree to which high performers are willing to share their techniques varies, it is understandable that some level of confidentiality will be in place. Finally, someone might simply feel a sense of exhilaration from not sharing because it provides a feeling of holding a secret.

Societal views of high performers have a lasting impact on the perceived performance ceilings we place on ourselves, and there are advantages of not revealing techniques that are known to help one overcome such beliefs. Fundamentally, it provides a potential competitive advantage to hold on to the "trade secrets" by allowing superior preparation and by keeping the competitive field smaller. What impact do these societal views and practices have on an individual?

The Impact of Societal Views on Mindset

Awareness of the societal factors discussed earlier in the chapter is important for understanding high performers and success as it is generally defined. It is understandable to wonder whether the overall societal view trickles down to the individual level to any significant degree. As with most matters of substance, the answer is "it is complicated." It is less likely that someone will place artificial ceilings on themselves in the most ideal of circumstances – adequate financial resources, interested or knowledgeable parents, access to great facilities, access to great coaches/educators, and similar advantages. As with many things experienced by the average person, these folks would be spared many of the disadvantages of life. However, the collective societal view of artificial performance ceilings can have a tremendous impact for most of us, resulting in a wide variety of outcomes.

Understandably, the societal factors described above resulted in many performers internalizing the message that they are not capable of achieving success. Such internalization had a tremendous impact on the lens through which these individuals viewed their performance ceilings. Consider Carson, a student at a rural high school, who is experiencing difficulty with one of his mathematics classes, viewing himself as "not a math person" who will never be able to grasp the concepts. Because of this view, Carson never makes an earnest attempt to learn the material. The situation was dire enough that a concerned teacher offered additional tutoring during Carson's dedicated study hour to help get things back on track. Believing that any additional effort was pointless, Carson ghosted the teacher and snuck out to join his friends in the parking lot instead. This decision results in a self-fulfilling prophecy, as Carson continues to both do poorly in the mathematics class and see himself as being bad at math. While Carson's story represents a single example, it captures the difficulty of getting someone to engage in activities to improve their performance when they have set artificially low ceilings on their performance and do not believe they can improve regardless of their preparation.

Recall from Chapter 1 that Stanford University's Carol Dweck coined the terms "fixed" and "growth" mindset while investigating the views one might hold about their own abilities (e.g., Dweck, 2006). Someone adopting a fixed mindset believe that they possess a given level of ability in an area and that they will be unable to move beyond that level. This view stands in contrast with a growth mindset, a viewpoint that arbitrary limits on performance are a fallacy, and one can always enhance their performance over time by taking appropriate steps.

Among Dweck's noteworthy findings were that, relative to those with a growth view, individuals possessing a fixed view were less likely to be comfortable with novel tasks or situations, exhibited less willingness to attempt challenging tasks, and were less willing to stay with a task following difficulties or failures. These tendencies were identified in children (Dweck & Leggett, 1988) and last into adulthood (Murphy & Dweck, 2010). It also appears that the view one holds is likely handed down by parents (Haimovitz & Dweck, 2016). In particular, parents who have a strong aversion to failure tend to focus on a child's performance rather than the possible lessons to be learned and/or performance improvements that could be made when things go wrong.

This hyper-focus on the performance aspect over possible learning opportunities can understandably lead children to also over-emphasize the performance component and adopt a fixed view of performance. To simplify the point – the children presumably come to believe that if growth and learning were the important parts of developing skills, then the parents would not be freaking out when things did not go well.

This transfer of mindset from parents to children can occur both implicitly, such as the example in the preceding paragraph, or explicitly, via the parent mentioning limitations directly. Perhaps influenced by the societal view, parents can have a tremendous impact when they place artificial ceilings on their children's potential by making limiting statements about the child. The potentially damaging statements are distinct from the practice of identifying what someone is not doing well (Chapter 10) or constructive feedback on performance to help improve (Chapter 14) – these are the possible learning opportunities described earlier. Rather, these potentially harmful statements are about the child themselves, and/or possibly the end results of performance (e.g., "Welp, you just are not a math person"). This dynamic potentially can be exacerbated when the parent has little experience in a domain, such as a nonathlete parent of an athlete or a parent of a first-generation college student.

Not Seeing Possibilities

A storm with hurricane level winds came through my current hometown and did considerable damage. There were at least six downed trees on my property as a result. Additionally, fallen limbs were scattered about and it looked as if someone had emptied giant matchboxes across my yard. It was quite a mess. I invested in a quality chainsaw and began sectioning the fallen trees for removal. Once that initial task was complete, the task of picking up the limbs commenced. It was arguably a more difficult task than cutting up the fallen trees because it felt endless. Eventually, it seemed as if the end was within reach, and I would be able to move on to another chore. However, it became obvious that there were almost as many medium and small limbs to remove once the largest, most obvious ones were cleared. It was fascinating to me was that I truly had not realized that the additional layer of medium and small limbs was there until the larger ones had been removed. This all happened while the planning of this book was in full force, and the parallels to the themes of the book immediately stood out. First, it reminded me that we often do not see the possibilities available to us, even when those opportunities are sometimes in plain sight. The second parallel is that sometimes it takes putting in a certain amount of effort to reach a given benchmark before we can psychologically see, or even be able to work on, the finer details.

This limitation can be exacerbated by being a first-generation anything. It is often a family member or trusted family friend that introduces one to a domain. A coach or teacher might take the reins following the introduction, but family members and friends often have some grasp of what one needs to do to get better, especially at these earliest stages. These folks often provide the primary or secondary guidance to get one well on their way. This can be a student attempting to qualify for a spelling bee, join a youth bowling league, play chess, or any other pursuit. The lack of more highly skilled guidance might hinder progress and ultimately feed into the idea of a fixed mindset – I guess I am just not good at X.

Thankfully, the difficulties of being a first-generation college student have garnered a good deal of attention. While it is true that one has already navigated a minefield of unknowns if they are enrolled in college, being unaware of possibilities can hinder someone well before reaching college enrollment. For example, a student could miss out on preparatory classes or opportunities to strengthen their chances to gain admission to college. While it is less likely to occur in the age of social media, an older sibling who is off the mark in understanding even the types of majors that could be pursued could really sideline their younger brother hoping to find the right college. The subset of norms for most domains take time to learn and learning them is enhanced by having someone *capable* of showing you the proverbial ropes.

An unfortunate consequence of being a first-generation college student is that the feeling of being out of place or inferior is a difficult one to overcome. We dedicated the entire preceding chapter, Chapter 3, to the phenomenon known as impostor syndrome, which is the feeling that one is a fraud regardless of accomplishments. Being a first-generation college student is one of the factors that increases the likelihood of experiencing impostor syndrome, as well as magnifying the feeling of stress when experiencing it (Holden et al., 2024). A first-generation college student might always battle the irrational fear of being "found out."

As we will discuss in Chapter 10 (acknowledging what you are not doing well) and Chapter 14 (seeking out feedback and criticism), these same folks can provide critical feedback on how well one is progressing. It is easy to overestimate, or underestimate, how well one will do at a given task – the now popularized Dunning-Kruger effect that we discuss in Chapter 10. Dr. Kevin Eva, a medical education scholar, noted that as much effort should be made to keep in place the qualified folks who do not yet recognize their potential as there is with correcting the erroneous perceptions of being good at something by the less capable. This certainly would apply here and to our discussion of highly capable first-generation students.

As a final consideration regarding seeing possibilities: it is not the fault of the person who is unable to see the possibilities. Again, the degree to which you do not see the possibilities can be greatly impacted by being a first-generation participant in something. The common feeling of being seated at a formal dinner and being unsure of which utensil to use, or the appropriate way to eat something, is something that you likely have experienced. Imagine having this feeling with almost everything you encounter. This is often the experience when you are the first in your family to enter college or a particular field. Disproportionate energy spent on figuring out the environment, while not standing out like a sore thumb, likely decreases the opportunities to recognize the possibilities available to you. We now share a potentially unexpected lens through which to view failure.

Failing to Win

What comes to mind when you think of "failure?" The concept of failure is one that is frequently misunderstood. Many of you might have imagined a desolate, miserable existence. Others might have envisioned a specific event that was particularly memorable, or something along the lines of the time you cost your team the win. While these conceptualizations certainly fall under the umbrella of the term, failure is an *integral* part of the process of getting better. You might make 300 attempts at something before finally getting it right or obtaining the desired outcome. The first 299 will be considered failures. But this is nothing more than the process of reaching your goals or the standards you have set for yourself. Someone giving up on a domain on the 79th attempt might rightfully consider it a failure in the way that the term is commonly used if it ultimately results in them ending their pursuit of their goals.

However, what if we reframed failure and what it means for you? As with the other topics of this chapter, we can consider the impact failure might have on your potential based on how it influences what you pursue, and this influence is dependent on your mindset. Someone with a fixed mindset will see failure as an embarrassment to be avoided because it will potentially expose their "limitations." In such cases, multiple failures will suggest that someone has reached the ceiling of their supposed limited abilities. In these cases, the person will pass on opportunities for which multiple tries (and failures) might be necessary. In contrast, someone with a growth mindset would focus on the process and would not see multiple tries (and failures) to be problematic (Murphy & Dweck, 2010). This is because someone with a growth mindset would generally believe that failure would not expose any existing limitations of their abilities.

We encourage you to adopt the approach of reframing failure as part of the process, regardless of your perspective on a fixed versus growth mindset or even if you are dismissive of the concept of mindset altogether. The bottom line is that you will not progress at anything, much less get really good, unless you experience failure repeatedly. Embrace the opportunity to use things that do not go as planned as a way to seek improvement. Failure in the sense that it is traditionally viewed occurs when this process is not allowed to play out and you drop a pursuit prematurely. We now consider a related consideration – not being afraid to attempt something new.

Not Being Afraid to Try

An important message gleaned from our interviews with high performers is that one should not be afraid to try something. This initially might sound like generic and overused advice repeated by self-help types ad nauseum. This is understandable. However, consider everything that we discussed above in this chapter – Galton's lingering influence, mindset, and self-imposing artificially low performance ceilings. The combination of these and other factors interacting in both major and subtle ways ultimately determines the trajectory of a given individual's efforts. Who knows what would have happened had Carson, our high school student struggling with math, taken the teacher's offer of additional assistance and spent additional time on his own working to improve? The researchers David Yeager and Gregory Walton stated it eloquently when they described the interplay of a myriad of factors allowing an object weighing several tons to achieve lift and fly. As noted in their quote below, subtle changes to any one component can have noticeable impacts on outcome:

> One reason planes fly is because their wings are sculpted to create an aerodynamic force ("lift") that elevates the plane. It is natural to wonder how a small change in the shape of a wing could make a heavy object fly. Basic laboratory research helps explain the principles of air flow and shows that the shape and position of wings cause air to flow faster below them than above them, lifting a plane beyond what might seem possible. In a similar way, hidden yet powerful psychological forces, also investigated through basic science, can raise student achievement. An engineer uses theories of fluid dynamics to fine-tune a wing, which in the context of other factors, makes a plane fly. Analogously, a social-psychological perspective uses basic theory and research to identify educationally important psychological processes and then subtly alters these processes in a complex academic environment to raise performance (Yeager & Walton, 2011, p. 274).

This is not unlike the shift that occurred once the upper limits of swimming performance changed because of the temporary swimsuit use described in an earlier section of this chapter. The swimmers recalibrated their perception of performance limits based on what had changed in relation to finishing times. You currently might have a mental barrier regarding a performance ceiling of which you are unaware. To reiterate the point, sometimes something seems impossible until it simply does not. This change in perception can occur at the broader societal level; other times it occurs at the individual level.

Once the swimmers adjusted their *idea* of what was possible, they consistently elevated their performance to a new level once the new bar had been set. It is worth repeating – it was the *idea* that changed. Other changes can be more subtle – a student improving academic performance or a bowler improving their game. Hopefully, the situation with the swimmers compels you to reevaluate any performance ceilings you have placed on yourself. Do not self-impose artificial limits, and do not be afraid to try something new because of perceived limitations.

Let us consider a few examples of real-world high performers not being afraid to try something new. Thomas Estrada has always loved to draw. He was a family man working in pest control when he got the opportunity to work in the film industry. Thomas has worked on major motion pictures for studios such as *Disney* and *DreamWorks*. As impressive as that is, the reason we are discussing his career in this section is that Thomas entered the career when everything was drawn manually by hand. The animation process changed tremendously several years into his career when computer-generated animation became prevalent in the industry. Thomas loved what he did and did not want to change careers despite the changes in production processes. The problem was that he did not know how to operate a computer at all. Seriously, Thomas did not even know how to set up his password because he was unfamiliar with the character part of the term, "special characters." Therefore, Thomas immediately went back to the pest control job and is doing very well.

As you might have suspected given the title of the subsection, that last sentence is not true. Thomas was understandably anxious at news of the transition. He considered finding a new career or at least a new job that would allow him to continue producing hand-drawn art. It was in those moments of reflection that Thomas had a moment of clarity – he realized that he already had *relearned* his art over and over throughout the years. He decided to view it as simply learning a new technique for producing art – and learn it, he did. Thomas has remained a respected feature film illustrator using the oft-changing techniques of the industry. This outlook of not placing artificial ceilings on himself continued to serve him well as the field continued to advance. Because of this initial leap into learning computer animation, Thomas viewed each new advancement in the industry as learnable. Thomas adds that this initial step was a "big deal," and the skills he honed along the way led to opportunities to also work in the video game industry.

Justin Causey, a manager in the music/entertainment and artist industries, went a step further to say that he embraces being uncomfortable. Causey, as he likes to be called, has worked in a variety of areas ranging from (the aforementioned) artist management to film production, even having designed a shoe for Nike. He shared that he makes it a practice to be ready to learn something new and figure out "How can I do this?" When someone reaches out to him with something new, Causey takes the leap, knowing the potential result is worth the attempt. This approach is an excellent example of one not artificially limiting their performance ceilings and missing out on opportunities.

Talon Beeson is an actor who experienced this firsthand when the stage manager of a play in which he was performing worked at a voice-over studio. After attending a show from their production, the owner of the voice studio was impressed with Talon's voice and suggested that he give voice-over a try. At the time, he did not even know that voice-over work was a thing. The owner of the studio offered to make a demo reel in exchange for Talon creating a website for the studio. The issue was Talon did not know how to create a website, but he was undeterred: "I said, 'yes,' anyway, and taught myself HTML over the weekend and built her website." Within a month, this exchange of a website for a demo tape led to a national spokesperson booking lasting two years.

Chapter Summary

In this chapter, we discussed how Sir Francis Galton's view of inherent performance ceilings persists and can cause us to place artificial performance ceilings on ourselves. A combination of such societal views of performance ceilings and not believing that one can improve by putting in the work can lead to many of us ultimately limiting what we accomplish. Such limitations are illustrated by a story of how a specialized type of fabric recalibrated what was thought to be possible for maximum human performance, and how the higher performance limits remained after the fabric was banned. These artificial limits we place on ourselves can lead to the pitfalls of not being able to see possibilities available to us, the fear of making mistakes, and not viewing mistakes as an opportunity to learn. Finally, we presented the way in which these factors can lead us to be afraid of even taking the first step within a domain.

I Did That?

Chapter 4: *Artificial Ceilings: This is Where I Top Out*

This exercise will help you identify some instances when you accomplished more than you thought possible, as well as some of your current fears about meeting your goals. In the **first part** of the exercise, you will be asked to write down at least one example of a time when you accomplished way more than you thought possible. The **second part** will ask you to identify some potentially frightening next steps.

1. Please provide at least one example of a time you accomplished something that surprised/shocked you.

2. What are some next steps that either frighten you or feel out of reach?

References

Campitelli, G., & Gobet, F. (2011). Deliberate practice: Necessary but not sufficient. *Current Directions in Psychological Science, 20*(5), 280–285. https://doi.org/10.1177/0963721411421922.

Davis, S. (2015, June). How Stephen Curry became the best shooter in the NBA. *Business Insider*. Retrieved from http://business insider.com/.

Dweck, C.S. (2006). *Mindset*. Random House.

Dweck, C.S., & Leggett, E.L. (1988). A social-cognitive approach to motivation and personality. *Psychological Review, 95,* 256–273. https://psycnet.apa.org/doi/10.1037/0033-295X.95.2.256.

Fadde, P.J. (2009). Expertise-based training: Getting more learners over the bar in less time. *Technology, Instruction, Cognition and Learning, 7,* 171–197.

Fadde, P.J. (2016). Instructional design for accelerated macrocognitive expertise in the baseball workplace. *Frontiers in Psychology, 7.* https://doi.org/10.3389/fpsyg.2016.00292.

Haimovitz, K., & Dweck, C.S. (2016). Parents' views of failure predict children's fixed and growth intelligence mind-sets. *Psychological Science, 27*(6), 859–869. https://doi.org/10.1177/0956797616639727.

Holden, C.L., Wright, L.E., Herring, A.M., & Sims, P.L. (2024). Imposter syndrome among first-and continuing-generation college students: The roles of perfectionism and stress. *Journal of College Student Retention: Research, Theory & Practice, 25*(4), 726–740. https://doi.org/10.1177/1521025121 1019379.

Krüger, A. (2006). Training theory and why Roger Bannister was the first four-minute miler. *Sport in History, 26*(2), 305–324.

Miller, S.D., Chow, D., Wampold, B.E., Hubble, M.A., Del Re, A.C., Maeschalck, C., & Bargmann, S. (2020). To be or not to be (an expert)? Revisiting the role of deliberate practice in improving performance. *High Ability Studies, 31*(1), 5–15. https://doi.org/10.1080/13598139.2018.1519410.

Murphy, M.C., & Dweck, C.S. (2010). A culture of genius: How an organization's lay theory shapes people's cognition, affect, and behavior. *Personality and Social Psychology Bulletin, 36*(3), 283–296. https://doi.org/10.1177/0146167209347380.

Robinson, M.A. (2022). Glimpsing the impossible: How artificially enhanced targets improve elite performance. *Journal of Sport and Exercise Psychology, 44*(3), 177–188. https://doi.org/10.1123/jsep.2021-0034.

Ward, P., Suss, J., & Basevitch, I. (2009). Expertise and expert performance-based training (ExPerT) in complex domains. *Technology, Instruction, Cognition and Learning, 7*, 121–146.

Yeager, D.S., & Walton, G.M. (2011). Social-psychological interventions in education: They're not magic. *Review of Educational Research, 81*(2), 267–301. https://doi.org/10.3102/0034654311405999.

Giving Up

5

I Should Just Quit

I don't think I would be an artist without the drive that I got. The drive never stops, and the want to create never stops. I don't think I've ever been in a position where I've gone, "I want to quit." I know I've been in a position where I've gone, "This is really hard, and I wish someone would help me."

– Katie Cole, touring member of *The Smashing Pumpkins* and singer-songwriter

I feel like there's times almost every round where everybody's ready to quit. It's, you know, it's kind of one of those things – you don't ever say it or put it on the table as an option. It's the same kind of mentality that successful marriages have of never putting divorce on the table – never putting it on the table as an option to even be able to turn to.

– Taylor Hull, Formula Drift professional driver

From Co-author Emily:

I had just finished my master's degree program and successfully defended my thesis with no revisions. When I entered my doctoral program, I was confident I would do just as well. About a year and a half into the program, I submitted my dissertation prospectus to my PhD. supervisor. It was returned with full pages marked with red Xs. The voices in my head were telling me to give up, that I was not cut out for this if I could not successfully write

DOI: 10.4324/9781003377542-5

a dissertation prospectus. My colleagues and family members encouraged me to not give up. I decided to work even harder and sought help with my writing and feedback from previous professors I trusted. I then submitted another draft, and this time, there were only a scattering of red marks. Had I listened to those voices telling me to quit, I would not have graduated with honors and become a successful researcher and professor.

We have likely all felt like Emily at some point. It is human nature to feel like giving up, at least sometimes, when something goes wrong. Giving up can feel much easier than facing the challenge head on. Maybe we determine that sticking with it just is not worth it. You might reach a level of performance and decide that you are okay with where things stand (recall the idea of satisficing discussed in Chapter 2).

We might also be afraid that our limitations will be revealed if we stay with something we are struggling with. As we discussed in Chapter 1, this consideration comes from the influence of a fixed mindset, the opposite of a growth mindset. Someone with a fixed mindset believes that they have a given amount of ability and that this level is mostly, or always, stable (e.g., Dweck, 2006). For example, someone may believe that preparing for the SAT is pointless because their score would be the same regardless of their level of preparation. This view of personal limitations also feeds into impostor syndrome (discussed in Chapter 3). Someone with a fixed mindset and/or struggling with impostor syndrome might give up so they are not perceived by those around them as a failure.

Such considerations are common, and impostor syndrome is a valid concern with very real consequences. However, as we proposed in Chapter 1, "you typically must work hard at the right things for some *time* in order to get really good at something." *Time* is a key component of this statement in our conversation. Getting really good at something almost always takes significant time. To be clear, we are not talking about only getting good enough to win the Thursday night bowling league at the local bowling alley. While anyone *consistently* placing near the top of the rankings likely has invested a notable amount of time, someone could feasibly become good enough to rank locally after a brief stint. Objectively, however, this would depend on the level of competition. As Anders Ericsson and colleagues noted (Ericsson,

Roring, & Nandagopal, 2007), we often reach a level of stable performance that allows us to perform well enough to maintain in a given area. An example of this would be golfing well enough to join your coworkers for a friendly game or playing table-tennis well enough to complete a game with friends. In these situations, you can easily get a false sense of how well you are doing. Being truly competitive at something almost always requires a much more intensive time investment.

More skeptical readers may think that the need to devote this extra time is not the case with the 99.9th percentile of performers. The argument could be that this 0.1 percent of performers might have natural abilities that preclude such time requirements. This may be the case. However, two considerations must be mentioned. The first is that we have no good way of separating the effort and time that the performers in the top 0.1 percent put in from their natural abilities. It is unlikely that someone with tremendous potential reached it without putting in work to develop it – athletes train, scholars think and write, entrepreneurs analyze and brainstorm, and so on. If they were lucky, some of them grew up in a household with parents blazing the trail – a musician, thinker, or athlete whose parents were good at each respective pursuit.

The second consideration is that, by default, there are not very many of us falling within the 99.9th percentile. That's inherently built into the concept. Broken down, the rate means that one person out of a thousand for whatever is being considered will be in the top 0.1 percent (1/1000). So, when you attend a sporting event or concert at the closest venue with a capacity of 50,000, you can expect there to be roughly 50 attendees with IQs in the top 0.1%. Cities with a population of around 500,000 will have 500 residents in the top 0.1%. Such rough estimates are strictly statistical considerations, but they illustrate how few of us would fall into this designation.

However, it is likely that the top 15.8 percent (the above-average threshold we will discuss in Chapter 10) of any domain will be the floor of your competition. In a city of 500,000, that equates to 79,000: at our 50,000-person event, that is almost 8,000. One of the points we are making is that even if the above-average performers are considered to have greater "natural abilities" than the average and below-average performers, the most common competitors for high-level performers likely will fall within the above-average group of performers. Their potential ability to accelerate the benefit from their training will be similar to other competitors at their level. We propose that the statement, "you typically must work hard at the right things for some time in order to get really good at something" holds.

Thus, we have maintained that putting in time is still of great importance, and this means that you will have to stick with something over time to be really good, which is the opposite of giving up. The remainder of this chapter will explore some of the research on not giving up. We primarily explore the work on perseverance, grit, and resilience. We then revisit some of the considerations first introduced in previous chapters on how aspiring performers can get derailed, including societal views of limited performance ceilings, lack of resources, and lack of awareness of techniques. Next, we explore the role goals might play in helping you not give up as easily. We discuss the concept of "fake it 'til you make it" and how the high performers we interviewed view the phrase. Finally, we introduce and share our thoughts on what is known as the sunken-cost fallacy.

Feeling Like Giving Up?

James was enrolled in one of the hardest courses he had ever taken. Up to this point, he had received A grades in all of his classes, but not in this class. He started doubting himself, and his self-belief kept diminishing with each assignment. These experiences led to a fear of failure and negative thinking, and he was losing patience with the assignments. He was ready to give up and accept that he would fail the course. However, when James shared his frustrations with friends, they told him to stop being overly critical of himself and focus on the task at hand. They also reminded James to focus on his accomplishments rather than his failures. While all of this was not easy for James to do, it did help. Once he changed his thinking about himself and the course, he saw it as a challenge to do better. In essence, his fear of failure became a motivator.

The road to success typically is not linear. Rather, it is a winding road with different potential setbacks at each curve. You might encounter a stretch that surprises you because it is curvy when you did not expect it, or you may be surprised at the number of curves you must navigate. Similarly, you might encounter a curve that seems to be particularly long. Such experiences with these metaphorical curves will sometimes test your patience. When we are dealing with difficult stretches, it is easy to forget what could lie ahead – progress towards completing our goal. Giving up might seem like the best option at times, but if you persevere and complete your goal, you will be proud of overcoming the obstacles to success. James passed the course with a B, and while it ended his A streak, he was very proud of the fact he did not give up.

Research into (not) giving up falls under labels such as perseverance, grit, and resilience, and it is extensive. Feeling as if perseverance was understudied as a predictor of performance (Duckworth & Quinn, 2009), Dr. Angela Duckworth and colleagues proposed the concept of "grit," and conceptualized it as perseverance, passion, and consistency of pursuing goals (Duckworth et al., 2007). Specifically, Dr. Duckworth and her colleagues described the concept: "Grit overlaps with achievement aspects of conscientiousness but differs in its emphasis on long-term stamina rather than short-term intensity. The gritty individual not only finishes tasks at hand but pursues a given aim over years (p. 1089)." Think of it as a combination of being a "go getter" with "stick-with-it"-ness.

The concept of grit is one way psychologists attempt to explain why two people of equal abilities, such as athleticism or intelligence, may have different levels of accomplishment. For example, one individual may have grit that keeps them going and helps them to persevere over the obstacles they face, while the other individual does not have this grittiness. Pertinent to the topic of giving up, Duckworth and colleagues (2007) state that those with grit have the stamina to keep going no matter what is thrown their way; those low in, or lacking, grit, will change their course or give up completely when curveballs are thrown their way. Because of this, grit is linked with leadership and high achievements.

The concept of grit has been the subject of a great deal of spirited debate since being proposed by Duckworth and her colleagues. While the concept has been effective in predicting retention in extremely demanding domains, including the United States Military Academy (Duckworth et al., 2007), there was a question as to how much overlap there was with existing measures such as conscientiousness and perseverance (e.g., Credé, Tynan, & Harms, 2017). Other scholars (e.g., Jachimowicz et al., 2018) proposed that passion was an underemphasized piece for understanding grit and must also be considered to best predict who will stick with something. Conversations about grit – what it is and what it can predict – ultimately became quite complex. The sheer number of differing interpretations and (mis)uses of the concept even led Duckworth to request a pause on claims related to grit until the issues to be resolved could be better organized (e.g., Dahl, 2016).

The critical point is that all of these terms allude to continuing with the pursuit – not giving up. While the intricacies of these encompassing terms will continue to be hashed out, the bottom line is that they all are intended to explain/describe the act of sticking with something. For our purposes, these broad considerations are inconsequential (or at least secondary) to the causes of why you choose to not give up – or the respective labels. In other words, we are not concerned with whether it is labelled grittiness, perseverance, resiliency, or something else. Although such distinctions are important for researchers to explore, the fact that you did not give up is our most important consideration. Let us revisit some of the obstacles introduced in the preceding chapters and how they might contribute to someone giving up on a pursuit.

"I do not have what it takes" – The Impact of Default Societal Beliefs

As we have mentioned in preceding chapters, Sir Francis Galton's views on individual performance ceilings heavily influenced our societal view of high performers. Adherents of such a view proposed that these performance ceilings were determined by inherent abilities, and such abilities could be improved only to a level predetermined by the performer's natural endowment. This view does not seem unreasonable on the surface, and we all have human limitations. This point can be considered to fall firmly on the "nature" side of the nature versus nurture continuum. These views directly influenced societal perceptions and actions for over a century.

Thus, it would be reasonable to attribute these views to someone giving up on a domain. If you are struggling to develop your football skills and have bought into the dominant societal view that Premier League players are there *strictly* because of natural ability, then you might assess your own struggles and determine that you will never reach that level. For the readers who potentially just took issue with making the nature versus nurture spectrum a dichotomy in the preceding statement – that was the point! The default societal view was creating a dichotomy all along: one that favored the nature side of the spectrum. It was so ingrained in the societal view that initial attempts to highlight the incredible work involved in being a top-level performer were jarring.[1] Thus, it is understandable that someone struggling within a domain would determine that they do not have what it takes to succeed and ultimately give up.

"I never have what I need" – The Impact of Lack of Resources

One of the frustrating parts of being a broke college student is needing auto repairs. This is especially true when the vehicle in question is likely on its last leg, and it is your primary means of transportation away from campus. It can seem as if there are a never-ending stream of repairs. We are sure many of you can relate to this experience – the need for ongoing resources to keep something going. This is particularly stressful if you have limited financial means. It also can be the reason that you choose to drop out of a pursuit. Compared to the other considerations, the aspect of resources available to us is more difficult to control as the amount we earn or have available varies widely. Our pursuits also require differing amounts of time investments depending on the domain. The best we can do here is to remind you of the other factors we cover in the book, such as having a growth mindset and setting achievable goals, which hopefully will increase the likelihood of being successful in a domain. If you stick with your pursuit long enough, there is a good chance something will break your way.

Obviously, there are no guarantees, but we have seen examples throughout the book of smaller opportunities leading to larger ones. These opportunities can make the difference. We address the conversation about not sticking with something for *too long* because you have already invested significant time and resources, a concept labelled the sunken cost fallacy, later in the chapter. However, we now discuss the potential impact of the lack of awareness of proper/appropriate techniques on choosing to give up.

"I keep being out of position" – The Impact of Lack of Awareness of Techniques

"I don't understand," I told my older sister, who was attempting to help me with math homework. I was very young, so the homework was elementary – the kind with pictures that look as if they belonged in a coloring book. We were working on multiplication, and it was not immediately clicking for me. Perhaps realizing that everything had been presented abstractly thus far, my sister decided to take a different approach. She went to the kitchen and gathered some objects – a spatula, a whisk, and the like. She put the items on the surface of our makeshift table, one of those old-fashioned wood console stereo systems. Placing three items on the top of the stereo, she asked me, "How many items are on the stereo?" I accurately responded that there were three items. Then, she did something that made *the* difference in my understanding. She placed another set of three of kitchen items on the stereo and asked me how many items were there. Though growing slightly frustrated with both my own struggles and the time my sister's demonstration was taking to unfold, I responded with exasperation that there were now six items on the stereo. And, it happened – it all made sense. She pointed out that six was the answer to the multiplication problem of 2 x 3 and then explained that the three items in each of the two piles she had created represented the "3" in the multiplication problem and that the two piles represented the "2." Then, she threw on the secret sauce – she pointed out how we could reverse these designations by making three piles of two items each. I got it! I understood multiplication conceptually. In the long term, that turned out to be a technique and a situation that provided me with a level of confidence that stopped me fearing math at the level that many do. Granted, I simply could have memorized the multiplication charts, but now I understood the concept at a very young age. It set me up for success.

We have discussed in earlier chapters how important an awareness of the techniques used by the best performers can be. These are often identified by researchers and coaches attempting to identify the activities the performer engaged in along their path in order to extract and share this information (Harris & Eccles, 2021). Having these techniques can be extremely valuable for both trainers and trainees. Techniques are vetted, and the ones resulting in performance gains are retained. The techniques not resulting in performance gains are discarded.

Performers might also develop their own techniques as they navigate domain requirements. However, this typically requires that the performer is already familiar with common techniques allowing them to reach a given level of performance. While this approach can be useful if the performer is able to identify techniques that improve performance, using the techniques already deemed successful might end up saving valuable training time. Knowledge of established techniques can come from the extraction processes mentioned earlier in this section or by informal channels from the performers themselves: for example, you have a conversation with them, and they are willing to reveal their techniques. However, as we discuss in Chapter 4, there are competitive reasons for performers not always sharing their techniques. It also is possible that these casual exchanges are attempts to sabotage your development (again, giving them a competitive edge).

Nevertheless, awareness of improvement techniques is critical. It is rare that someone will improve without some basic knowledge of what to do. Even my earlier example of learning to play tennis with limited resources, playing at a public park with a discarded, outdated tennis racquet, was supplemented by the poster of proper technique. My friend and I had to "wing it" and never really knew if we were doing it correctly, but we did have the picture with a description of what it should look like. The bottom line is that limited or no awareness of the techniques required for a domain will make it more likely that you give up.

"I didn't make it to 12, but I got 11" – The Potential Impact of Goals on Not Giving Up

Goal setting and whether we end up giving up can go hand in hand. On one hand, if we accomplish a goal, we feel satisfied, and we likely will move on to the next goal. On the other hand, if we fail at accomplishing a goal, we may get stuck in a negative frame of mind where giving up feels like the only way out. We discuss the process and benefits of goal setting extensively in Chapter 9. The discussion in Chapter 9 includes the importance of feedback in assessing goal progress, the different types of goals, and the ongoing discussion as to the benefit of goal-setting. For the current chapter, we will discuss goal-setting through the lens of how it has been used for some time.

One way we can attempt to help prevent giving up on a pursuit is to create small goals leading to the larger, final goal and outcome. Dr. Edwin Locke and Gary Latham are the pioneers of goal-setting theory, which defines a goal as something we are consciously trying to do (Locke & Latham, 1990), and they spent decades studying the impact of goals and goal-setting on performance (e.g., Locke & Latham, 2002). You are making goals almost nonstop, even when you do not recognize it – brushing your teeth, making a sandwich for lunch, and stopping to refuel are all goals. We often do not recognize them as such because they are typically achievable within a short timeframe. You are likely to only recognize them as goals when something goes awry. For example, you run out of toothpaste on a holiday and cannot find a store, or you cannot get to the place you had calculated being able to reach because you are out of fuel. *Are you kidding me?!*

Suddenly, these typically simple tasks are recognized as goals because you now have to figure out how to reach them while working around an unexpected obstacle. Granted, most of us are talking about goals of a different type when we mention our goals, but it is important to recognize the scope of the term. Let us now consider goals in the traditional sense and how goal-setting might help us stay with our pursuits.

One way is that goals often increase motivation, especially when smaller steps – goals along the way – are successfully completed while working toward a larger goal, sometimes the end result. However, goals should have specific features to increase the likelihood that they strengthen our performance (Locke & Latham, 1990). Goals should be specific, be difficult but attainable, and have deadlines. Examples of this would be Jamal writing at least 20 pages of his dissertation by the end of every week for 11 months, or Kimberly increasing her running distance by one mile every month until she reaches the 26.2 miles (42.195 km) required to run a marathon. Again, we dig more deeply into the process of goal setting in Chapter 9. For now, we will mention that it can be a great feeling when we finally accomplish one of our goals!

This sense of accomplishment can serve as motivation to continue our pursuits, and we likely will continue to create and work on future goals.

A Little Bit of This and a Lot of That – The Impact of Competing Goals

I remember standing on the stage, thinking, "A standing ovation. Wow! Maybe there is something to me doing this stand-up thing." I was excited. Later that evening, the headlining comic who followed my performance inquired whether I would be interested in becoming a full-time stand-up comic. She offered to connect me with her management team. Needless to say, I was very flattered. A career in comedy had always been on my radar. I reveled in making my friends and classmates laugh throughout my childhood, and I was pretty good at doing so. After a debate broke out over who was the most hilarious classmate in sixth grade, it was ultimately resolved by a student-led vote. I came in as second funniest classmate. It stung a tad to not be in first place, but I was happy with it. My peers voted me second, after all. It would be over a decade before I attempted to transfer this penchant for getting laughs into the art of stand-up comedy on stage, when I finally made my debut in front of an audience after honing my set of jokes for months with a karaoke machine. A fellow comic who would go on to be a writer for NBC's *Saturday Night Live* pulled me aside to tell me how well written my jokes were and encourage me to stick with it. So, when I finally got the offer to do stand-up comedy for a living while simultaneously being offered access to a management team, I declined.

You presumably found the conclusion of the previous scenario to be jarring. Why would I turn down such an opportunity? It was very difficult not to consider the potential upside of taking the offer – eventually performing at arenas and making feature films. However, I was within a couple of years of earning my doctorate and had already invested a tremendous amount of time in rigorous academic programs. This meant moving across multiple states and living on the earnings of a graduate student and whatever employment my wife had secured. I was leaning toward dedicating my time and energy to finishing my PhD. At least this way, I likely would be earning a consistent paycheck in a few years. Besides, there already had been a tremendous investment made in pursuing the PhD. On top of that, road comics must travel long distances to performance venues and may only be on stage for an hour or less. This would obviously require significant spans of time away from home. And, finally, overhearing a headliner with recognizable credits in the entertainment industry asking for additional gigs just to cover living expenses solidified my decision to decline the offer.

This example might seem counter to the message of the book. Specifically, why did I not take the opportunity if I had wanted to be a stand-up comic in the past? The short explanation is that I had already made significant strides toward a different goal by the time I received the offer to become a professional stand-up comic. I was fully immersed in obtaining my doctorate and knew that I could not pursue both goals. If anything, I felt that I had a better chance of pursuing both academia and comedy if I finished the doctoral program first.

This situation with competing goals illustrates how conflict can arise as we work toward goal attainment. Researchers have identified two types of conflict relevant to the current discussion: inherent conflict and resource conflict (Segerstorm & Nes, 2006). When creating goals, typically we have more than one goal we are working toward. Inherent conflict occurs when we are progressing toward one goal, which in turn, increases difficulty in attaining another. In other words, some things cannot happen simultaneously because of the inherent nature of it – think of the phrase "it is black and white." Something cannot simultaneously be both black and white, and someone cannot be the class clown and also be the quiet one. Resource conflict, however, arises when there are limited resources to attain a specific goal. Any goal pursuit consuming the available resources will reduce the capacity available to pursue a different goal. Time spent on the road travelling to stand-up comedy gigs will diminish time available to be successful in the doctoral program or even be at home with family. How can these conflicts be resolved?

"I Don't Mess With That Stuff Anymore" – Resolving Goal Conflicts

Ian had always dreamed of playing in football's (soccer's) highest level, The Premier League. He had been under development since he was a very young player. Moreover, he had performed very well on the pitch against the early competition he faced growing up. Unfortunately, Ian did not grow as tall as he had hoped. He was staying roughly the same size while the other players were hitting growth spurts or adding weight to match their newfound height. Ian was a skilled enough player to continue advancing, even though he was losing ground as the others grew taller and stronger. However, he realized it was becoming increasingly unlikely that he would move much higher than his current tier. Ian had watched players he dominated when they were younger become physically dominant players in their current tier and ultimately advance. He did not want to give up on football altogether and used his contacts to secure a coaching gig working with a respected head coach.

Ian's example of pivoting his goals from being a player at the highest level to coaching demonstrates an idea referred to as accommodation of a goal pursuit (Brandstädter & Renner, 1990). The players who continued on their original path were undoubtedly presented with ever increasing demands required to continue to advance. Successfully encountering and navigating such increasing requirements can be referred to as assimilation in a goal pursuit. Scholars think of these as tendencies we demonstrate – either accommodative or assimilative tendencies. With the assimilative tendency, we try to modify the situation to line up with our goal. In general terms, we stick with our initial plan/goal as much as possible and absorb (assimilate) the new demands as we encounter them: for example when facing speedier competition, we focus on improving our own overall speed or reaction time. The pre-med student encountering difficult courses might develop new study strategies or carve out additional time for a particularly difficult class (we are looking at you, *Organic Chemistry*). They might also seek out other ways to enhance the chances of reaching their goals, for example, by seeking opportunities to engage in high impact practices to further hone their skills or fostering relationships with faculty who could provide coaching or helpful insight.

Pivoting to a different goal would represent the accommodative tendency. This often happens when we determine our original goal is not realistic for us or we no longer are willing to invest in pursuing it. Ian disengaged from the goal of being a footballer in The Premier League and redirected his resources to becoming a coach. The pre-med student could disengage from the goal of attending medical school and change their major to a similar subject area of interest. A more extreme pivot would be giving up on any pursuits related to the original goal. An example of an extreme pivot would be leaving the domains of football and academia altogether and becoming a customer service representative for a major cell phone company. No wonder this accommodation process has been proposed to result in disorientation and depression (e.g., Brandstädter & Renner, 1990). Presumably, the newly refined goals will be the least disruptive when they end up as close to the original goal as possible – Ian coaching rather than playing football or Kevin being able to insert humor into his lectures rather than being a stand-up comic.

However, the decision to pivot or abandon goals is often a lengthy process that unfolds over time. The scholarly work on this process was spearheaded by the same researcher leading the research discussed in the preceding paragraphs, Jochen Brandstätter (Brandstätter, Hermann, & Schüler, 2013). We often will encounter an action crisis when working toward our goals. Action crises can be thought of as circumstances in which you have invested a great deal of effort and resources into your goal, but suffer from ongoing or major setbacks. We may go from being optimistic to pessimistic, and have an increase in goal-related doubt and a decrease in psychological and physiological well-being. The conflict arises between having invested just enough to not want to take the losses resulting from giving up, but being unsure about or unwilling to continue to sink further resources into the goal. This situation can lead to either reducing the value we place on the goal or assessing whether goal attainment is even a realistic possibility.

"Sure, I Can Do That" – Fake It 'Til You Make It?

My stepfather decided to teach me to drive a vehicle with a manual transmission (a stick-shift), which typically requires some practice to get the hang of. I was growing a little frustrated with the process. Around the same time, he was painting a storage building and placed a stepladder in the back of his pick-up to reach the walls located just below the apex roof (*disclaimer: do not attempt anything described in this scenario yourself*). As if that was not unorthodox enough, he wanted me to drive the truck around the building while he stood on the ladder in the truck bed. I honestly hoped he was trying to get a laugh, and I was thinking there was no way this would actually happen. I was not yet comfortable or skilled, and the jerking from not releasing the clutch smoothly would surely not have a good outcome. Fearing the worst-case scenario, I vehemently protested but found myself sitting behind the wheel preparing to move the truck – with my stepdad standing on the ladder in the back. "I trust you," he said. Shockingly, I released the clutch with absolutely no issues, and I was both surprised and relieved. From that day forward, I was able to drive a stick-shift vehicle.

What about *fake it until you make it*? We have likely all heard this phrase. If we have doubts about an upcoming situation or are not prepared to do something, this is a fairly common piece of advice. But, what exactly does it mean? We turned to the high performers we interviewed to help us uncover what the phrase meant to them. Three themes emerged from the interviews: a) pushing beyond your comfort zone, b) keeping yourself/trainee in a domain or situation long enough to gain self-confidence, and c) a negative connotation of putting up a front or being "fake."

The first interpretation, situations in which you are being asked to do something new or just above your current level, was explained by Thomas Estrada, the film and video game animator, through an example from when he was asked to produce a piece of art for the legendary band, the *Foo Fighters*:

> I got a gig working with the Foo Fighters, and they needed the artwork I was doing in a particular format for their production needs that I had no idea about. I was like, "Absolutely." And then I hung up the phone. I was like, 'okay, what does that mean?' I jotted that down. I'm like, okay, how do I do this? I had no idea. But, I thought 'I'm not going to let that stop me.' Fortunately. we live in the information age where I can get online. And so yeah, I don't know if that ever, if that ever stops, you know. So, there's always those times when things come up like that where it's like, "I'm just going to have to figure this out." You know?

Mark Johnson, cofounder of Hobnail Trekking Co., shared a similar example of combining his songwriting experience with his upbringing on a farm to produce a writing sample needed for a job interview with a national farming magazine. These examples suggest that, while we might initially feel uncomfortable with new or unknown aspects of the situation, successfully moving forward with completing the task can reduce or remove the feeling of "faking it."

The second interpretation is to keep yourself, or a trainee, in a domain long enough to gain self-confidence or reduce self-doubt. Often, when we are starting a new position or a new sport, or performing for the first time, we do not necessarily "know" with confidence whether we are doing something correctly or not. It is critical to not allow this lack of confidence to derail us because putting in the time to get better is critical to becoming really good at something. High-performance researcher, Joe Baker, noted, "Competence comes from participation." These early stages can be thought of as applying what we have learned to new situations; essentially, we are faking it (by taking what we have previously learned) until we make it (becoming confident in doing what we are doing; Gunder, 2010).

Fundamentally, this is a way of persevering through the early stages of an endeavor (Nielsen, 2015). We are figuring out what works for us in real-time – faking it until we make it our own. We might know where we want to get, but we have a long way to go. The amount of time you choose to invest or the long-term choice not to give up a pursuit will begin with these initial experiences. Joe Baker adds, "Get them coming back the next day because they love what they're doing. They enjoy what they're doing, because if they do that, you probably have solved the competence. The "fake until you make it" [concept] sounds like the same kind of a thing – you fake it because it keeps you coming back. And you coming back is the thing that eventually leads to you making it, which from one perspective, is straight-up deliberate practice."

The third interpretation of putting up a front or "being fake" is the interpretation with a negative connotation. Hip-hop artist Brian Brown captured this sentiment:

> Try that or just make it look like this, make it like that. But, it's like, why would you? Why would you not make it real, so somebody can know what they're dealing with? You faking? Anybody who might be trying to follow in your footsteps, or is in the same world, might not know exactly what's coming to them.

He added, "To me it's lying, and I don't like lying. I have no reason to fake anything."

In the context of facing challenges that could lead to giving up, we encourage you to heed this solid advice. You might experience self-doubt or feel unqualified when encountering new tasks or opportunities. These thoughts can lead to you experiencing some unpleasant feelings/emotions (see Chapter 8 on how our perceptions of these feelings can influence the outcome). Pushing through these thoughts and feelings or sticking around until you realize that you are capable is key. The feelings of self-doubt should be minimized once we achieve some small successes. Many of us will be prone to self-doubt as we discussed in the chapter on impostor syndrome (Chapter 3). However, if it happens to a Nobel Laureate, then it can happen to anyone at any phase. It is not a cue to stop.

"Year 43 of Acting Will Finally Be My Big Break"

Being good at something takes a lot of work and investment of resources. At the very least, you will have invested your time. Some performers will exit a domain quickly, and others will stick with it for a long time. In any domain, there will be a tremendous amount of competition and rejection (Chapter 7) along the way. The investments into and experiences of pursuing success in a domain can lead us to feel that we cannot give up because we do not want what we already have invested, or the experiences we endured, to be in vain. The numerous stories we have shared demonstrate how individuals overcame obstacles they faced to find success. We highlighted the experiences of a variety of folks accomplishing some amazing things – world tours, successful businesses, and renowned scholarship. Your favorite professor? It is likely they did not get their job on the first try. Rather, they most likely went through many interviews at different schools before landing a job. It would not make sense for you to drop out of college a credit short or bail on your business without giving it time to flourish. However, as we discussed, sometimes we must make accommodations for our goals when things do not go as planned.

Sometimes, such accommodations can be just what we need. Ian was able to coach football even though he could no longer play. So, we can think about the term "giving up" in a different way. While often stigmatized, it can lead to a positive, if unforeseen, outcome. If we truly know that something is not for us, we should consider moving on. For example, being miserable in a career but sticking with it is not healthy. While we may give up on a specific iteration of a goal, we are also able to decide that we would like to set a new goal. The accommodative tendency allows us to step back and determine a new path. We ultimately should be as happy as possible with the decisions we are making.

The aforementioned conflict that comes with shifting goals when we have invested time and resources. This can lead us to sometimes stick with a pursuit longer than we reasonably should because we want the sacrifices to be worth it. This phenomenon has been dubbed the "sunk cost fallacy" by scholars (e.g., Friedman et al., 2007). We often feel a need to recoup our investment, despite the negative impact it might have on us. For example, if you have invested life savings in a failing business, you may try to keep it open when, by objective measures, it should have been shuttered. Hopefully, you would eventually recoup your investment, right? To be clear, we encourage you to stick with your plans during the tough stretches. That can be considered part of the process. However, sacrificing your well-being would not be worth it, and it is up to each individual to determine when that point has been reached.

It makes sense that we are prone to thinking this way. If you have spent years or decades pursuing something, it can be an odd experience to suddenly give up. We often see examples of those who stayed with something "just long enough" for it to work out. Despite such examples, there are also individuals stuck in perpetual "near-success experiences." Hobnail Trekking's Mark Johnson described such an experience:

> I was on a trajectory. I was working with big producers and publishing companies in Nashville, so when I rerecorded my last album, everybody that was involved with me thought that this was going to be the thing that was going to get me a major-label record deal. And then, things were going to move on from there. That didn't happen, and it disillusioned me to the point at which I said, 'you know what, I'm done with the music industry. I've given it everything, and I was just wiped out.'

Mark had to decide whether he should stick with his original goal of becoming a musical artist signed to a record deal or move on. He ultimately decided to move on, "Either I'm going to stop and do something else, or I'm going to be an old guy playing *Brown Eyed Girl* and *Margaritaville* in clubs when I'm 60 years old, and I don't want to do that. I do not want to be that guy. So, I quit that." As a reminder, he is now a successful entrepreneur

Chapter Summary

In this chapter we discussed the importance of not giving up and the variety of terms used to describe sticking with a goal over the long term. We also revisited how the lingering default societal views of high performers, the access to resources, and the act of setting goals can each influence whether we do give up. We discussed the concept of "fake it 'til you make it" and shared the themes identified when we asked the high performers what the concept means to them: a) pushing beyond your comfort zone, b) keeping yourself/trainee in a domain or situation long enough to gain self-confidence, and c) a negative connotation of putting up a front or being "fake." Finally, we considered that it is sometimes healthier to give up on a pursuit, even when there already have been significant investments.

Keep Pushing!

Chapter 5: *Giving Up: I Should Just Quit*

This exercise is intended to help you identify some "bail out" phrases to help you get past the inevitable moments when you will consider giving up. In the **first part** of the exercise, you will be asked to write down instances where you were successful prior to reaching the point of wanting to give up. The **second part** will ask you to identify some phrases you can use when the voices in your head start telling you to give up.

1. You have done many things well to get to the point at which you might consider giving up. Please provide at least three examples of things you have done well that preceded feelings of wanting to give up.

2. Think of at least one phrase you can use to replace the thoughts of quitting as they begin to appear.

Note

1 In the spirit of transparency, there were equally strong attempts to attribute the performance abilities of the highest-level performers to the nurture side of the spectrum (e.g., Ericsson, Roring, & Nandagopal, 2007). Most scholars in this area, ourselves included, have proposed that we move on from these types of comparisons (e.g., Hambrick et al., 2016; Ward et al., 2017) and work to uncover the subtleties of how the world's best performers get to where they are.

References

Brandtstädter, J., & Renner, G. (1990). Tenacious goal pursuit and flexible goal adjustment: Explication and age-related analysis of assimilative and accommodative strategies of coping. *Psychology and Aging, 5*(1), 58–67.

Brandstätter, V., Hermann, M., & Schüler, J. (2013). The struggle of giving up personal goals: Affective, physiological, and cognitive consequences of an action crisis. *Personality and Social Psychology Bulletin, 39*, 1668–1682. https://www.doi.org/10.1177/0146167213500151.

Credé, M., Tynan, M.C., & Harms, P.D. (2017). Much ado about grit: A meta-analytic synthesis of the grit literature. *Journal of Personality and Social Psychology, 113*(3), 492–511. https://doi.org/10.1037/pspp0000102.

Dahl, M. (2014) Don't believe the hype About grit, pleads the scientist behind the concept. *New York Magazine: The Cut.* https://www.thecut.com/2016/05/dont-believe-the-hype-about-grit-pleads-the-scientist-behind-the-concept.html. Accessed January 24, 2024.

Duckworth, A.L., & Quinn, P.D. (2009). Development and validation of the Short Grit Scale (GRIT–S). *Journal of Personality Assessment, 91* (2), 166–174. https://doi.org/10.1080/00223890802634290.

Duckworth, A.L., Peterson, C., Matthews, M.D., & Kelly, D.R. (2007). Grit: Perseverance and passion for long-term goals. *Journal of Personality and Social Psychology, 92*(6), 1087–1101. https://doi.org/10.1037/0022-3514.92.6.1087.

Dweck, C.S. (2006). *Mindset.* Random House.

Ericsson, K.A., Roring, R.W., & Nandagopal, K. (2007). Giftedness and evidence for reproducibly superior performance: An account based on the expert performance framework. *High Ability Studies, 18*, 3–56. https://doi. org/10.1080/13598130701350593.

Friedman, D., Pommerenke, K., Lukose, R., Milam, G., & Huberman, B.A. (2007). Searching for the sunk cost fallacy. *Experimental Economics, 10*, 79–104. https://doi.org/10.1007/s10683-006-9134-0.

Gunder, M. (2010). Fake it until you make it, and then …. *Planning Theory, 10*, 201–212. https://doi.org/10.1177/1473095210387542.

Hambrick D.Z., Macnamara B.N., Campitelli G., Ullén F., Mosing M.A. (2016). Beyond born versus made: A new look at expertise. In Ross B.H. (Ed.), *The psychology of learning and motivation* (Vol. 64, pp. 1–55). San Diego, CA: Academic Press.

Harris, K.R., & Eccles, D.W. (2021). Training derived from expert performers: The extractable components of deliberate practice and the expert performance approach. *Journal of Expertise, 4* (2), 234–247. https:// www.journalofexpertise.org/articles/Volume4_issue2/JoE_4_2_Harris_ Eccles.pdf.

Jachimowicz, J.M., Wihler, A., Bailey, E.R., & Galinsky, A.D. (2018). Why grit requires perseverance and passion to positively predict performance. *Proceedings of the National Academy of Sciences, 115*(40), 9980–9985. https:// doi.org/10.1073/pnas.1803561115.

Locke, E.A., & Latham, G.P. (1990). *A theory of goal setting and task performance*. Prentice Hall.

Locke, E.A., & Latham, G.P. (2002). Building a practically useful theory of goal setting and task motivation: A 35-year odyssey. *American Psychologist, 57*(9), 705–717. https://doi.org/10.1037/0003-066X.57.9.705.

Nielsen, K. (2015). "Fake it 'til you make it": Why community college students' aspirations "hold stead". *Sociology of Education, 88*, 265–283. https://doi. org/10.1177/0038040715601889.

Segerstrom, S.C., & Nes, L.S. (2006). When goals conflict but people prosper: The case of dispositional optimism. *Journal of Research in Personality, 40*(5), 675–693. https://doi.org/10.1016/j.jrp.2005.08.001.

Ward, P., Belling, P., Petushek, E., & Ehrlinger, J. (2017). Does talent exist? A re-evaluation of the nature–nurture debate. In J. Baker, S. Cobley, J. Schorer, & N. Wattie (Eds.), *Routledge Handbook of Talent Identification and Development in Sport* (pp. 19–34). Routledge. https://doi.org/10.4324/ 9781315668017-3.

Limiting Your Scope   **6**
Think Like a Kid

I didn't have anyone telling me to think of a realistic goal. People never put limitations on me.

– Lauren Regula, Olympian and professional athlete
(on *The Path Distilled* podcast)

Create the highest, grandest vision for your life because you become what you believe.

– Oprah Winfrey

Josh was interested in starting his own clothing line, which would feature original designs to market in the highly competitive clothing market. He began securing funding, sourcing materials, designing the clothes, and identifying a manufacturer. Josh's clothes finally hit the market after much initiative, planning, and work – the critical thing is that Josh is 14 years old. There were plenty of voices throughout this process telling Josh not to continue with his plans, or to wait until he was older. Josh obviously did not listen.

The opening vignette is based on an actual event. In this chapter, we discuss the obstacle of limiting your scope, or setting the bar too low for yourself, and the power of thinking like a child. This does not mean that one should flippantly pursue any impulse that comes to mind, but often, the voices telling us to lower our bar are those inside

DOI: 10.4324/9781003377542-6

our own head. We often discourage those around us from thinking too grandiosely when deciding what they want to accomplish. Phrases like "pie in the sky" are used to describe ambitious pursuits, and the pursuits themselves often are dismissed as child-like naivete. Despite such dismissals, it is often the performers who never let go of grandiose pursuits who end up accomplishing them. Because we discuss both imposing limitations on oneself and goal-setting in this chapter, let us take time to distinguish the purpose of this chapter from those of Chapter 4: Artificial Ceilings and Chapter 9: Being Vague, which focus heavily on goal setting, before fully diving in.

The most straightforward way to think of the distinctions between the content of the chapters would be that Chapter 4 focuses on how perceptions of artificial ceilings shape beliefs about one's own limitations and whether a pursuit should even be undertaken. While there is overlap between Chapter 4 and the current chapter, the emphasis of this chapter is not aiming too low once embarking on a path. For example, Chapter 4 might consider that Jason thinks that he would never be capable of sewing well enough to be the costume designer for the local high school play (the artificial ceiling). The present chapter, Chapter 6, considers that Jason should not limit his scope and can reasonably consider pursuing a goal that most consider unrealistic – becoming a Hollywood wardrobe designer or creating his own clothing line. Finally, Chapter 9 emphasizes that, in addition to lofty ambitions and the ability to create amazing clothing, Jason also will need a roadmap to success.

It is not surprising that we often end up limiting the scope of our ultimate goals. There are multiple reasons for this ranging from individual differences in achievement seeking (see Chapter 2) to the shaming of someone with ambitious goals. As noted in the earlier chapters, societal views, fixed mindsets, and a lack of knowledge about how to get there are also limitations. Additionally, we will discuss the stigma and misunderstandings that have accompanied the concept of "ambition" in the sections below – the differences in how ambition has been viewed throughout human history are noteworthy and the magnitude of the disdain was surprising. The chapter also includes discussions about how we might go about comparing ourselves to others to gauge our own status and the risk of not taking opportunities we deem to be beneath our current status.

"Too Big for Your Britches" (and My Tattered Self-esteem)

A fellow graduate student of mine, Monte, shared a story of having grown up on a farm. He worked the farm with his family throughout his childhood and was mostly neutral about the line of work. However, Monte felt a drive to attend the nearby Florida State University to try his hand at preparing for a different line of work. He submitted his application and waited as patiently as he could; any day could be the day that the admittance letter arrived. Finally, it came. Monte had been accepted! As he began walking the long gravel driveway back to his house, he was thinking about whom he should tell first after his parents. About that time, a neighbor driving down the road slowed to a stop to chat with Monte. Monte decided in the moment to go ahead and share, "I was just accepted to Florida State," while holding up the letter. The response from his neighbor left him speechless, "I thought you were a good boy!"

There is something embedded in the fabric of the culture of the southeastern region of the US that discourages sharing lofty goals. This is likely also the case in other places, but this example is one with which I am intimately familiar. Although it could also refer to someone – often a child – misbehaving, the phrase, "too big for your/ their britches" was commonly used when someone shared aspirations that seemed too grand for others in that particular community. Its meaning is similar to the pejorative phrase "forgetting where you came from" if success is realized. These examples illustrate that not everyone is rooting for the success of others. Could it be that observing someone achieve great accomplishments, or even express aspirations to do so, is a threat to the self-esteem of some witnessing it play out?

One of the world's best-known scholars, Roy Baumeister, and his colleagues spent considerable time studying a version of this question, fundamentally asking, what are the consequences of both low self-esteem, and more generally, what happens when someone's self-esteem is threatened? Their work could provide insight into why not everyone is rooting for you to be successful. In an extensive review, the scholars countered the view that low self-esteem was a primary cause of violent behavior by arguing that threats to someone's positive view of themselves were more likely a cause of violence and aggression

(Baumeister, Smart, & Boden, 1996). This explanation makes intuitive sense on an interpersonal level and likely can explain the tenuous relationship with, and often negative societal perception of, ambition described in the coming sections.

In a follow-up laboratory test of the idea that violence and aggression were likely to result from a threat to someone's positive self-view (egotism), researchers either boosted or diminished the participants' egos by providing either positive or negative fake feedback on an essay that was written by the participant (Bushman & Baumeister, 1998). Relative to praised participants, the insulted participants subsequently aggressed the person believed to be the source of the feedback by blasting them with an unpleasant noise at a higher decibel level and for longer. Thus, it is not a stretch to assume that observing someone else do well, potentially accomplishing things that the observer may have strived to accomplish themselves, could be a threat to one's ego. Someone doing particularly well, with a collection of accumulated accomplishments, could threaten the ego of many.

More generally, ambition has historically been met with scorn. For example, Timothy A. Judge and John D. Kammeyer-Mueller, two scholars whose work falls at the intersection of business and psychology, provided a brief historical overview on how ambition has been historically viewed (2012). Their analysis suggests that lofty ambition has historically been seen as a negative. Perhaps naively, we found this negative connotation surprising – after all, this is a book on not limiting yourself! Nevertheless, some comments they collected for their work suggest that ambition generally might have been viewed as a vice, at least among philosophers. However, Judge and Kammeyer-Mueller sought to distinguish the role of ambition from achievement motivation for success. The scholars believed that much of the controversy stemmed from the lack of a clear definition of the terms.

To summarize their assessment, ambition is considered to be a general aspiration for success in life, which is distinct from achievement motivation, a desire to be good at something regardless of external rewards. Much of the prior work on the distinction between achievement motivation and ambition suggested that achievement motivation enhanced the likelihood of satisfaction as compared to ambition, presumably because the desire is to be good at something without consideration of what will come from our efforts. However, the need to make the distinction might not be as strong as initially proposed, as the researchers found that greater ambition led to greater educational and work success, which appeared to enhance overall life-satisfaction (Judge & Kammeyer-Mueller, 2012).

Discovering that this distinction had been made so adamantly, and has been the center of a debate lasting centuries, came as another huge surprise. Understandably, too much or misaligned ambition falls within the realm of mental health disorders (e.g., Yager & Kay, 2023). However, we will be using ambition in a positive sense – *without* the historical baggage. For us, ambition is not limiting your scope when deciding what might be possible. An aspirational author or baseball player should not feel shame when stating that they hope to have a best-selling book or make it to the major leagues, particularly if they are willing to take the steps to move closer to such a goal. As noted by Olympian and professional athlete Lauren Regula in her opening quotation (Harris & Tashman, 2021), limitations were not placed upon her, and she ultimately benefitted from it. It is remarkable that her sibling, Jason Bay, was a long-time professional baseball player. It is relatively unusual to have two siblings from a small town both reach the pinnacle of their domains, particularly in sports. Thus, the distinction between wanting to be the best at something and desiring the outcome associated with being the best will not be made for our purposes.

Aiming for the Stars and Hitting the Trees – The Role of Counterfactual Thinking

Standing on the platform as they drape your bronze medal around your neck, the feeling of pride washes over you. You did not end up with a gold or silver medal, but you *did* medal. Not to mention the field of competitors you bested to make it to this point. It is one of the biggest accomplishments of your life. You look around with the hope of remembering as much of this moment as possible. The gold medalist appears to also be taking in the moment and seems as proud as you are. Moving your gaze beyond the gold medalist, you see something surprising – the silver medalist is almost inconsolable. Rather than celebrating and savoring the moment, they are emotionally distraught.

This counterintuitive scenario was the topic of a series of research studies that determined that bronze medalists were typically happier than silver medalists with their placement (Medvec, Madey, & Gilovich, 1995). The reason? Their frame of reference. The silver medalists felt that they just missed finishing in first place – "second place is the first loser." On the other hand, the bronze medalists were using the frame of reference that they were the last competitors to reach the threshold for being awarded a medal. To reiterate, the silver medalist (second place) bested a greater number of opponents than the bronze medalist (third place) but felt comparatively less enthusiastic.

This example begs the question as to how someone generally compares themselves to others to ascertain their status and potentially gauge progress toward their goals. The evidence strongly suggests that we tend to compare ourselves to those with higher status – an upward comparison (Weingarten, Davidai, & Barasch, 2023). This is understandable as most of us are aspiring to move to a better position in relation to our goals, with the possible exception of your slacker cousin and similar others. Because we are seeking to move up the pro-verbial ladder, these comparisons allow us to judge where we currently stand in relation to others. However, this line of research on upward and downward comparisons is vast, and the direction of comparison depends on a variety of factors.

Let us discuss a limited selection of the relevant factors in this vast array of research. We have already discussed the impact placing second versus third can have on which direction a comparison is made. Another determining factor of whether someone will make an upward or down-ward comparison is where they fall in the general tiers (upper, middle, bottom) of a particular field (Weingarten, Davidai, & Barasch, 2023). For example, we tend to want to avoid being last at anything – dubbed "last place aversion" (Kuziemko et al., 2014). As with the medalists, this phenomenon does not always make logical sense. For example, the last pick of the National Football League (NFL), a professional American-style football league, is noted each year; the pick is dubbed, "Mr. Irrelevant." However, there are thousands of other free agent or unsigned prospects on the market for a spot who would have loved to be drafted in any position.

Thus, it seems that benchmarks of any kind can serve as demarca-tion points influencing those we select for comparison. Presumably, this would function within the tiers themselves in the sense of asking, "where do I fall?", when reflecting on your place within the upper, middle, or lower tiers. Many of us will strive to be at the top of our respective tiers, which would keep the next closest tier within reach. Someone presently in the top tier would be striving to be the best of all competitors. However, as already mentioned, there is a strong mental component to how the comparison is made. Thus, in alignment with ideas underlying "last place aversion," someone ranking near the bottom of a tier might make a downward comparison instead (e.g., Garcia, Tor, & Gonzalez, 2006). This could be the performer in the 95th slot looking at the 96th–100th performers. Similarly, even someone who is typically nonchalant with their performances might make an all-out effort to avoid being last – the aforementioned last place aversion (Kuziemko et al., 2014).

This downward comparison might also be a buffer that minimizes the blow to someone's self-esteem that could occur from relatively low performance. By making the comparison to performers ending up in a worse position than themselves, one can convince themselves that they were at least better than someone else – the "at least I am not that guy" approach. The good news is that this type of comparison can work to reduce the blow to self-esteem. However, keep in mind that success is a relative concept – the second-place finisher was ahead of all but one competitor, but as discussed, can feel less successful than the third-place finisher.

The relative nature of success was made crystal clear in a conversation I had with Katie Cole, who appears throughout the book. Katie is a successful singer-songwriter and touring member of the legendary rock band, *The Smashing Pumpkins*. I commented that the podcast I created and cohosted, *The Path Distilled*, had, at the time, just reached its 66th country for listeners. Katie had been a guest on the podcast, and I wanted her to know our reach was strong. Katie's response was something along the lines of "do not be discouraged by the reach." I was initially puzzled but quickly realized that she tours the world with one of the better-known bands of all time. Not only that, their reach through online streaming services and sales would extend to all of the countries of the world – roughly tripling that of *The Path Distilled* podcast. Her sincere and supportive comments were based on her experiences in the upper tier of the music industry. The message of this story is that the reach of the podcast still can be celebrated while striving to land listeners in the remaining countries. Success does not exist in a vacuum. There are myriad factors at play as to how we view our own success and how others view us. It is inevitable that some will be threatened by our success while others will not. Similarly, some will be supportive of our success, and others might actively attempt to counter it.

The bottom line is that focusing on others, regardless of whether they are supportive or not, can be counterproductive. The best approach is to focus on the tasks in front of you – the ones that you must do to get to where you want to be. Recording artist Stephanie Quayle shared this sentiment – a great metaphor – on *The Path Distilled* podcast:

> I remember running the marathon, and it was mile 19 [of] 26.2. I remember it so vividly because I remember there was a moment where it was just like, 'OK should I just call it? No one's going to really know if I finish.' You go through all these things in your mind where you convince yourself it's okay to quit, and I remember I'm slowing down a little bit. And I looked to my right, and I looked to my left now. Not quick, like, I turned my neck both ways, and it slowed me down, paying attention and focusing on the people passing me (Harris & Tashman, 2020).

This also could factor into the collective shaming described earlier, as each person from your own personal environment accomplishes something impressive, another can be demoted in the accomplishment hierarchy – Jamal overtook you in annual sales, or you lose your top spot in the local table-tennis rankings. This will lead some "competitors" to actively root against you. In extreme cases, competitors might go as far as attempting to sabotage your performance. Such examples reflect explicit efforts to shame, or even damage, the standing of other performers.

However, a related consideration is that this compulsion to shame might not even be recognized by those attempting to shame you. Humans are really good at maintaining a positive self-view, even when the evidence doesn't support it – "I'm [cute, funny, attractive, athletic, charming, a great conversationalist]," or too many more to list. A clever study by Yu Niiya and colleagues demonstrated just how seemingly inclined we are to maintain this positive self-image when it is associated with something of importance to us (Niiya, Brook,

& Crocker, 2012). Their surprising findings suggest that individuals with growth mindsets, who are personally invested in a domain, will engage in behaviors that minimize the blame they would attribute to themselves if they were to fail. For example, when presented with very difficult problems, participants whose academic performance was important to their self-worth were more likely to self-handicap by intentionally selecting music labelled as "highly distracting" or pass up practice opportunities altogether. Such choices provide an opportunity to blame poor performance on the distracting music, or lack of practice. These unexpected findings – that individuals with a growth mindset were eager to protect their self-worth when the tasks were related to areas that were personally relevant and the task was difficult – changed the way that scholars viewed the differences between those with fixed versus growth mindsets.

The findings of Niiya and colleagues make sense when considered within the realm of high performance. If one is participating in a competitive domain, a tremendous investment of resources is to be expected. The competition only increases as one progresses through the ranks. Making your way through the competitive ranks is tough – really tough. Impostor syndrome (Chapter 3) and self-doubt are real phenomena. One must become comfortable with the necessary level of work (Chapter 1) and repeated rejections (Chapter 7) – all while allowing for rest and recovery (Chapter 11) and forgiving oneself when things do not go as planned (Chapter 12). Thus, it makes sense that, when we are heavily invested in an area and a task is presented as a *key* step for success in that area, even someone with a healthy growth mindset potentially would engage in actions to protect their self-worth, like foregoing practice or causing a distraction to have something else to blame. If this form of self-handicapping happens, hopefully it will buffer the impact that not performing well might have. In the long run, this might be the desired outcome if it enhances the perseverance of the performer. In other words, we all are human. The obstacles we encounter can take a tremendous amount of courage, a lot of "guts," and the right mentality to overcome. These factors providing a buffer can mean the difference between persevering to reach our goals and making an earlier-than-anticipated exit from the domain. We now turn to the opposite end of limiting one's scope – not taking advantage of small opportunities.

Smaller Opportunities Leading to Larger Opportunities

The bulk of this chapter is about not limiting one's scope, and the pushback that can be experienced when someone states aspirations that exceed the comfort level of others, which can lead to threatening their self-esteem. We must also be mindful of not minimizing more subtle opportunities that could lead to new contacts or help us in some other way. It is not unreasonable to be skeptical of opportunities that, upon first glance, do not seem to fit into the upward trajectory one is seeking. However, smaller opportunities almost always lead to larger opportunities. Let us turn directly to the content of our interviews to highlight some examples of this.

Kevin Rapillo, musical director and drummer for country music star Rodney Atkins, noted how progress often requires a series of smaller events:

> It's always the smaller things. It's never some gigantic thing, lottery-winning situation. It never is. It may seem like that from the outside. Oh, they just won a Grammy – like somehow, that just happened magically out of nowhere. It's all those little opportunities, even playing with someone like Rodney came from a smaller opportunity of a friend. I was playing with this folk singer in Nashville. He knew Rodney before he had anything, and I just did it as a one-off gig – one weekend, like the millions of other one-off gigs I did in Nashville. Here I am, 20 years later, still playing with that guy. It's all small things; I think the mistake is people don't listen to the small things, right? They just sort of blow them off, waiting for this gigantic thing to happen, where all these small opportunities just keep spreading out into more. Nashville being a perfect example of that... it's all, 'Oh, I played with this guy or this woman, and that led to that, led to that,' even if it was four years later. It sort of circles back around, you know. So that's very much the Nashville scene. I think people ignore that, especially now, I think, because [Nashville] became so popular. Younger people move to town and just are upset that Keith Urban hasn't called them in the first month.

The anonymous gold-record musician we interviewed reiterated this by noting that smaller opportunities leading to larger opportunities:

> usually happens by meeting someone that leads you into a new door. The industry is an infinitely overlapping network of individuals that know each other, from big acts to small acts. If someone wants to help you, for whatever reason, then they can easily propel you to bigger opportunities. Small opportunities can sometimes lead to events that change the trajectory of your entire life.

Rondal Richardson, philanthropist and former musician manager, shared how his multi-decade career in the entertainment industry began with what he perceived to be a summer gig with "a single raising of my hand at my high school." A visitor was recruiting someone to sell merchandise for Ricky Skaggs during summer concerts. Rondal recalls that the visitor was looking for someone who, "isn't overly infatuated with country music artists. Who can go out on the road and be around them. Eat dinner with them in a way that's not in their faces or in the way." Rondal thought he was an excellent candidate. He shared, "I was the perfect kid for that. I was nervous to ask my parents. They were first to say, 'you're crazy if you don't do this.' But I remember raising my hand in one small way, and that moment changed my life." And that is no exaggeration. Rondal went on to work with some of the best-known musical artists of all time.

Comedian Henry Cho took the approach of the beneficial combination of putting in the work and taking advantage of the subsequent opportunities arising from it. He told us:

> So that's how it works. Work breeds work. I tell my openers that all the time. They'll go, 'Hey. So, they want us to do this thing, but it only pays X.' Or it's a six-hour drive or eight-hour drive. I go, 'Do it. Work breeds work.' I get more work being on stage than I do not being on stage.

The advice is crystal clear. Take the opportunities you might consider to be small ones. It often will be these smaller opportunities putting you in a position to eventually land that larger opportunity you were hoping to get.

Chapter Summary

In this chapter, we discussed some of the factors that can lead us to limit the scope of what we hope to accomplish, such as the historical negative connotation associated with ambition and societal norms. Research suggests that an observer can experience a blow to their self-esteem when witnessing someone accomplish something remarkable, especially if they are similar to the observer. As a result, we begin to limit our goals in order to better fit in with others instead of thinking like a child and not limiting ourselves. We also unpacked how we compare ourselves to others to gauge how well we are doing, and how someone who just missed reaching a goal can feel worse than those not making it as far. Finally, our high performer interviewees shared the importance of taking the small opportunities that come your way and how they can lead to larger opportunities.

You Wanna Do What?!?

Chapter 6: *Limiting Your Scope: Think Like a Kid*

This exercise is intended to help you identify what you would attempt to do if you were not afraid to try and/or had unlimited resources. In the **first part** of the exercise, you will be asked to write down some things you would love to try if there were no risks. The **second part** will ask you to identify your specific fears and some possible solutions.

1. What are some things you would love (have loved) to attempt if there were no risk involved and you would be guaranteed to accomplish it?

2. Thinking about the previous question, list at least three thoughts/things that kept you from pursuing the things you wanted to attempt. What are some potential ways to get past such thoughts?

References

Baumeister, R.F., Smart, L., & Boden, J. M. (1996). Relation of threatened egotism to violence and aggression: The dark side of high self-esteem. *Psychological review*, *103*(1), 5–33. https://doi.org/10.1037/0033-295X.103.1.5.

Bushman, B.J., & Baumeister, R.F. (1998). Threatened egotism, narcissism, self-esteem, and direct and displaced aggression: Does self-love or self-hate lead to violence? *Journal of Personality and Social Psychology*, *75*(1), 219–229. https://doi.org/10.1037/0022-3514.75.1.219.

Garcia, S.M., Tor, A., & Gonzalez, R. (2006). Ranks and rivals: A theory of competition. *Personality and Social Psychology Bulletin*, *32*(7), 970–982. https://doi.org/10.1177/0146167206287640.

Harris, K.R., & Tashman, L. (Hosts). (2021, May 2). Lauren Regula [Audio podcast episode]. *The Path Distilled*. https://podcasts.apple.com/us/podcast/the-path-distilled-podcast/id1511069681?i=1000519697850.

Harris, K.R, & Tashman, L. (Hosts). (2020, August 9). Stephanie Quayle [Audio podcast episode]. *The Path Distilled*. https://podcasts.apple.com/us/podcast/the-path-distilled-podcast/id1511069681?i=1000487566447.

Judge, T.A., & Kammeyer-Mueller, J.D. (2012). On the value of aiming high: The causes and consequences of ambition. *Journal of Applied Psychology*, *97*(4), 758–775. https://doi.org/10.1037/a0028084.

Kuziemko, I., Buell, R.W., Reich, T., & Norton, M.I. (2014). "Last-place aversion": Evidence and redistributive implications. *The Quarterly Journal of Economics*, *129*(1), 105–149. https://doi.org/10.1093/qje/qjt035.

Medvec, V.H., Madey, S.F., & Gilovich, T. (1995). When less is more: Counterfactual thinking and satisfaction among Olympic medalists. *Journal of Personality and Social Psychology*, *69*(4), 603–610. https://doi.org/10.1037/0022-3514.69.4.603.

Niiya, Y., Brook, A.T., & Crocker, J. (2010). Contingent self-worth and self-handicapping: Do incremental theorists protect self-esteem? *Self and Identity*, *9*(3), 276–297. https://doi.org/10.1080/15298860903054233.

Weingarten, E., Davidai, S., & Barasch, A. (2023). Who's on first? People asymmetrically attend to higher-ranked (vs. lower-ranked) competitors. *Journal of Experimental Social Psychology*, *104*, 104405. https://doi.org/10.1016/j.jesp.2022.104405.

Yager, J., & Kay, J. (2023). Ambition and its psychopathologies. *The Journal of Nervous and Mental Disease*, *211*(4), 257–265. https://doi.org/10.1097/NMD.0000000000001644.

Facing Rejection 7

Taking "No" as a Cue to Stop Grinding

Over the years, I've gotten better at trying to separate myself from the rejection, because most of it isn't personal.
  – Kandle Osborne, artist, singer, and actress

I hate it when people are like, "Oh, I love failure. I love rejection." No, you don't. You're lying. We are hardwired [whereby] that kind of criticism creates an error signal in your brain, which is meant to be profoundly aversive… right?… to tell you something's wrong. Pay attention. So, it's never going to feel good. That's not the point. But what you're really trying to do is, get better at things that matter to you.
  – Todd Rose, bestselling author and thought leader

Jaylen moved to Los Angeles to make it as a performer in the music industry. He arrived in an older model Honda Accord with two changes of clothes and eight dollars to his name. Jaylen quickly got to work and was making or performing music almost every day. He settled into a routine and decided he would give himself at least three years to "make it" in the music business. After the second year, Jaylen's hopes were realized, and he was signed to a major label. Unfortunately, he was dropped from the label after only one year. The years that followed were a dizzying roller coaster of interest, ultimately followed by rejection. Jaylen stayed the course and is now a successful performer touring nonstop with a worldwide fanbase.

DOI: 10.4324/9781003377542-7

We have all faced rejection at some point in our life – at school, at work, or in our personal lives. The thing about rejection is that it stings. Really stings. There is evidence that social rejection results in the same activation of the brain responsible for physical pain (MacDonald & Leary, 2005). While this claim has been heavily debated (e.g., Woo et al., 2014), there are distinct areas of the brain dedicated to processing social rejection. Rejection can cause one to think less of themselves, magnify fears of being an impostor (the topic of Chapter 3), or give up all together (the topic of Chapter 5). However, rejection is quite commonplace – something that *everyone* experiences. In fact, most successful people experience rejection multiple times, so we must recognize rejection for what it is and learn to live with it. If Jaylen had given up after he was dropped from his label, he would not have become a successful performer. In this chapter, we will share examples of both high-profile and everyday people, and their experiences with rejection. We will then discuss the science on the pain of rejection, look at some of its consequences, and ultimately suggest ways to move past it.

"We Regret to Inform You" – Rejection Is Commonplace

Lainey Wilson, a Grammy-winning country singer shared that she was rejected seven times by the televised singing competition, American Idol (Norwin, 2024). Seven times! Let us consider another example – the beloved Walt Disney. What if he had given up after having his Mickey Mouse idea rejected? The cartoons we know and love today, the Disney movies, and the theme parks never would have come to fruition (Johal, 2020). Legendary boxer Muhammad Ali failed all of the tests assessing a boxer's skill level when he first started out, but he continued training and became one of the greatest boxers of all time. Similarly, Michael Jordan was cut from his high school basketball team!

Whew! That sounds like a lot of rejection. It seems a little jarring to read because we tend to avoid discussing our rejections because of the associated stigma. Rejection is justifiably considered a bad thing. However, as many of you have already experienced, the likelihood of experiencing rejection increases as you strive to accomplish more and advance to the next level. We do not have videos of college applicants getting word of their acceptances into the most competitive schools because the majority of applicants tend to be accepted. To the contrary; the majority of applicants are rejected. The same applies to what many consider to be dream jobs. On *The Path Distilled* podcast, Logan Mize shared his experience of being rejected by every record label in Nashville (Harris & Tashman, 2020). Logan has certainly found success in the music industry but has experienced repeated rejections over the course of his career.

Similarly, the number of athletes competing at a professional level is minuscule. For US athletes having gotten through the winnowing process to make it to the collegiate ranks (roughly 500,000 out of eight million high school athletes; National Collegiate Athletic Association [NCAA], 2013), the odds of reaching the highest professional level are still slim at around 1 percent for basketball and football (NCAA, 2015). Even making it on a team prior to a season does not come without rejection or the fear of it. Consider the National Football League (NFL), the most prestigious league for American football. On the final day of cuts to determine who makes the roster, 1,187 players are released from the roster of the team for which they managed to survive the initial rounds of releases. This is a large number for a mass rejection by any standard. The cuts have to be a gut punch for each and every player who experiences this. Granted, some players end up making it on an NFL team's final roster or being signed to a practice squad. Others will play professionally in lower-tier leagues. However, the majority of players will have played for the last time.

Rejection is certainly not limited to domains that already seem like a long shot, such as entertainment or professional sports. Applicants to prestigious universities, medical schools, top law firms, or other highly competitive jobs face similarly high likelihoods of rejection. One of the coauthors of this book was rejected from five PhD programs, and the other coauthor tallied eight of them – a combined 13 rejections! And, they are not alone – far from it. Getting the rejection letters does not mean you are unworthy of entering a graduate program or obtaining a job. The reality is that hundreds of applicants apply; only a few are selected. According to the American Psychological Association (APA), the average acceptance rate during the 2022–2023 academic year for doctoral programs was 11 percent, and the average acceptance rate for master's programs was 44 percent (2023).

And, the rejections keep coming. Social psychologist Dr. Josh Ackerman counted his rejections to share with attendees at a symposium he was leading (Jaremka et al., 2020). He later found the exercise of compiling his rejections to be helpful (more on this in a later section) but was initially rattled by the results:

> It was a little disheartening to relive my rejections and to recognize how small the chances are of not being rejected in some pursuits. For instance, across the various academic jobs for which I have applied, I have a 5.1 percent success rate of moving from application to on-campus interview and only a 2.9 percent rate of receiving an offer. Also apparent were the rejection valleys, where negative experiences cluster together (e.g., a very successful colleague reports having 10 manuscripts rejected in a row and knowing another scholar who had around 20 such repetitions). By the time I finished documenting these failures, I was having serious doubts about my life choices (p. 525).

Those are long odds. And these rejection rates are not limited to academic jobs. Desirable jobs in any field are in high demand. It is not uncommon for experienced professionals to submit well over 100 applications to secure just three to five initial interviews. We discuss ways to make yourself more competitive and increase the likelihood that you will make the initial cut in Chapter 13. The point here is that all of us have faced rejection – we have, you have, your cousin Katrina has – and the rejection hurts.

"Ouch, That Hurts!" – The Physical Pain of Rejection

The chirping birds outside the window of your dormitory seemed to be encouraging you to head outside to the quad. It was not only the center of life on campus; the trees and other foliage were breathtakingly beautiful. Especially on a day like today – sunny and slightly breezy. Although you could not stop thinking about the paper due this week, a spring day like this does not come around very frequently. Just as you are about to decide to take a study break and head out for some sunshine, your suitemates pop in and ask if you want to head to the quad to toss a flying disc (the one with the trademarked name).

Definitely! Everyone is able to position themselves quite nicely to toss the disc despite the collection of fellow classmates who also could not pass up the opportunity to be outside on such a beautiful day.

It starts out well enough as the three of you toss the disc around pretty traditionally, with each getting the disc roughly every third throw, except when it ventured off course. Then, you get skipped when it was supposed to come to you. "No big deal," you think after the first time it happens. The disc comes to you the next time you expected it. You are relieved. Then… skipped again. Now, you are puzzled. Initially they are skipping you here and there, but eventually, you are left out altogether. This goes on for at least 20 minutes until they decide to wrap up and head back in. It is certainly confusing, but it also hurts … truly hurts.

The pain you felt in the preceding example is not hyperbole. Rejection – social ostracism in this case – has been found to activate the same brain areas responsible for physical pain (MacDonald & Leary, 2005). As mentioned, the specifics of how this works have resulted in ongoing debate about whether the activation occurs in the same brain pathways as, or ones adjacent to, those activated in physical pain response, but it is clear that we react neurologically in a similar way (e.g., Woo et al., 2014). Rejection hurts!

Much of the research in this area uses a computerized version of the flying disc example at the beginning of this section – a ball tossing game called "Cyberball" (Williams, Cheung, & Choi, 2000). The game, created by a team of Australian researchers, has been particularly helpful in studying the effect of rejection on a variety of measures. A review of hundreds of studies with more than 11,000 participants revealed that the game was very effective at generating a perception of being ostracized (Hartgerink et al., 2015).

Possible Causes of Rejection

Someone once tried to give me a house. Granted, it needed a lot of work. Oh, and the property taxes were due soon. After a very brief contemplation, I decided to decline the offer. Between the expense of completing the work needed to make the house viable and paying the property taxes for the past year, it just did not seem worth it. Not to mention the fact that the current owner was *giving* the house away.

Literally, not metaphorically. Needless to say, the demand was low for that particular house. Contrast this experience with some of the home purchases made in the recent housing market. Many sellers are receiving multiple offers above asking price. Potential buyers are writing letters to the sellers to secure their favor. Many good offers were rejected because of the large number of interested buyers for a given property. The point illustrated in this example is that rejection can be associated with pursuits involving a notable amount of competition. This competitiveness can arise from the intrinsic value of the end-goal, scarcity, or both.

Another hard truth is that how to gain an advantage over others is not always common knowledge (see Chapter 2 for more on this aspect). What separates you from the hundreds of other applicants vying for the same position? Many applicants prepare themselves in similar ways and have similar selling points (check out Chapter 13 for some ways to distinguish yourself). The majority of this collection of generally qualified but indistinguishable applicants will be rejected, and they are likely unaware of how underwhelming or average they actually appear among the applicant pool. The applicants who have learned to stand out will likely not share their techniques with potential competitors. This is the concept of "gatekeeping" – once granted entry to some fields or achieving a certain level, some performers are not inclined to share how they, themselves, were successful.

The hard truth is that some gatekeeping is necessary for many fields. One of the advantages of social media is that some have been able to circumvent the traditional gatekeepers such as record labels. A currently viable model is to record your music, using readily available software, and release it on the platform(s) of your choice. This new model has led to some really great musicians gaining an audience that would have been more difficult to gain in years past. However, there are a lot of promotional videos for musicians that appear on my social media feeds, and many of them are not ready to be heard by the masses. While being a horrible singer or mediocre band is perfectly fine if you choose to stand on the sidewalk to perform, being a horrible singer or mediocre band is unacceptable if my company is footing the bill (give us back the cheese tray you ordered for your dressing room). Moreover, you certainly would not want the surgeon to operate on you before their mentors have given the greenlight that they are ready, and we certainly want the pilot of our cross-country flight to have been sufficiently gatekept. In other words, while some gatekeeping is superficial or competitive, it also can serve a legitimate need.

Unfortunately, rejection is sometimes the result of biases – some are well-known, such as those based on race or gender, but there could be other biases active. For example, the way you speak could lead to rejection. This could be because of improper grammar or the regional accent or dialect of the speaker. Other potential biases that can contribute to rejection are based on height (e.g., Habibov et al., 2020) and weight (e.g., Roehling, 1999). It has been found that taller people are more likely to be employed and earn more than shorter people – a 5 percent salary increase for men and 12 percent salary increase for women (Habibov et al., 2020). Relatedly, evidence suggests women are more likely than men to experience weight bias (Hebl & Mannix, 2003). The list of biases potentially contributing to rejection is probably endless. Such biases combined with other potential causes of rejection, already discussed, combine to create a realistic idea of how common rejection actually is. We discuss in a coming section how this realization of the pervasiveness of rejection can be used to help us better cope with rejection and its aftermath.

Consequences of Rejection – "I Know You Are But What Am I?"

We discussed some of the causes of rejection in the preceding section. It should not be considered an exhaustive list, and there also will be other factors that undoubtedly contribute. In this section, we now will consider some of the very real consequences of rejection. These include anger and depression, and an increase in the stress hormone cortisol (Blackheart, Eckel, & Tice, 2007). There is also the aforementioned physical pain associated with rejection (e.g., MacDonald & Leary, 2005; Woo et al., 2014). And of course, rejection ultimately can increase feelings of self-doubt/being an impostor (Chapter 3), stall progress of what you are working toward, or ultimately lead someone to decide that they do not belong in a certain domain or field and dropping out (quitting was covered in Chapter 5).

Each person can be located on a continuum of rejection tolerance, ranging from tolerating a few of them to facing as many rejections as it takes to get where they want to be. Many will take rejection as a cue to give up on their pursuits. Some will never take the risk at all and will therefore (perhaps intentionally) face minimal rejections. Others will take a risk but drop their pursuits after the first rejection they experience. This continuum matters because, as we discussed in Chapter 1, you have to do the right things for the appropriate amount of time to get good at something. By dropping out prematurely (Chapter 5) because of rejection, we certainly prevent ourselves from contributing the amount of time needed to advance in the endeavor and miss out on opportunities that would eventually arise

"It Does Not Hurt Anymore" – Ways to Move Beyond Rejection

I worked with a colleague for months on a conceptual paper applying the work on expertise to the specialty area of the colleague. It was essentially a guide for helping the specialty area of this colleague identify unanswered empirical questions that needed to be addressed to increase the likelihood that the practitioners were operating at the highest level. I received an email notifying me that it had been submitted to a particular journal with a line added, "I submitted the manuscript today. I am not confident they will take it." The uncertainty was over whether the journal accepted any articles that were strictly theoretical considerations and not empirical studies for which data were collected. Nevertheless, the comment demonstrated the recognition that rejection is a possibility – we know that rejection is commonplace and a part of the process of our work.

We shared some well-known names who overcame rejection, along with how commonplace rejection is, earlier in the chapter. Awareness of how common rejection is should be one of the first tools we use to move beyond its negative impacts. Dr. Lisa Jaremka's article on a variety of topics, including rejection, was intended to help with destigmatizing such issues as they typically have not been openly discussed. Two of the contributors, Drs. Sweeney and Molina, echoed the sentiment that rejection is part of the process. We should add that it is part of the process for most pursuits – especially competitive ones.

In this regard, the academic environment is useful because we sometimes are able to count the specific rejections, as Dr. Ackerman did (discussed earlier), in order to share the frequency. The American Philosophical Association (APA; 2023) reported that, from 2015 to 2019, the acceptance rate of paper submissions to be presented at their annual convention was 25.3 percent across all divisions. This means roughly three-quarters of applicants who submitted a paper to be presented at professional conferences were rejected. When it comes to publishing research in a journal, the acceptance rate drops to roughly 10 percent. This means that the most common decision when submitting a manuscript is a rejection. However, there is also a plus-side to this. When your manuscript is rejected, you get feedback on ways to improve. This can help if you then want to try again by submitting to a different journal. These examples underscore the point that rejection will be more commonplace than acceptance. If we know we will be getting more rejections than acceptances, we can lessen the sting and move forward more easily.

Had we taken our own rejections to our PhD program applications as a cue that graduate school was not for us, we would not be the professors we are today. Rather than ending our pursuits, we both continued our path with some slight modifications. One of us applied to master's programs, was accepted, and actually had several to choose from. While the rejections and need to pivot really stung at first, it was the best possible outcome. The pivot led us to network more extensively than we otherwise would have, meeting mentors and peers who shaped our careers.

Again, recognizing how commonplace rejection is and viewing it as an expected part of the process are some ways to cope with the experience. Musical artist Kandle Osborne echoed this sentiment during our interview with her:

> Over the years, I've gotten better at trying to separate myself from the rejection, because most of it isn't personal." However, the road of getting to this realization was quite difficult, "I have people that are amazing label heads and managers. They come to my shows and sing along, but they won't sign me. And, I've had

very strange things happen – like a couple of years ago, a very big, major label said they were sending me a contract the following week. My lawyer was ready for it. 'We are excited,' they said. I was going to be the focus artist of the next year, and all the plans. We had many hours of phone calls, and [I] never heard from them again. But, that's happened enough times in my career, where you just kind of, you know nothing's a sure thing until it's actually happening. And, that's harder to learn when you're younger, because you know 22-year-old me being told that I was the next big thing – I believed it. I was excited, and then each disappointment just really breaks your heart.

Logan Mize shared with *The Path Distilled* podcast (Harris & Tashman, 2020) that he also was put through the wringer with rejection before sticking with it long enough to realize success. He spent years getting close to being signed by many major record labels just to be rejected, repeatedly. Ultimately, he stuck with it and is a very successful musician. Kandle and Logan were able to stick around, in part, because they withstood the ongoing experiences with rejection. Such rejection can lead to you feeling as though you are a fraud, you will never be good enough, and that you cannot produce quality work.

Recognizing how common rejection is can be helpful for beginning to change the way you view rejection. It can also help to consider rejection as an opportunity to gain feedback and possibly learn something to improve upon. As mentioned earlier, whenever an academic manuscript is rejected, the reviewers provide feedback for improvement. Co-author Emily learned to accept such rejections as learning experiences after her PhD advisor would tell her, "It's okay; we will find it a home." That guidance reframed her mindset.

Using feedback as a learning experience dovetails with the continuous learning angle of resilience (Pulley & Wakefield, 2001). Resiliency can be thought of as two processes: being exposed to adversity and having a positive adaptation (Fletcher & Sarkar, 2003). When we face an obstacle we do not think we can overcome, but we do, that is resiliency. The question becomes – how do we get from point A to point B when we face obstacles that make us want to give up, such as rejection? The short answer: do not give up. Face each battle head on and become more resilient each time. When we face rejection, whether it be from a job interview or a potential promotion, learn from the experience. What can we fix or change to increase our chances of an acceptance for the next time? We learn what works (or not) with each scenario we face, and we develop courage to keep going, and strength and experience to overcome future rejections. This approach aligns well with the second component of resilience, reflection (Pulley & Wakefield, 2001). Many of us will want to move right to the next thing after being rejected. However, if we do not take the time to reflect on the experience, we cannot expect to learn and grow from it.

Another method of reframing proposed by Dr. Ackerman (Jaremka et al., 2010) is to examine other factors besides you or your work that may have contributed to the rejection. On the surface, this seems to be at odds with taking a close look at what *you* need to improve upon. While you still need to be open and honest in seeking out what you can do better, sometimes there are things out of your control that have nothing to do with you or you work. Consider the biases mentioned above, the limitations on number of acceptances possible, or even how well you slept the night before. Bottom line – continue seeking continuous improvement, but be aware that sometimes "stuff happens."

Relatedly, rejection should be viewed as impersonal, which is often difficult. Remember Kandle Osborne's view on rejection: "most of it isn't personal." We are fairly certain that the reviewers were not criticizing us personally when they rejected our manuscripts. Similarly, there might be three amazing candidates for a single position within a company. This means that two outstanding candidates will experience rejection. From the employers' perspective, there are often candidates in high demand for competing employers. These candidates may receive multiple offers but can only accept one, and then, the employers will experience rejection. Again, these candidates likely did not make their decision as a personal affront to their suitors.

Not taking rejection personally might be more difficult when it comes to promotions with an existing employer or after extended time within a domain. This is because there actually is a history with the person rejecting you. After months or years in a position, you may be turned down for a promotion or raise. This type of rejection can trigger feelings of not being good enough or of being a fraud (see Chapter 3 for more on impostor syndrome). This happened to one of our interviewees who was asked to serve in a senior leadership position at a company on an interim status. They absolutely loved serving in the position. When it came time to find a full-time person for the position, they thought they would be the obvious choice to fill the position permanently, but the company selected a different candidate. The rejection stung, and they felt like giving up on the company altogether. As mentioned, it was the track record with the organization and key players that made the decision feel so personal.

"You sure are sensitive"

Nobody likes the feeling of being rejected. So, why do some of us continue to pursue our goals and dreams when experiencing repeated rejections, and others drop out when it happens? One reason that researchers have discovered is that there are differences in how sensitive individuals are to rejection – some of us are impacted more severely than others. This phenomenon was dubbed rejection sensitivity (e.g., Downey & Feldman, 1996). Our sensitivity to rejection falls on a continuum from rejection having very little impact to having a tremendous impact. Those with a high rejection sensitivity experience rejection more intensely and anxiously expect rejection, which would presumably impact performance and perception. For example, coming across as "on edge" could create the opposite vibe from what you are hoping to achieve, particularly if you end up coming across as hostile or defensive.

Researchers were able to capture the impact of rejection sensitivity in a study in which participants were led to believe that they had been rejected by a peer (Ayduk, Gyurak, & Luerssen, 2008). The same participants were later allowed to deliver a variable amount of hot sauce to the person they thought had rejected them. The participants were led to believe that the person did not like spicy foods. Rejected participants who rated high in rejection sensitivity applied a significantly greater amount of hot sauce compared to the other rejected participants, even more when the rejection was unexpected.

Presumably, even those who have high rejection sensitivity can overcome such tendencies, but it is also possible that someone with high rejection sensitivity would drop out of a domain. This being the case, we propose that viewing repeated rejection as part of moving up the ranks might help. We both see rejection as part of the cost of existing in academic positions. As the examples throughout the chapter illustrate, it is the same with other domains. Staying in the mix despite the rejections is critical for getting where you want to be.

Chapter Summary

In this chapter, we discussed rejection and the tremendous impact it can have on someone striving to become a high performer. Rejection is commonplace, and we shared examples of both high-profile and everyday people experiencing it, ranging from hypothetical job applicants to Nobel Laureates. Research suggests that social rejection activates the same, or possibly adjacent, neural pathways as when we experience physical pain. Nevertheless, rejection mimics physical pain – it hurts. Other consequences include anger and depression, and an increase in the stress hormone cortisol (Blackheart, Eckel, & Tice, 2007). Rejection ultimately can result in increased feelings of self-doubt/being an impostor (Chapter 3), stall progress of what you are working toward, or ultimately result in someone deciding that they do not belong in a certain domain or field and dropping out (quitting was covered in Chapter 5). Suggestions to move past rejection include being aware of the high rate of rejection in most domains and coming to view it as part of the process, even learning from it.

"You'll Never Make It In…!"

Chapter 7: *Facing Rejection: Taking "No" as a Cue to Stop*

This exercise will help you realize that rejection is normal and reduce the stigma. In the **first part** of the exercise, you will be asked to provide examples of times you have personally been rejected. The **second part** will ask you to recall what the ultimate outcome was for each example of rejection you provide.

1. Provide three (or more) examples of rejections you have experienced.

2. High performers typically continue their pursuits despite multiple rejections along the way. Reflect on the rejections you provided in the previous question and describe the outcomes on the goals you were pursuing. Did you give up altogether or were you ultimately successful?

References

American Philosophical Association (APA) (2023). APA paper submission guidelines: Paper acceptance rates. https://www.apaonline.org/page/papersubmission. Accessed November 21, 2023.

American Psychological Association (APA) (2023). Graduate education data tool: Applications, acceptances, and enrollments. https://www.apa.org/education-career/grad/survey-data/graduate-education-data-tools. Accessed November 21, 2023.

Ayduk, Ö., Gyurak, A., & Luerssen, A. (2008). Individual differences in the rejection–aggression link in the hot sauce paradigm: The case of rejection sensitivity. *Journal of Experimental Social Psychology*, *44*(3), 775–782. https://doi.org/10.1016/j.jesp.2007.07.004.

Blackhart, G.C., Eckel, L.A., & Tice, D.M. (2007). Salivary cortisol in response to acute social rejection and acceptance by peers. *Biological Psychology*, *75*(3), 267–276. https://doi.org/10.1016/j.biopsycho.2007.03.005.

Downey, G., & Feldman, S.I. (1996). Implications of rejection sensitivity for intimate relationships. *Journal of Personality and Social Psychology*, 70(6), 1327–1343. https://doi.org/10.1037/0022-3514.70.6.1327.

Fletcher D. & Sarkar M. (2013). Psychological resilience: A review and critique of definitions, concepts, and theory. *European Psychologist, 18*, https://doi.org/12–23.10.1027/1016-9040/a000124; https://doi.org/10.1027/1016-9040/a000124.

Habibov, N., Auchynnikava, A., Luo, R., & Fan, L. (2020). Influence of height on likelihood of employment, occupational sorting, and earnings in 27 post-communist countries. *American Journal of Human Biology*, *32*(6), e23422. https://doi.org/10.1002/ajhb.23422.

Harris, K.R., & Tashman, L. (Hosts). (2020, May 24). Logan Mize [Audio podcast episode]. *The Path Distilled*. https://podcasts.apple.com/us/podcast/the-path-distilled-podcast/id1511069681?i=1000475563956.

Hartgerink, C.H., Van Beest, I., Wicherts, J.M., & Williams, K.D. (2015). The ordinal effects of ostracism: A meta-analysis of 120 Cyberball studies. *PloS One*, *10*(5), e0127002. https://doi.org/10.1371/journal.pone.0127002.

Hebl, M.R., & Mannix, L.M. (2003). The weight of obesity in evaluating others: A mere proximity effect. *Personality and Social Psychology Bulletin*, *29*(1), 28–38. https://doi.org/10.1177/0146167202238369.

Jaremka, L.M., Ackerman, J.M., Gawronski, B., Rule, N.O., Sweeny, K., Tropp, L.R., Metz, M.A., Molina, L., Ryan, W.S., & Vick, S.B. (2020). Common academic experiences no one talks about: Repeated rejection, impostor syndrome, and burnout. *Perspectives on Psychological Science, 15*(3), 519–543. https://doi.org/10.1177/1745691619898848.

Johal, S. (2020). Bouncing back: 6 stories of triumph after rejection. *LinkedIn.* https://www.linkedin.com/pulse/bouncing-back-6-stories-triumph-after-rejection-shawn-johal. Accessed November 22, 2023.

MacDonald, G., & Leary, M.R. (2005). Why does social exclusion hurt? The relationship between social and physical pain. *Psychological Bulletin, 131*(2), 202–223. https://psycnet.apa.org/doi/10.1037/0033-2909.131.2.202.

National Collegiate Athletic Association (NCAA) (2013). Probability of competing beyond high school. https://www.ncaa.org/sports/2013/12/17/probability-of-competing-beyond-high-school.aspx. Accessed February 20, 2024.

National Collegiate Athletic Association (NCAA) (2015). Estimated probability of competing in professional athletics. https://www.ncaa.org/sports/2013/12/17/probability-of-competing-beyond-high-school.aspx. Accessed February 20, 2024.

Norwin, N. (2024) Lainey Wilson's past 'American Idol' rejection shocks judge Luke Bryan: "Don't always get it right." *Y! Entertainment.* https://www.yahoo.com/entertainment/lainey-wilson-past-american-idol-093545138.html#:~:text="I%20tried%20out%20seven%20times,it%20past%20the%20first%20round. Accessed February 23, 2024.

Pulley, M., & Wakefield, M. (2001). *Building Resiliency: How to Thrive in Times of Change.* Center for Creative Leadership.

Roehling, M.V. (1999). Weight-based discrimination in employment: Psychological and legal aspects. *Personnel Psychology, 52*(4), 969–1016. https://doi.org/10.1111/j.1744-6570.1999.tb00186.x.

Williams, K.D., Cheung, C.K., & Choi, W. (2000). Cyberostracism: Effects of being ignored over the Internet. *Journal of Personality and Social Psychology, 79*(5), 748–762. https://doi.org/10.1037/0022-3514.79.5.748.

Woo, C.W., Koban, L., Kross, E., Lindquist, M.A., Banich, M.T., Ruzic, L., Andrews-Hanna, J. R., & Wager, T. D. (2014). Separate neural representations for physical pain and social rejection. *Nature Communications, 5*(1), 5380. https://doi.org/10.1038/ncomms6380.

Aiming for Perfection   **8**

Identify Your Threshold and Dive In

When you realize how many people would love this job [Disney], and to do what you're doing, it can be really a lot of pressure to keep up and to be perfect; and to do more even than you are expected to, just to compete.
— Thomas Estrada, film and video game animator

If everybody's a perfectionist, you never make it on the racetrack, because the car's never perfect. It's as much as you want it to be. Things happen. Cars happen. We push them really hard. All of them almost are over 1,000 horsepower, and parts just aren't designed to last long-term making that kind of power, taking that kind of abuse. So, perfection is relative to some degree.
— Taylor Hull, Formula Drift Pro driver

While mindlessly scrolling through a popular social media site one day, an image captured my attention. It was a picture of a camel climbing a steep sand dune. The most intriguing part was that the camel appeared to be crawling. The camel's neck was extended parallel to the steeply angled dune with front legs bent as if crawling with its front knees. While this technique certainly could not be considered elegant, it must be quite effective. This got me thinking about perfectionism.

In many instances, we are afraid to take the initial steps or want to wait until we are just a little better. In some cases, we will wait for a perfect moment to launch, or until we have experienced a perfect performance. This approach is flawed for many reasons. As we will

DOI: 10.4324/9781003377542-8

discuss below, perfectionism is often maladaptive. Just as the camel uses a seemingly awkward technique to climb dunes, sometimes we must jump in to get something done with what we have or know at the time. We also discuss how these opportunities might lead to mistakes along the way, how these mistakes can help us in the long term, and how not taking the leap with small opportunities can lead to missed larger opportunities.

Perfectionism in the Traditional Sense

When Malik entered his master's degree program, he was given a set timeframe in which to complete his thesis. As he reviews it in preparation to submit, Malik is not sure what is bugging him about the manuscript. He just cannot bring himself to submit a draft for his advisor to review. The thesis is objectively well written. However, Malik finds something to revise every time he reviews – changing a word on one page or deleting a sentence on another. Making matters worse, he is already several months behind schedule. It makes sense that the tardiness of the submission is stressful but not nearly as stressful as the current state of his paper. It just is not... something. It just is not... perfect. Ultimately, Malik exhausted his window of eligibility and never earned his degree.

Malik's example illustrates one of the potential negative consequences of perfectionism. For example, perfectionism has been associated with a long list of negative outcomes, including increased stress, burnout, and depression (Moate et al., 2016). Additionally, work by U.K. scholars Thomas Curran and Andrew Hill suggests perfectionism has been on the rise since the 1980s (Curran & Hill, 2019). Their meta-analysis of American, British, and Canadian teens found that present-day teens are more prone to perfectionism. The researchers determined that present-day teens experience greater societal demands and are more demanding of themselves, and they themselves contribute to the increased societal demands. A later empirical study by the same scholars identified that parental criticism had also increased over time, and it contributed directly to the increased perfectionism identified in the teens (Curran & Hill, 2022).

While there are proponents of perfectionism because it can improve performance in certain circumstances, such as the adaptive perfectionism helping medical students meet the rigorous demands of medical school (Enns et al., 2001), there also is evidence that perfectionism leads some to limit their scope (the topic of Chapter 6). For example, a team of Canadian researchers expanded the work on the impact of perfectionism to college professors and found that perfectionism stymied productivity (Sherry et al., 2010). In particular, professors holding themselves to standards of perfectionism tended to avoid situations in which they might fail or receive criticism – sounds much like one of the potential consequences of a fixed mindset that we introduced in Chapter 1. This led them to both think less creatively and to produce fewer deliverables than someone not striving for perfection.

You might have found yourself in a similar position if you have perfectionist tendencies. Even for those without the perfectionist tendencies, criticism and failure are not pleasant. Anecdotally, this reminds me of a common refrain among musicians and artists about the pressure they can feel once they experience some degree of success. Their early artistic work likely was produced based on what the musician or artist enjoyed or were drawn to create. Their original album might have been written over several years. However, once some success is attained, there often is pressure to maintain the momentum of their original success in a much shorter window of time. There is nothing inherently problematic with attempts to maintain momentum. However, perfectionism, or perfectionism-like tendencies, might enter the picture given the higher expectations.

Evidence for such pressure to maintain success, and its potentially limiting impact on creativity, was provided by a clever study conducted by a group of researchers analyzing the stylistic originality of songs released by musical artists following Grammy nominations (Negro et al., 2022). Artists who won a Grammy subsequently released music that was noticeably stylistically different from their peers. The researchers labelled this "artistic differentiation." Grammy winners subsequently exhibited increased differentiation from other artists with their releases when compared to their music prior to the Grammy nomination. Critically, the artists who were nominated for a Grammy but ultimately *did not win* ended up sounding *more like their peers* with subsequent releases. This illustrates the impact that the lens through which one is viewing performance can ultimately have on the outcome – including pressure to maintain momentum and perfectionist tendencies. It takes an understanding of the potential value of both criticism and failure to begin appreciating the usefulness of each, and perfectionist tendencies complicate this process.

"You Sure do Train a Lot and Keep Working on Improving"

There are many examples to choose from when highlighting the intensity of the training of world-class performers. You might have seen videos of high-level athletes training in sandpits to add an extra layer of difficulty. Presumably, running on a typical field or pitch would seem easy after attempting to go full speed in the sandpit. Another version of this type of training is having the athlete sprint up steep inclines or while wearing additional weights. Brandon Payne, a basketball skills trainer who has worked extensively with NBA player Steph Curry, shared with *The Path Distilled* podcast that he uses a similar training technique by creating situations that exceed what might be expected in an actual game (Harris & Tashman, 2020). By doing so, the game can seem much slower to a player trained in such as way.

These intense training techniques are not limited to physical pursuits; Chapter 1 opened with the model of Joyce Carol Oates writing practice novels to be thrown away (Kellogg, 2006) and acclaimed screenwriter Jonathan Goyer noting that you will need to have written numerous screenplays before they begin turning out well (Donelly, 2005). While this writing is quite distinct from physically training in a sandpit, writing a full novel or screenplay to improve your craft is intense. Almost any domain with high levels of performance will have some version of this intense training.

An observer of such training could very easily, and understandably, be prone to labelling what they are witnessing as prime examples of perfectionism. The person being observed might be working iteratively to get the best possible line in a novel or consistently make a shot on the basketball court. Moreover, they typically are consistently striving to reach the next level of performance. These observed behaviors could easily appear to be one and the same as perfectionism in action. However, there is a term that better encapsulates what typically occurs with world-class performers – *excellencism*. Patrick Gaudreau and colleagues have spent considerable time distinguishing perfectionism from excellencism (Gaudreau et al., 2022). While both perfectionism and excellencism involves the pursuit of high levels of performance, a key distinguishing feature between the two is flexibility.

In other words, excellencism can be thought of as striving to be your best without the baggage that frequently accompanies perfectionism. Pursuing excellencism allows you to work toward your goals, presumably with a reduced risk of being derailed by unrealistic expectations or failing to reach perfection. Having said that, the expectations one might have for themselves can still be set very high and the performer's expectations of themselves extremely demanding. The flexibility allotted in striving for excellencism, as opposed to perfectionism, comes in part from providing the mental space that will allow for mistakes to be made. At least, that is the way it should be approached. While such mistakes are typically not made intentionally, taking advantage of the opportunity to analyze and learn from them is advantageous for improving performance

Never a Perfect Time to Launch – Embrace the Uneasiness

Chace and Tina were bonding over coffee at a local bistro. When he got home, Chace could not stop thinking about Tina. He thought that there might have been some romantic interest. Always self-conscious about his appearance, he wanted to drop at least ten pounds before asking her on a date. He figured that he could hit the gym and be ready to ask her out in a couple of months. Unfortunately for Chace, Tina was beaming at their weekly coffee meet-up three weeks into Chace's plan – she had met someone! Chace realized in that moment that his window of opportunity was closed, and he could kick himself for not asking Tina out much sooner.

Pay very close attention to this next statement. *There never will be a perfect time to launch.* This applies to almost anything. There will always be something that could be better or improved. Chace lost out on his chance to ask Tina on a date over a perceived issue with his weight. In the previous section, Malik lost out on his chance to earn a graduate degree because he felt his thesis could always be improved. He was concerned about perceived mistakes that may never have been noticed by the committee reviewing his work. Another common fear is of making mistakes, especially when attempting to enter a domain or move up in a hierarchy. As we will see in the next section, the mistakes one makes can be excellent learning tools. Hooman Rahini, PROSPEC Formula Drift driver, noted the advice he received from his father about making mistakes:

> There's no chance that I don't mess up eventually. I'm going to make a mistake. But something my dad taught me early was, you can make a million mistakes. Just learn from them. If you learn from every mistake, then it's a mistake, but it's not the end of the world. You can move on; you can grow from it and actually become better.

We dive a little deeper into the potentially surprising benefits of failure in a coming section. We also discuss, in a separate upcoming section, how you also could miss out on some of the smaller opportunities that eventually lead to the larger opportunities by waiting on the sidelines too long. Now, let us discuss the somewhat paradoxical experience of the anxiety and other negative feelings induced by doing something that we really want to do – and some research-based potential ways to overcome them.

It is often unrecognized that doing something new can be unnerving, even if you really want to do it. This could be standing on a stage with a microphone attempting to make a crowd laugh by performing stand-up comedy. It could be competing in a local tennis tournament or making a pitch to secure funding for your start-up. It could be anything that you really want to do but still gives you butterflies. Rondal Richardson, philanthropist and former musician manager, was part of Garth Brooks' management team when Brooks played Central Park in the 1990s. Rondal shared the story of Brooks – despite already performing at sold-out stadiums across the globe – having his breath taken away upon observing the size of the crowd. Many of you reading this book aspire to accomplish great things. Some level of discomfort will always remain. Consider Brandon Flowers of the legendary band, *The Killers*. Brandon shared with the *Smartless* podcast hosts that he still gets butterflies before taking the stage over 20 years into his career (Batemen, Hayes, & Arnett, 2024).

There are some techniques to counter the jitters that are used by those consistently in the thick of it. For example, Darryl McDaniels, aka DMC of the legendary hip-hop group Run-DMC, revealed in a recent documentary about the group that he adopted the persona of a superhero to help him get past the performance jitters that never went away (Simmons et al., 2024). Beyoncé revealed some time ago during an interview with Oprah Winfrey that she adopts the persona of an imaginary person when she is performing – Sasha Fierce, who is fearless (Winfrey, 2008). This persona can handle the demands of performing with ease and without the jitters commonly accompanying them. Doing this allows Beyoncé or DMC to not fret about the jitters they are experiencing too much – Sasha and the superhero can handle it. Many of the first steps you, as well as most anyone, take will feel uncomfortable, at least in the beginning. Lean into this. Recognize it for what it is and move past it. Let us consider some examples of why this is possible – if you understand the combined psychological and physiological components at play.

Empirical studies support the position that to what we attribute our physiological experiences can play a huge role in our interpretation of the situation, and ultimately, our performance. The official line of research is called misattribution of arousal. In the classic study, participants were injected with epinephrine, which causes physiological arousal (e.g., increased heartrate), or a placebo before engaging in staged interactions with actors, who were either angry or jovial. Participants injected with the epinephrine labelled their arousal differently, based on the scenario in which they were involved (Schacter & Singer, 1962). In other words, participants interacting with the jovial actor interpreted their arousal as meaning they were having a good time. The arousal was interpreted as anger when they were interacting with the seemingly angry participant.

Later findings suggest that misattribution of arousal can even play a role in sexual attraction whereby physiological arousal is attributed to a person who is present. For example, physiological arousal from music can lead participants to provide comparatively higher attractiveness ratings of a face as compared to physiologically non-aroused participants (Marin et al., 2017). These examples show how prone we are to misinterpreting our own physiological responses and reminds us that we are interpreting the responses based on cues in the environment.

Can awareness of the misattribution of arousal phenomenon actually make a difference in your performance? Absolutely! Let us consider two examples. Researcher James Olson found empirical support for this conclusion. In his well-known study, when participants were told that the sound being piped in through their headphones would make them "unpleasantly aroused" while giving a speech, the participants made fewer errors than participants who were told the music would make them relax or there would be no effect (1988). Why was this the case? They were able to attribute their jitters to the noise coming through their headphones instead of doubts about their own abilities. Being able to attribute their jitters to something other than the task allowed the participants to functionally trick themselves – "if the task is not making me nervous then maybe I got this."

This phenomenon was made even more applicable when a different group of researchers, Jessi Smith and Meghan Huntoon, conducted a variation of this study by asking women in college to write an essay explaining why they deserved a scholarship (Smith & Huntoon, 2014). When the women were told that subliminal noises occurring while writing their essays would make them uncomfortable, they engaged in greater self-promotion (a topic covered in Chapter 15) compared to women who were not informed that the noises would make them uncomfortable. Once again, having something other than the task, or their own thoughts about the task, to account for their discomfort led to higher performance. Our own experiences have been that high-level performers eventually learn to recognize feelings of discomfort as part of the process. The need for an external source to which the uneasiness can be attached goes away, and it is deemed part of the experience.

Failing to Win

In Chapter 2 we discussed Tony Hawk's tremendous dedication to getting better at skateboarding. This dedication to improving included experiences with some pretty extensive injuries in the pursuit of mastering his craft. The anecdote was used to provide an example of someone not becoming complacent and attempting to move on to the next performance level. Implicit in this scenario is the willingness of

Tony and his fellow skateboarders to repeatedly fail in their attempts to pull off a particular maneuver. This repeated failure occurs frequently in most every domain. In some cases, such as the skateboarding examples, the failures have physical consequences. In other domains, the failures take different forms – a computer coding failure or a recipe not being what was expected. These failures can teach us tremendous lessons.

In many pursuits, it is this repeated failure that eventually leads to large gains for the performer. More specifically, attempts to move beyond current levels of ability lead to multiple failures, but these failures eventually lead to successful performance increases. These increases arise, in part, from the lessons learned during the iterative process of attempting something, mostly failing at it, and then repeating the attempting/failing cycle until performance stabilizes. Anders Ericsson (who coined the term deliberate practice and is mentioned throughout the book) and his coauthors used figure skating as an example to illustrate this principle in action (Ericsson, Roring, & Nandagopal, 2007; see also Deakin & Cobley, 2003). The authors highlight the high frequency of failed attempts when attempting to master skills required for high-level figure skating. And, just like Tony Hawk attempting to master his moves on the skateboard, failed attempts in figure skating can be painful as they often result in physical falls. Critically, the most elite skaters spent the majority of their training attempting the moves they had yet to master while the skilled, but lower status, skaters spent the majority of their practice time working on moves they were already good at performing. In other words, the most elite performers were not only comfortable with failure, they expected it. It was part of the process. Thankfully, failures in many domains are not painful, but they still provide tremendous opportunities for learning.

The Soviet chess training academies introduced in Chapter 2 provide another example of learning from failing. A practice they employed was to study in-game positions of previously played games and identify why a trainee's selected move differed from the higher-level grandmaster in the actual game. The trainee then moved on to other in-game positions to repeat the process (Shadrick & Lussier, 2004). While mistakes in chess are not physically painful, the process is similar – identify mistakes and use them to improve performance on subsequent attempts. The goal again would be to reach stable performance on the skill originally out of reach and then turn attention to reaching the next level of performance.

Major League Baseball's (MLB) Alec Mills shared:

> There's a lot of times where I've learned more things from a bad outing than I have from a good outing. I think that's life, period, you know. I think we learn from our mistakes, and that's how we get better from our mistakes. Mistakes are something that we know we've done wrong, and a lot of times when things are going well, it's hard to learn from that, because nothing's going wrong. I'm learning more from losing or learning more from doing poorly. Take when things don't go well and learn from that, and leapfrog that into your next outing, or next day, or even next hour.

Andrew Lang, founder of Leatherwood Distillery, shared a similar sentiment, "I'm also of the mindset you can't win every time. There's going to be downfalls. You're going to trip and fall. And, as long as you learn from it and fix it the next time, things will work out."

Thus, failure is part of the process of becoming really good at something. Those of you who have made it to a high level are already aware of this. However, the collective societal views discussed in Chapter 1 come back into the picture with regard to failure. When someone drops out of a domain because of failure, it feeds the societal views by maintaining the belief that they could not make it. In reality, there is a pretty good chance that the person dropping out was impacted by the issues highlighted throughout this book, including the impact this view can collectively have on mindset in combination with a lack of resources available for some.

Researchers Ronnel King and Jose Eos Trinidad (2021) analyzed the data for over 15,000 middle school students and confirmed that a growth mindset was predictive of success for wealthier students but not for students on the lower end of socioeconomic status. Such findings make intuitive sense. Believing you can get better at something is not particularly helpful if you do not have the resources needed to do so (more on these factors can be found in Chapters 1 and 2). Thus, it seems that we tend to drop or rise to the level of our surroundings.

Small Opportunities Leading to Larger Opportunities

Another consideration related to waiting for things to be perfect is the consideration that we have already discussed in Chapter 6 – that small opportunities often lead to larger opportunities. Implicit in this is that you are involved in the domain of interest at some level. Relevant to the current chapter, this could be making sacrifices to get initial opportunities, or it could be just showing up (which you cannot do if you have dropped out). Let us consider some examples of this playing out by turning to some of the experiences of our interviewees.

Brian Bates is a stand-up comedian and co-host of the very successful *Nateland* podcast. He discussed this premise as a guest on *The Path Distilled* podcast (Harris & Tashman, 2020). Brian mentioned that, despite still working a full-time job, he would hang out at the local comedy club. The club is well known and features nationally touring comedians – many of them household names. The goal was to get as much stage time as possible and to gain exposure to other comics. Brian got to know many of the comedians, and opportunities began to pile up. In addition to his podcast hosting gig, he currently tours nationally as a stand-up comedian. These opportunities arose, in part, by his immersion in the local scene and willingness to take less glamorous opportunities for years.

Presumably, Brian was viewing each opportunity as a building block for the next. Mark Johnson, co-owner of Hobnail Trekking Company, echoed this sentiment, "You rarely get presented large, big, fat, hairy opportunities at the beginning. My experience has been that, for every success that I've had, it's been a progression of small opportunities to big ones." As a reminder, these smaller opportunities can be derailed by perfectionistic tendencies. Nothing in this chapter should be taken as guidance to jump into something when you are definitively subpar at whatever the domain is – you have to at least be on par with the performance expected at your current level of the domain. Instead, it is a reminder to not keep yourself on the sidelines once you have reached a reasonable level of performance by seeking perfection. Our world-touring, gold-record selling, anonymous musician reminds us how taking the smaller opportunities can potentially change our lives:

> This usually happens by meeting someone that leads you into a new door. The industry is an infinitely overlapping network of

individuals that know each other, from big acts to small acts. If someone wants to help you, for whatever reason, then they can easily propel you to bigger opportunities. Small opportunities can sometimes lead to events that change the trajectory of your entire life.

These examples illustrate the ultimate impact that taking what are considered to be small opportunities can have – leading to larger opportunities. Critically, withholding yourself from a domain by waiting for things to be perfect can obviously hinder this progress. Even if your hesitation does not reach the level of perfectionism in the traditional sense, you might be hesitant to begin. Though you should not jump into something when you are so unskilled that you will damage your reputation, you should not wait too long to immerse yourself in a domain you strive to enter. As stated earlier in the chapter, there *never* will be a perfect time to start.

Chapter Summary

In this chapter, we discussed the pitfalls of perfectionism and how it is on the rise. Perfectionism can stall our progress by causing us to feel that we are not ready or convincing us to wait on the "perfect" time to launch. Either of these approaches can either hinder our progress or lead to us not participating because we never identify a time to launch. Watching the training of high performers can be intense and they can appear to exhibit perfectionism to an observer. However, a relatively new concept called "excellencism" is a better term to describe the intense commitment of high performers and their attempts to be the best version of themselves possible. Excellencism is the pursuit of excellence rather than perfection. We also proposed that feeling anxious when performing, especially early on, is a normal part of the process and should not discourage us from continuing. Rather, we can learn from our mistakes if things do not go as planned, and as we discussed in the previous chapter, small opportunities can lead to larger opportunities. Waiting until we no longer feel anxious or for the "perfect" moment is counterproductive.

Let's Go Now

Chapter 8: *Aiming for Perfection: Identify Your Threshold and Dive In*

This exercise is intended to help you counter the idea that circumstances should be "perfect" before proceeding on a path. In the **first part** of the exercise, you will be asked to provide examples of things you have wanted to do but have postponed. The **second part** will ask you to specify what is holding you up.

1. Provide at least one example of something you have wanted to do but have postponed and/or you feel anxious about doing.

2. High performers often still feel anxiety about performing, even
   when they really want to do it. Reflect on the examples you provided
   in part 1. Specifically identify what is holding you up or making you
   anxious. Finally, make a plan outlining how you are going to proceed
   despite feeling anxious. (Note: ensure you meet minimal safety / performance thresholds.)

References

Bateman, J., Hayes, S., Arnett, W. (Hosts). (2024, February 5). The Killers [Audio podcast episode]. *Smartless.* https://podcasts.apple.com/us/podcast/the-killers/id1521578868?i=1000643216888.

Curran, T., & Hill, A.P. (2019). Perfectionism is increasing over time: A meta-analysis of birth cohort differences from 1989 to 2016. *Psychological Bulletin, 145*(4), 410–429. https://psycnet.apa.org/doi/10.1037/bul0000138.

Curran, T., & Hill, A.P. (2022). Young people's perceptions of their parents' expectations and criticism are increasing over time: Implications for perfectionism. *Psychological Bulletin, 148*(1–2), 107. https://psycnet.apa.org/doi/10.1037/bul0000347.

Deakin, J.M., & Cobley, S. (2003). A search for deliberate practice: An examination of the practice environments in figure skating and volleyball. In J.L. Starkes & K.A. Ericsson (Eds.), *Expert Performance in Sports: Advances in Research on Sport Expertise* (pp. 115–135). Human Kinetics.

Donnelly, S. (2005, June). How to: write a screenplay. *Maxim, 90,* 56.

Enns, M.W., Cox, B J., Sareen, J., & Freeman, P. (2001). Adaptive and maladaptive perfectionism in medical students: A longitudinal investigation. *Medical Education, 35*(11), 1034–1042. https://doi.org/10.1111/j.1365-2923.2001.01044.x.

Ericsson, K.A., Roring, R.W., & Nandagopal, K. (2007). Giftedness and evidence for reproducibly superior performance: An account based on the expert performance framework. *High Ability Studies, 18*(1), 3–56. https://doi.org/10.1080/13598130701350593.

Gaudreau, P., Schellenberg, B.J., Gareau, A., Kljajic, K., & Manoni-Millar, S. (2022). Because excellencism is more than good enough: On the need to distinguish the pursuit of excellence from the pursuit of perfection. *Journal of Personality and Social Psychology, 122*(6), 1117–1145. https://psycnet.apa.org/doi/10.1037/pspp0000411.

Harris, K.R., & Tashman, L. (Hosts). (2020, May 10). Brandon Payne (TPD developing high performers series) [Audio podcast episode]. *The Path Distilled.* https://podcasts.apple.com/us/podcast/the-path-distilled-podcast/id1511069681?i=1000474135647.

Harris, K.R., & Tashman, L. (Hosts). (2020, September 13). Brian Bates [Audio podcast episode]. *The Path Distilled.* https://podcasts.apple.com/us/podcast/the-path-distilled-podcast/id1511069681?i=1000491079368.

King, R.B., & Trinidad, J.E. (2021). Growth mindset predicts achievement only among rich students: Examining the interplay between mindset and socioeconomic status. *Social Psychology of Education, 24*(3), 635–652. https://doi.org/10.1007/s11218-021-09616-z.

Kellogg, R.T. (2006). Professional writing expertise. In K.A. Ericsson, N. Charness, P.J. Feltovich, & R.R. Hoffman (Eds.), *The Cambridge Handbook of Expertise and Expert Performance* (pp. 389–402). Cambridge University Press.

Marin, M.M., Schober, R., Gingras, B., & Leder, H. (2017). Misattribution of musical arousal increases sexual attraction towards opposite-sex faces in females. *PLoS One, 12*(9), e0183531. https://doi.org/10.1371/journal.pone.0183531.

Moate, R.M., Gnilka, P.B., West, E.M., & Bruns, K.L. (2016). Stress and burnout among counselor educators: Differences between adaptive perfectionists, maladaptive perfectionists, and nonperfectionists. *Journal of Counseling & Development, 94*(2), 161–171. https://doi.org/10.1002/jcad.12073.

Negro, G., Kovács, B., & Carroll, G. R. (2022). What's next? Artists' music after Grammy awards. *American Sociological Review, 87*(4), 644–674. https://doi.org/10.1177/00031224221103257.

Olson, J.M. (1988). Misattribution, preparatory information, and speech anxiety. *Journal of Personality and Social Psychology, 54*(5), 758–767. https://psycnet.apa.org/doi/10.1037/0022-3514.54.5.758.

Schachter, S., & Singer, J. (1962). Cognitive, social, and physiological determinants of emotional state. *Psychological Review, 69*(5), 379–399. https://psycnet.apa.org/doi/10.1037/h0046234.

Shadrick, S.B. & Lussier, J.W. (2004). *Assessment of the Think Like a Commander Training Program.* (ARI Research Report 1824). U.S. Army Research Institute for the Behavior and Social Sciences.

Sherry, S.B., Hewitt, P.L., Sherry, D.L., Flett, G.L., & Graham, A.R. (2010). Perfectionism dimensions and research productivity in psychology professors: Implications for understanding the (mal) adaptiveness of perfectionism. *Canadian Journal of Behavioural Science/Revue Canadienne des Sciences du Comportement, 42*(4), 273–283. https://psycnet.apa.org/doi/10.1037/a0020466.

Simmons, J., McDaniels, D., Masterson III, W., Hunt, B., Goodman, D., Lehman, M., & Blamoville, E. (Producers) (2024). *Kings from Queens: The RUN DMC Story* [Television Series]. Believe Entertainment Group.

Smith, J.L., & Huntoon, M. (2014). Women's bragging rights: Overcoming modesty norms to facilitate women's self-promotion. *Psychology of Women Quarterly, 38*(4), 447–459. https://doi.org/10.1177/0361684313515840.

Winfrey, O. (2008). Beyoncé is Sasha Fierce. *Oprah.com.* https://www.oprah.com/oprahshow/beyonces-alter-ego/all. Accessed February 28, 2024.

Being Vague

9

Evaluate Your Own Path/Needs

I think the concept is the same of trying to identify, "Okay, what do I need to do to improve in this situation or to do better?" And then setting yourselves goals and targets, and then working on how you can achieve that goal and target.

– A. Mark Williams, world-renowned expertise researcher

If you can have those little goals that [you can say], "Okay, I hit that goal," It's mentally a hurdle that you can get over and say, "Okay, I got there."

– Alec Mills, pitcher, Major League Baseball (MLB)

Nina wanted to take a beach vacation, so she hopped in her car and started driving. She despised travelling via the interstate system, so she was taking as many secondary roads as possible – following any that held the promise of being scenic. Nina was having little luck finding a place to stay at night because of the isolated locations of the roads she was taking. When she did find a hotel, there would be no vacancies. By the third day of her trip, Nina had been sleeping in her car each night. She also was now out of gas and flat broke. This might seem like an extreme example of failing to plan, yet it is a surprisingly common approach to reaching one's goals. In this chapter, we discuss the importance of evaluating one's goals and identifying actionable steps that can be taken to move closer to reaching them.

DOI: 10.4324/9781003377542-9

What did, or do, you want to be when you grow up? Those initial aspirations are likely well behind you. (Granted, some of you have ended up becoming astronauts, physicians, professional athletes, farmers, or anything else you considered very early on in life.) Some of this shift can be chalked up to ambitions naturally shifting – the thought of working with blood ultimately ending the medical career ambitions. However, as we begin to solidify our interests, it is still important to know where you want to ultimately end up – world champion or local star. Thankfully, there is a history of studying goal-setting that we can pull from to better understand how setting goals can benefit us.

There has been a significant amount of research in the past century on goal-setting and identifying how performers can best benefit from making use of goal-setting strategies. This work generally has been very informative and has led to an excellent structure for considering the issues. Also, much like some of your stated relationship statuses – "it's complicated." For example, an Olympic Gold medalist shared on *The Path Distilled* podcast that he finds goal-setting to be counterproductive (Harris & Tashman, 2020). Frankly, this stance surprised me, as goal-setting is an integral component of the framework for both studying expert performers and developing expertise. I subsequently learned that there is a contingency of practitioners who question whether one should engage in goal-setting and decided to dig a little deeper.

Although we will dive into some of the specific research on goal-setting in coming sections, we begin with some overarching facets of goals that we believe to be uncontentious. First, you must have some general idea of what you want to achieve – essentially, which direction you will start moving. Second, goals generally can be broken down into smaller pieces / sub-goals. Third, there are many different types of goals. The three that seem to have the greatest amount of agreement on how they are defined and used are: outcome goals, performance goals, and process goals.

Cooking with a Recipe Versus Winging It

I have rarely seen my mother use a recipe when she cooks. She is an excellent cook and tends to cook by instinct – the proverbial, "a little bit of this and a little bit of that." This is an ability that I have not developed yet. It is unclear whether the comfortable feeling of having a recipe to follow is the culprit. Winging it would drive my anxiety level sky high – "let me see the recipe!" Surely, there will be many cooks who prefer to wing it, as well as many who will want a recipe with precise measurements. This example of cooking with a specific recipe versus winging it sets the stage to discuss the benefits of goal-setting.

The first useful comparison of goal-setting with cooking is that the desired outcome is important. This could be a delicious pan of lasagna or stepping on stage to a sold-out crowd. In other words, you must know what dish you intend to make to move toward the end product. Someone is unlikely to utter the phrase, "I have a goal of making lasagna," or "I have the goal of making delicious lasagna," but the goal is inherent in deciding to make lasagna. Ditto for other desired outcomes. We include these when considering the term, "goal(s)." This does not imply that there is not an extensive body of research on goals with some very specific considerations. Nevertheless, we are taking a broad approach and consider any desired status or end result to be a goal.

As we will see in the upcoming sections, there are many ways that we can move ourselves closer to the goals we set for ourselves. For instance, we can get ourselves to the goal of a final dish by using a recipe to prepare and cook the meal versus winging it in the lasagna example. We obviously have similar leeway in determining what our own life-goals will be – a certain occupation, performance level, financial status, or living in a certain city. A critical point is that it is advantageous, if not a requirement, to know where you want to end up – you cannot earn a college degree without identifying at least one university you want to apply to.

You must have some general idea of what you want to achieve. This idea can be extremely vague or short term, but it must exist. These ideas should be considered initial goals – losing weight, earning an A, shaving a minute off your running time, making money, or any other idea of something you want to achieve. Go ahead and call that a "goal." Identifying the things that you want to achieve need not be very specific in this initial stage, although it could be. One of the benefits is that it potentially allows you to identify the needed and/or next steps.

Prominent goal-setting theorist, Edwin Locke (Locke et al.,1981; see also Weinberg, 2013) argued that goal-setting is generally an effective practice, in part, because goals serve to direct attention and action. He also proposed that it provides a target for your efforts. Even these initial, potentially ill-defined or vague, goals should allow you to begin developing or refining strategies on how to move closer to the identified goal.

Mowing in Chunks

As newlyweds, my wife and I found a fixer-upper in the country. The yard was larger than a push lawn mower could accommodate. We had hardly any money and ended up with a push mower anyway. It seemed like a never-ending task to use the push mower to get the job done, so I began using crude mental tricks to make the task more bearable. One of these tricks was to focus on a chunk of the yard at a time. While this is nothing novel, it did allow me to identify sizeable tasks that could be accumulated to eventually get me to the final goal. The task was made more manageable by focusing on mowing smaller chunks of the overall yard.

The concept illustrated here could be applied to almost anything. Alec Mills, an MLB pitcher, stated it well:

> [A goal] needs to be attainable. A lot of times for me, it's something that's measurable and attainable within two weeks. Okay, so then you get that, go, 'Okay, let's do another one.' In two weeks, you get that goal. If you keep stacking goals, then eventually that long-term goal is going to become a lot closer and a lot more attainable than it was before.

Consider something that you want to achieve as a long-term goal – a raise, weight-loss, a recording contract, or anything else. What are some potential, attainable short-term goals you could set to get you closer to the overall goal? To use Alec's terminology, how will you be stacking goals? These examples you just came up with illustrate the individualized nature of goals. However, there are commonalities across goal categories.

Three Common Types of Goal

In a well-known psychology study, Elizabeth Loftus presented to participants a video of a car accident and asked them to provide an estimate of how fast the cars were going when they "smashed" into one another (Loftus & Palmer, 1974; Loftus, 1975). The participants estimated that the cars were travelling at approximately 64.65 km/hr (40.8 mph). While this estimate is unremarkable by itself, something fascinating happened when a different group of participants was asked how fast the cars were going when they "contacted" each other. This time, the participants estimated the cars were travelling at approximately 51.17 km/hr (31.8 mph). The implication was that the way the question was asked ("smashed" versus "contacted") influenced the answer. This example illustrates the importance of specificity of language.

There has been considerable debate about the success of goal-setting and one of the root causes could be the variety of meanings when using the term, "goal." Joe Baker, a researcher who studies high performers, conveyed this sentiment in our conversation with him:

> It comes back to the same problem we have with talent as well. How do we clearly define this concept that we're talking about? Because I doubt that they're not goal-setting. It's just they're not seeing it as traditional sort of SMART (Specific, Measurable, Achievable, Realistic, Timebound) goal, or whatever; that sort of overly simplistic old school goal-setting that we think about.

We will now consider the three particular types of goal, mentioned earlier, that can be differentiated based on their scope – outcome goals, performance goals, and process goals (Locke et al., 1981; Weinberg, 2013). A quick note before getting to what they are – it took a great deal of effort to track down the definitions. The terms were showing up frequently in the sizable amount of goal-setting research, but none of the articles actually defined them. However, I finally came across the work on goals by the esteemed scholar, Robert Weinberg. Weinberg spent much of his career studying athletes' goals and how best to use goals to improve performance.

The least specific of the three types of goal, in terms of actions to take, would be an *outcome* goal. As the name suggests, an outcome goal refers to the "end result" of something (a goal related to the outcome). Weinberg described it as referring to "winning or losing" (2013, p.171), but we will be using it more broadly. Specifically, an outcome goal could be to reach a specific weight, win an art contest, or win a marathon. Using the example earlier in the chapter, graduating from college would be considered an outcome goal. You might have noticed that some of these outcome goals happen on vastly different timelines. For example, an outcome goal for a college degree could be years in the making, while a different outcome goal could potentially be reached in months (or sooner).

The second type of goal we cover are *performance* goals. Weinberg describes these goals as "one's actual performance in relation to their own standard of excellence" (2013, p.171). These are the goals for which we ask ourselves if we are performing where we want to be and if we need to attempt to improve our performance. You might be asking yourself if you should improve your walking time by three minutes, increase your sales by 20 percent, or write an additional 20 pages a week of your manuscript (asking for a friend). Performance goals can be thought of as providing some specificity to the outcome goals – "I will be salesperson of the year by increasing my sales by 20 percent."

Finally, *process* goals have an even greater level of specificity and focus on the specific process that you will engage in. Weinberg described these goals for athletes as, "how an athlete performs a particular skill, displays a certain technique or carries out a specific strategy" (2013, p.171), such as using proper form when batting or returning a tennis serve. However, we also consider process goals in a broader sense. Process goals can be thought of as the specific things you will do to increase your sales by 20 percent (follow up with all leads), improve your walking time by three minutes (stay hydrated, use proper form, and improve nutritional value of diet), or write an additional 20 pages of your manuscript (allot blocks of time and write anything that comes to mind for later editing).

You likely noticed that these definitions represented a hierarchy. The outcome goals were overarching in scope; the performance goals were used as a mechanism to move closer to the ultimate outcome goals; and the process goals also could be considered as the means to work toward reaching the performance goals and ultimately the outcome goal(s). However, this hierarchy is not a requirement. Feasibly, these can work independently of one another. However, it certainly seems that it would make a lot of sense to direct all of these goals towards the same end. Consider each of these levels when you complete the *I Need to Start Doing...* exercise (Expert Performance International Collective [EPIC], 2023).

"I Wanna Be a Judge When I Grow Up" – The Individualized Nature of Goals

Being a judge was never a personal goal of mine. Chances are, some of you actually did have a childhood goal of becoming a judge. As is the case with any type of goal, the goals themselves and the way that we reach them are quite individualized. Let us assume that you have established your end goal – where you want to end up and/or what you want to accomplish. Now give some thought to how things are right now. Spend some time thinking about the steps that will be needed to reach your end goal. Really dig into these last things (the *I Need to Start Doing...* exercise at the end of the chapter will help you do this). These will be your sub-goals. They could take the form of the performance, process, or even multiple, progressing outcome goals (Weinberg, 2013), described earlier in the chapter. As you embark on this path, it is critical to identify what suits you as you work toward reaching the goals you have set for yourself. Ways to do this include seeking feedback on your performance by being honest about what you are not doing well (covered in Chapter 10) and seeking feedback/criticisms of your performance (covered in Chapter 14). We will not do a deep dive into these topics in this chapter since the topics have dedicated chapters. However, we want to reiterate the importance of personalizing your goals.

We learned relatively recently that there is a measurable contingency of researchers and practitioners who advocate *against* goal-setting. This stance surprised us as goal-setting is an integral component of the framework for both studying expert performers and developing expertise. One of the core tenets of improvement is identifying a current level of performance and striving to move to the next one that is currently out of reach. As noted earlier in the chapter, we count this as a goal. Presumably, the argument against goal-setting includes at least two considerations. Echoing Joe Baker's earlier comments, we assume one of the arguments against goal-setting is disagreement with the *rigid approach* specified in the academic realm about goal-setting.

It turns out that much of the second issue has been with large, overarching goals – becoming a professional athlete or winning the Boston Marathon. Olympic Gold-medalist Joe Jacobi shared this sentiment on *The Path Distilled* podcast (Harris & Tashman, 2020). This makes sense given the discussion of the types of goals in the earlier section. Such outcome goals without the specific steps to accomplish them – the performance or process goals – are of limited value. However, our use of what is considered goal-setting is much broader than what is typically inferred Stating you want to go to college or make enchiladas will count. These are statements of a goal. This illustrates how someone can say that they do not practice goal-setting but also state a variety of personal goals. Some will argue that these are plans or ambitions. For our purposes, same difference. As with other concepts presented in this book, at its core, goal-setting is identifying where you want to be/what you want to achieve. Identifying how to get there can be called your plan, your steps, your aspirations, or anything else. Fundamentally, they can be considered goals. Even having lunch today is a goal.

A final consideration related to goals is that success builds momentum and leads to new goals. As you immerse yourself in a domain, you likely will be made aware for the first time of new possibilities. As we noted in earlier chapters, one of the hindrances to domain involvement includes lack of awareness of techniques and lack of resources. We do not always know what to aim for until we are immersed in a domain. You likely will adjust your goal pursuits upward as you become more successful. Such success often affords us with a greater awareness of both effective techniques and possibilities. You might even end up finding yourself in the role of "gatekeeper;" a role determining who among the next "generation" of aspirers is granted access to your domain.

Chapter Summary

In this chapter, we presented some of the seminal work on goal-setting and considered the impact goal-setting can have on becoming a high performer. Recently, there have been instances in which the importance of goal-setting has been questioned. However, goal-setting should be considered more generally as there are some overarching facets of goals that we believe to be uncontentious. First, you must have some general idea of what you want to achieve – essentially, which direction you will start moving in. Second, since goals generally can be broken down into smaller pieces/sub-goals, doing so can make the overall goal seem more attainable and allow for progress to be gained. The three types of goals that seem to have the greatest amount of agreement on how they are defined and used are outcome goals, performance goals, and process goals. Using these hierarchical goals can allow one to personalize goals, gauge progress, gain momentum, and ultimately identify new goals.

I Need to Start Doing…

Chapter 9: *Being Vague: Evaluate Your Own Path/Needs*

This exercise is intended to help you identify the steps required to get where you want to be and how to take those steps. In the **first part** of the exercise, you will be asked to provide some of the requirements of the domain you are pursuing. The **second part** will ask you to assess where you currently are in relation to the requirements and develop a plan to get there.

1. What are some of the domain requirements of what you hope to accomplish?

2. Reflect on where you currently stand regarding the requirements noted in part 1. What are some specific ways you can close the gap between where you currently stand and what you hope to accomplish?

References

Expert Performance International Collective (EPIC) (2023). *I Need to Start Doing...* [Exercise]. Nashville; New York City.

Harris, K.R., & Tashman, L. (Hosts). (2020, September 20). Joe Jacobi [Audio podcast episode]. *The Path Distilled.* https://podcasts.apple.com/us/podcast/the-path-distilled-podcast/id1511069681?i=1000491859964.

Locke, E.A., Shaw, K.N., Saari, L.M., & Latham, G.P. (1981). Goal-setting and task performance: 1969–1980. *Psychological Bulletin, 90*(1), 125–152. https://psycnet.apa.org/doi/10.1037/0033-2909.90.1.125.

Loftus, E.F. (1975). Reconstructing memory: The incredible eyewitness. *Jurimetrics Journal, 15*(3), 188–193. https://www.jstor.org/stable/29761487.

Loftus, E.F., & Palmer, J.C. (1974). Reconstruction of automobile destruction: An example of the interaction between language and memory. *Journal of Verbal Learning and Verbal Behavior, 13*(5), 585–589. https://doi.org/10.1016/S0022-5371(74)80011-3.

Weinberg, R.S. (2013). Goal setting in sport and exercise: Research and practical applications. *Revista da Educação Física/UEM, 24*, 171–179. https://doi.org/10.4025/reveducfis.v24.2.17524.

Sugarcoating

10

Acknowledge What You Aren't Doing Well

Sometimes, there are workouts that aren't that great even when you're dealing with the greatest shooter that's ever played. There are days when the ball doesn't go in as much as we want it to in our workouts. How we improve is we've got to look deeper. What causes us not to have a great shooting day?

– Brandon Payne, Stephen Curry's basketball skill development coach (on *The Path Distilled* podcast)

Honest feedback is very important. It's difficult nowadays, where it seems the culture has kind of shifted where everything is affirmed. No matter what you're doing, you're great at it. This is what most people will tell you. It can be tough. Because when you get out there in the real world and you start applying for jobs, it can be tough when suddenly someone tells you this stuff isn't that great. And what are you going to do with that?

– Thomas Estrada, feature film and video game animator

Trent was a rising star in the world of high-school football. The quarterback was named Mr. Football for the state of Texas his senior year. Now playing for a large state university, coaches felt that Trent would be the unquestioned starter if he worked to correct two issues with his game – holding the ball too long and his foot placement. Having thrown for just under 5,000 yards in high school, Trent was not keen on changing anything about his game. He transferred after sophomore

DOI: 10.4324/9781003377542-10

year to a different school but never became the starter. Trent now owns a landscaping company in his hometown. Trent's example illustrates the unwillingness and/or blind spots that most people have regarding recognizing what they are not doing well along with the devastating consequences. The frequency of such blind spots is surprisingly common. In fact, you might be shocked to discover how large your own blind spots are. We now unpack some of the psychological factors leading to these blind spots.

"I'm Pretty Good at This – At Least Better Than Most"

How do you feel about your driving skills? Would you say that you are an average or above average driver? If you are like most people, you will tell us that you are an above average driver – even if you recently caused a crash. In fact, almost 90 percent of respondents declared that they were above average drivers (Svenson, 1981, as cited in Dunning, Meyerowitz, & Holzberg, 1989). Not only is this hard to believe, having driven on public roads recently, but it does not line up with the way statistics actually work. When something is said to be normally distributed, it takes the shape of a bell – the bell curve. Let us break this down in common language before you decide to skip to the next section or chapter because we are talking about statistics so early in this chapter.

Consider the average height of women in the United States of America, which is around 161.3 cm (5 ft 3.5 in), according to the National Center for Health Statistics (2024). Obviously, not every woman is 161.3 cm, and it only takes looking around a crowded place to notice a variety of heights. In fact, because we know that the standard deviation is 5.59 cm (2.2 in) (National Bureau of Economic Research), we also know that 68.2 percent of women in the crowd can be expected to be between 155.71 cm and 166.89 cm (5 ft 1.3 in and 5 ft 5.7 in). This breaks down as roughly 34.1 percent above 161.3 cm (5 ft 3.5 in), and 34.1 percent below. This entire 68.2% of women represent what we consider to be the range of "average." Because we are accustomed to thinking of average in terms of the single number, 161.3 cm (5 ft 3.5 in) in this example, it can be easy to forget that it is an actual range. Consider IQ scores – the IQ test scores for many common tests, such as the Wechsler Adult Intelligence Scale (WAIS; Wechsler, 1997), are calculated using a special technique such that 100 will always be the average IQ. However, average "intelligence" is represented by the range created by adding and subtracting the standard deviation, typically 15, resulting in 85–115 being the typical range for what is considered an average IQ score.

Getting back to the height example, some of you might be wondering about the really short or really tall people. They are represented, too. There just are not as many of them. As we go to the extremes of anything normally distributed, there are fewer and fewer of them – geniuses with an IQ greater than 145 or women who are 178.07 cm (6 ft 1.6 in) tall. These extremes are two standard deviations above the mean, exceeding 99.9% of women in height or 99.9% of others regarding IQ. This also works in the opposite direction, such as there are relatively few women shorter than 160.12 cm (4 ft 11.1 in) or individuals scoring less than 70 on the WAIS.

This brings us back to the driving example. For anything on a true bell curve, only 15.8 percent of anything is above average. Full stop. However, most of us tend to see ourselves as above average in some, or possibly many, aspects of our lives. For example, almost two-thirds (65 percent) of Americans believe that they possess above-average intelligence (Heck, Simons, & Chabris, 2018). Again, only the top 15.8 percent of Americans could actually be above average. The finding that 94 percent of college professors consider themselves to be above average (Cross, 1977, as cited in Dunning, Meyerowitz, & Holzberg, 1989) never fails to generate a hearty laugh among our colleagues. However, the reality is that the majority of us will likely retreat back to our own thoughts, confident that we are not among those inflating our actual performance or standing.

This phenomenon originally was labelled the "above average effect" and was found to be very common. For example, in a now classic survey of over a million high school students conducted by the College Board in the late 1970s, only 2 percent of students judged themselves to be below average in leadership ability (70 percent rated themselves above average) and only 6 percent rated themselves below average for athletic ability (60 percent rated above; as cited Dunning, Meyerowitz, & Holzberg, 1989). It appears that we are very ill-suited to gauging our abilities and relative performance. Analysis of this line of thinking evolved into what is now known as the Dunning-Kruger effect.

The concept of the Dunning-Kruger effect eventually reached the mainstream, and you likely have heard it mentioned outside of academic conversations. The initial findings were that the majority of us overestimate our actual performance capabilities (Kruger & Dunning, 1999). Justin Kruger and David Dunning had Cornell students estimate their ability to perform a variety of tasks such as grammar and logic tasks. All but the highest performing students overestimated their performance. Critically, the lowest performing students had estimated their performance would be well above average. In a particularly illustrative variation of the original study, students were asked just before taking an exam how they would rank compared to their classmates once the exam had been graded. The predictions were all on the higher-end of percentile rankings – everyone estimated that their performance would be near the top. All but the very top performers had overestimated their performance. The highest performers had slightly underestimated theirs. This was one of the original studies examining the Dunning-Kruger effect.

When we say that the Dunning-Kruger effect reached the mainstream, it did so in a huge way. Having been in the field for decades, we know that something is huge when the concept starts showing up in everyday conversations with those not working with it daily. The Dunning-Kruger effect has joined the list of psychological science concepts that have permeated popular culture, such as situation awareness, "the 10,000-hour rule," growth mindset, and cognitive dissonance. Typically, the original meaning of a concept is diluted, or lost altogether, when this happens. An interesting layer of consideration with the Dunning-Kruger effect is that we all still tend to overestimate our performance – even when we are aware of the concept and this exact risk. You likely did consider yourself to be an above-average driver, but so did the thousands (millions?) of other readers.

However, we must remember that only a small percentage of you can actually be above (or below) average. Just over two-thirds of us are statistically average on a variety of things. The remainder is divided into being above (or below) average by one standard deviation or by two standard deviations. As you likely have already determined, the difference between being one standard deviation versus two standard deviations above or below the mean can also result in noticeable differences. Recall from the earlier discussion that it is a difference between being in the top 15.8 percent and being in the top 0.1 percent. This would translate into the difference between being noticeably bright and being a true genius.

The Chicken or the Egg?

As noted in the previous section, one of the key findings related to the Dunning-Kruger effect was that most of the performers overestimated their actual performance. In some cases, the overestimation of performance is minimal; in others, the estimates are off by "miles." However, a finding that generally receives less attention is equally intriguing. In particular, the top performers slightly underestimated their actual performance. Obviously, this stands in contrast to the findings related to the low-performers, who consistently overestimate their status or abilities. As you know by this point in the chapter, this high-performing group also represents a much smaller percentage of performers. It does raise a fascinating empirical question of whether being better at assessing your own performance increases the likelihood of being a top performer? Or is that being a top performer then allows you to better assess others by comparing your own performance? There are two studies that could provide some insight.

Researchers investigating the accuracy of surgical interns when estimating their own skills found that the interns generally *underestimated* their performance compared to their actual outcomes (Karnick et al., 2021). A quick note on this finding before we proceed. Although this finding of underestimation is obviously out of line with the predictions expected of performers on the lower end of performance based on most discussions of the Dunning-Kruger effect, the finding that this accomplished, highly selective group (by proxy of succeeding in a highly specialized, complex, and demanding field) is likely the high-performing group that would underestimate their own abilities, as found in some of the original Dunning-Kruger effect studies. They literally are the top-performers who tend to underestimate their performance. As the researchers noted, these interns could rate themselves on the higher end of performance and still be underestimating their actual performance – akin to predicting a 95 on the exam and making a 100 in the traditional examples of the Dunning-Kruger effect.

It is worth noting that the interns with the best performance tended to be relatively harsher in their self-assessments than the relatively lower performing ones. The interns who were most accurate at self-assessment showed the greatest improvement, which suggests that it is possible that the greater self-assessment accuracy could be one of the mechanisms ultimately leading to better performance. If this were the case, it would represent a potentially trainable component, meaning that they were able to identify their "weak spot" and develop ways to improve that could be taught to others.

An alternative explanation is that the highest performers have yet to recognize their ability. This fits the original finding of the Dunning-Kruger effect with roughly a flat line for estimates of performance, with the observed differences arising from the actual performance. Momentarily venturing into the realm of creativity, researchers discovered an interesting breakdown when students across a variety of years/grades in school were asked to first give estimates of their creativity and then subsequently were tested for creativity (Urban & Urban, 2021). While over half of the overall participants were found not to be creative based on the test, only half of that group recognized their lack of creativity. The more interesting finding is that almost half of the participants (44.3 percent) were actually creative but did not realize it – a category the researchers labelled "skilled and unaware." Taken as a whole, these findings fit the general pattern of Dunning-Kruger results as only a quarter of the students were accurate in esti-mating their ability – creativity in this example. However, the number of participants who are actually creative but unaware of it begs the question of how common this underestimation could be. What are the factors that impact how accurate a performer will be at identifying how well they perform?

We Are Horrible at Self-assessment. Now What?

There are at least two layers of acknowledging what you are not doing well that are relative to high performance. The first is being aware of the tendency for most people to overestimate their performance – the Dunning-Kruger effect described earlier in this chapter. Such awareness might not necessarily prevent you from overestimating your own performance. However, being aware of the tendency to overestimate our own performance can put you on a path to identifying better ways to obtain insight into your own performance. We dedicate a chapter to seeking out feedback and criticism (Chapter 14) but will introduce some considerations here.

In their work related to medical training, Kevin Eva and Glenn Regehr (2008) provided excellent analysis of some of the relevant issues. While the entire analysis is thought provoking, there are some key points that are most applicable to our discussion. The authors remind us that we all are vulnerable to this inaccuracy and suggest that we treat it as a "we" problem rather than a "they" problem. In other words, we all are prone to inflating how well we think we perform compared to how well we actually perform. It is not a case of just getting to someone via an intervention in order to have them try to get better at self-assessment. Rather, the authors recommend that training and educational systems should be set up so that assessment is a built-in part of the process. Moreover, reliance on measures of self-assessment, without other evidence, should be minimized: "The empirically derived conclusion that humans are generally poor at self-assessment merely indicates that we are inaccurate as often as not and that, as a result, one should not rely on self-assessments to provide valid indications of ability" (Eva & Regehr, 2008, p. 17).

While minimizing the use of self-assessment might seem like an extreme stance, it might be better stated with the qualifiers of "at least for now," and certainly "as the sole measure." As we have established, we are not very good at assessing our own performance, particularly when there are no other, corroborating external measures. Eva and Regehr also point out that knowing how well we are doing is a continuum (2008). We might be very attuned to how well we are doing (poorly or well) for some things, and way off base for others (poorly or well). Eva and Regehr use the example of someone commenting that self-assessment is easy because they knew they would never make it as a professional athlete. The authors used this comment to point out that this is one of the low-hanging fruits of the aforementioned continuum – the odds of anyone becoming a professional athlete are slim. It does not take a great amount of self-assessment skill to make such a call. It is the subtler calls that we often struggle with. How well did you do with the last presentation/talk that you gave? An interviewer once asked me how well my job presentation went, after they had attended it. While my answer was that it went well, my actual thoughts were that they should be telling me.

However, many situations provide other means of indicating how well you are doing, including some type of external feedback – a patient stabilizing, opposing players unable to return your tennis serve, or a critique from a thesis advisor. It is the examples used during the discussions of the above-average effect that are most prone to misjudgments – relative ranking as a driver or professor. There are vague measures on which to base such judgments, such as frequency of accidents or student feedback. Unfortunately, such measures still leave a great deal to be interpreted, and these interpretations tend to be unreliable. Thus, we suggest acknowledging that there are things you might not be doing well and seeking out other sources of feedback to assess further. You also should continue monitoring beyond the initial assessment by seeking ongoing feedback. We will expand on this in Chapter 15.

"I'll Have the Truth – No Sugar, Please"

Taking your 928th free throw shot in basketball or taking a tumble for the 56th time on the half-pipe can provide organic feedback. However, akin to my job presentation mentioned earlier, there are situations where you just do not know what you are doing well or not. It could be that you are too new to the domain to recognize the indicators. The competition might also be too low level to get a good sense of how well you are doing in a broader sense. We are sure that many of you have been embarrassed playing a video game because you were pretty good at the game against the computer as an opponent but found that a skilled human opponent outplayed you. Someone once shared that he was considered one of the best local football (soccer) players in his hometown. As a result, he was pretty confident in his performance. It was not until his cousins visited from a country with a much more ingrained football culture that he realized he was not really very good at football – at least not as good as he thought.

Identifying what it is that you are not doing well is one of the keys to reaching the next level, and potentially the top level. We have already mentioned in Chapter 8 that the best figure skaters, relative to the mid-level skaters, spent a greater amount of their practice on what they were not doing well. The Chapter 8 discussion was to suggest that you should not let waiting on things to be perfect sideline you for too long. However, another aspect of this is that you must also be able to identify those areas, commonly called "weak spots," before you can work to fix them. Obtaining appropriate feedback is the topic of Chapter 14. However, there also is a psychological component at play when we acknowledge what we are not doing well.

It can be uncomfortable for us if we are able to see around our "blind spot" or use other feedback to recognize that there are things we are not doing well. In some instances, this can cause you to have to reassess how you will proceed. However, as we noted earlier, it is *more* common for the best performers to target their weaknesses. This makes perfect sense. Once you reach a level of stable high performance at a task within a domain, you can turn your attention to the weakness in your performance. As long as you do not completely neglect what you were already good at, you should continue to improve by targeting identified weaknesses.

You also might find yourself reaching the level of performance at which an observer would consider your refinements to be overkill. Stephen Curry's personal skills trainer, Brandon Payne, provided an excellent example of such refinement on *The Path Distilled* podcast, "you have to be tough enough, mentally, to be able to dissect your performance on a daily basis to locate why things went badly or went well. And that's a big part of improvement as well. So, it's this idea of incremental improvement" (Harris & Tashman, 2020).

Brandon's example of ongoing refinement should be encouraging to all of us. It shows that even the most elite performers are still working on what they can improve. Some of you are likely discouraged by what might sound like a never-ending process. However, think of it as illustrating how much you can still accomplish. We encourage you to condition yourself to hear the hard truth. Acknowledge what you are not doing well and develop a strategy to work on that piece. Chapter 15 is dedicated to seeking feedback and some specific strategies that you can use to assess performance and the effectiveness of any interventions.

Chapter Summary

In this chapter, we introduced the research on how poorly we do in assessing our performance and how this blind spot can hurt our progress toward becoming the best performer possible. Most people believe themselves to be above average at most things – driving ability, intelligence, most anything. However, this assessment does not match up with reality as the amount of us who could be above average is statistically limited. This "above average" effect evolved into the well-known Dunning-Kruger effect, a tendency for underperformers to be unaware that they are underperforming. This phenomenon occurs, in part, because we tend not to seek feedback or acknowledge it when it is available. High performers actively seek out the things that they are not doing well and attempt to improve upon them. Therefore, we should all heed the message of the importance of seeking as much feedback as possible, including evidence of the things that we are not currently doing well.

"I Am Really Bad At..."

Chapter 10: *Sugarcoating – Acknowledge What You Aren't Doing*

This exercise is designed to help you identify areas in which you could improve your performance and to normalize looking for room to improve. In the **first part** of the exercise, you will be asked to identify some areas you need to improve. The **second part** will ask you to identify some potential ways to go about this (it could be combined with the Chapter 9 exercise, *I Need to Start Doing…*).

1. Please identify three (or more) things that you are not doing well or could do better.

2. Reflect on the areas of potential improvement you identified in part 1. What are some specific ways you can go about improving?

References

Dunning, D., Meyerowitz, J.A., & Holzberg, A.D. (1989). Ambiguity and self-evaluation: The role of idiosyncratic trait definitions in self-serving assessments of ability. *Journal of Personality and Social Psychology, 57*(6), 1082–1090. https://doi.org/10.1037/0022-3514.57.6.1082.

Eva, K.W., & Regehr, G. (2008). "I'll never play professional football" and other fallacies of self-assessment. *Journal of Continuing Education in the Health Professions, 28*(1), 14–19. https://doi.org/10.1002/chp.150.

Harris, K.R., & Tashman, L. (Hosts). (2020, May 10). Brandon Payne (TPD developing high performers series) [Audio podcast episode]. *The Path Distilled.* https://podcasts.apple.com/us/podcast/the-path-distilled-podcast/id1511069681?i=1000474135647.

Heck, P.R., Simons, D.J., & Chabris, C.F. (2018). 65% of Americans believe they are above average in intelligence: Results of two nationally representative surveys. *PloS One, 13*(7), e0200103. https://doi.org/10.1371/journal.pone.0200103.

Karnick, A., Limberg, J., Bagautdinov, I., Stefanova, D., Aveson, V., Thiesmeyer, J., ... & Fahey III, T. J. (2021). Can general surgery interns accurately measure their own technical skills? Analysis of cognitive bias in surgical residents' self-assessments. *Surgery, 170*(5), 1353–1358. https://doi.org/10.1016/j.surg.2021.04.008.

Kruger, J., & Dunning, D. (1999). Unskilled and unaware of it: How difficulties in recognizing one's own incompetence lead to inflated self-assessments. *Journal of Personality and Social Psychology, 77*(6), 1121–1134. https://doi.org/10.1037/0022-3514.77.6.1121.

National Center for Health Statistics (2024). *Body Measurements.* https://www.cdc.gov/nchs/fastats/body-measurements.htm. Accessed January 20, 2024.

Urban, M., & Urban, K. (2021). Unskilled but aware of it? Cluster analysis of creative metacognition from preschool age to early adulthood. *The Journal of Creative Behavior, 55*(4), 937–945. https://doi.org/10.1002/jocb.499.

Wechsler, D. (1997). *Wechsler Adult Intelligence Scale--Third Edition (WAIS-III)* [Database record; APA PsycTests]. https://doi.org/10.1037/t49755-000.

Not Allowing for Rest/ Recovery

11

Make Rest a PRIORITY

But when you're not rested, you're going to make bad decisions. Your judgment doesn't work.

– Major General Walter Lord, US Army (Ret.)

The default is to think about and prioritize the training, and not consider resting and recovery efforts. Particularly from a psychological perspective, that was often overlooked. So once again, if you're an athlete, it's much more likely that you're considering ice baths, foam rolling, staying off your feet, massage, very light exercise to get the ball moving on rest days, these kinds of things. But you're not considering trying to avoid your training facility on your rest day, not continuously hanging out with your teammates all day on a rest day.

– Dr. David Eccles, professor and world-renowned scholar on expert performance and rest

John comes from a long line of farmers. His grandfather bought the land that John farms over 70 years ago, and it has been in the family ever since. The farm is comprised of over 600 acres but at least a quarter of it is currently lying fallow – not being used for a predetermined span to allow the soil to recuperate and replenish critical nutrients. This rest is critical for the longevity and health of the soil. We also need these periods of dedicated rest/recovery for both our physical and mental health. This chapter will focus on the importance of rest, how to rest, and the consequences of not incorporating rest into our routines.

DOI: 10.4324/9781003377542-11

"Lying fallow." This idea in relation to human performance can be thought of as the concept of "rest." Rest is one of the commonly overlooked components of the expertise literature (Eccles et al., 2022). Although rest was heralded as an essential component of becoming a world-class performer by some of the early researchers, such as Anders Ericsson (Ericsson, Krampe, & Tesch-Römer, 1993), it did not gain as much traction as the other components – the type of practice or amount of practice. There are numerous instances of evidence suggesting that rest should be a priority for anyone seeking the highest levels of excellence. For example, the amount of time allocated to the rigorous mental demands of writing should be limited to a window of one to four hours for most professionals (e.g., Kellogg, 2006), and daily naps are common among world-class performers (Ericsson, Krampe, & Tesch-Römer, 1993). However, the importance of rest was commonly left out of the conversation when the idea of putting in a great deal of work over a period of time began gaining traction. We rarely, if ever, heard anything about the importance of rest as part of the equation whenever the idea of the so-called "10,000-hour rule" (see Chapter 1 for more on how this amount is actually quite variable) began creeping into everyday conversations. Despite the neglect, rest is a critical part of becoming a high performer.

Rest, Rest, Where Art Thou?

"Rest? If I rest, I won't have enough time to finish everything on my to do list!" Does this sound like you? How about someone you know? Or how about the opposite – you feel as if you have so much to do so you rest to avoid work? Either way, our body could be telling us something: it is time to take a break. How will you respond? We hope that you will make time to rest and recuperate. However, the concept of rest can be tricky. Rest does not come easy for many of us. We might feel we will get further behind if we rest. Still, others may not realize that rest is more than just physical. It is not difficult to read the signs when we are physically fatigued. Our paces might become slower or our performances decline markedly. Ignoring the signs of physical fatigue can result in our body shutting down – many of us have observed the common sight of a marathon runner moving awkwardly toward the finish line because their limbs will no longer obey the brain's signals to perform correctly. The marathoner might even be on the ground crawling toward the finish line. Mental and psychological fatigue is often less obvious to observers than physical fatigue but is just as important to recognize.

Dr. David Eccles is a well-known researcher in the field of expert performance and performance psychology, and has worked with athletes internationally. He has worked extensively on conducting research to help us better understand how the best performers develop their skills across a variety of domains and what we can learn from them to potentially apply to training. These efforts include attempts to make the proposed tools for understanding expert performance as user-friendly as possible.

While carrying out his scholarly work, Dr. Eccles realized that the idea of rest as part of the training process was commonly overlooked (Eccles at al., 2022). While physical rest and sleep are important for consolidating memories, learning, and other biological processes, mental rest is not discussed as frequently. When many people hear rest, they might think of taking a nap or taking a breather from a basketball game. However, mental rest is also critically important. Recall that becoming a high-level performer is a demanding process, both mentally and physically, but it is not a given that rest will be prioritized despite the intensity of mental and physical exertion. The performer might be fearful of losing ground to the competition or drawing the ire of their coach. This is one of the reasons Dr. Eccles has emphasized the need to make rest as much of a priority as the other aspects of becoming a high-level performer. As highlighted by Dr. Eccles and his colleagues, it was considered an integral component in the early days of studying high performers.

You probably have experienced the benefit of prioritizing rest and recuperation – a spa day or just a random "mental health" day. These often result in some level of restoration. Thankfully, there are multiple ways to benefit from spontaneous rest. For example, it could be resting your mind by partaking in a mundane task where your mind is not focusing on anything specific. This could be video games for you and painting for someone else. Along these lines, when Dr. Eccles asked athletes what rest meant to them, common responses were time away from the sport or time not thinking about the sport.

Mental rest can be thought of as a psychological state that is sub-jective to each individual; therefore, there is no one definition or experience that can inform people on when mental rest is important. However, there are warning signs that indicate you may not be performing at your best, and your mental abilities are showing you need to rest. Let us consider the case of Nikki. Nikki realized that she was always feeling tired, lacked motivation to continue with what she was doing, was applying very little effort, and was finding less joy in things she used to enjoy. She could not figure out what was going on, but when she started to talk about this with her family, they told her it was a sign she needed to rest mentally and recuperate. But what does mental rest look like? What constitutes mental rest can be quite individualized. For example, mental rest for Emily could be sitting in the recliner with her favorite television show on in the background – where she is not actively engaging in anything, whereas mental rest for Kevin could be taking a walk through nature. Dannelle Whiteside, an attorney, shared that for her:

> Self-care looks different depending on the day. Besides a demanding career, I have a busy family. I'm not always able to go and treat myself to a massage or something like that. But, I can get to say, 'Okay, I will take time journaling, meditating, that kind of thing, every day.'

Therefore, we can consider the determination of how to rest and recu-perate to be something that you must identify as being effective for you. While the exact approach to being able to rest will be personalized, we now consider some the commonalities of mental rest.

"But I Didn't Work Out This weekend" – The Considerations of Mental Rest

The movement to return rest to its rightful place in the development of high-level performance is still in its infancy. The majority of research related to this push has been focused on mental rest in athletes; how-ever, these tactics can apply outside of the world of sports. Dr. Eccles and colleagues outline six wakeful resting experiences to help us recuperate mentally: (1) taking a break from always thinking about work, school, or one's sport; (2) getting a break from any effortful thinking; (3) getting a break from feeling like your life is controlled by work, school, or sport; (4) getting a break from the daily monotony of your routine; (5) being able to catch up on important work tasks; and (6) being able to have a personal life outside of work, school, or sport (Eccles et al., 2021).

We need to be able to psychologically detach from our schooling, work, sports, or anything else with which we consistently engage that is a potential stressor. Think about it – even things you initially find enjoyable potentially would be causing you distress during the ninth month of intense engagement. Such involvement can be consuming to the point that we are always thinking about something related to it. This is why the psychological detachment is important; it refers to our ability to be mentally away from what we are immersed in. Using the analogy of an on/off switch, this detachment would be turning the switch "off" in our minds. This detachment can be an important way to allow you some level of recuperation.

The issue is that most of us have difficulties, at least some of the time, being able to turn off the switch. This might translate into thinking about what needs to get done or how you can improve some aspect of your performance during what are supposed to be "off" times. Perhaps we need to start practicing "turning off" thinking about our obligations. However, this might be easier said than done. I have spent many nights trying to get back to sleep because a thought enters my mind and leads to a deluge of all of the related things that need to get done. You might have similar experiences. Someone once told me that a project is not truly yours until you are thinking about it in the shower. Thus, we might have difficulties with being able to psychologically detach.

This can be especially difficult if we feel as though we are not accomplishing everything we should in a given time period. However, it is important to remember that if we run ourselves until we feel as though we are on "empty," we will not be producing quality work. We might even cause ourselves more work in the long-run when accounting for the extra effort needed and the potential errors resulting from being at less than full capacity, compared to if we had incorporated rest into our schedule in the first place. Our colleagues who specialize in industrial-organizational psychology frequently emphasize the importance of a work-life balance, and that is essentially the takeaway from this first point. If you are able to use that on/off switch, switch it to "on" when you are at work or school, or playing your sport, and then turn it back "off" once you leave the campus or field.

But it can be hard to turn our brains off, especially when we have been working intensely toward a goal. Whether we are at work, at school, or on the field, we are prone to adopting a mentality of just doing what needs to be done to be successful. This is especially the case when you are striving to compete on a world stage. When interviewing Dr. Eccles for this book, he shared that when asked what rest meant to them, National Football League (NFL) athletes stated that rest was time away from the sport or time to not think about the sport. This is a prime example of the aforementioned psychological detachment, accomplished in this case by not engaging in any effortful thinking, whether it be about your sports team, work, or school. This sometimes can be as simple as immersing yourself in a book, movie, or hobby. We have heard of gardening referred to as "dirt therapy" because the focus of your thoughts can be blissfully limited to the task at hand – the decision of when to prune or adjust the soil occupies your mind. One specific way to potentially decrease our engagement in effortful thinking is through mindfulness. Researchers have found that when we practice mindfulness-based techniques, we can detach from work, have an increased satisfaction with work-life balance, and have decreased psychological conflict over time (Althammer et al., 2021).

We have all believed or have been told at some point in our life that our schooling, work, or sport should come first so we can put in our best-efforts. However, this mindset is essentially allowing the task to control us, either explicitly or subconsciously. In these orbits, we can be controlled by deadlines, goals, assignments, or meetings. It can come to consume our thoughts, and we may feel an unhealthy obligation to accomplish our goals and meet those deadlines. If we do not meet our goals or deadlines, we fear we will be seen as a failure or even see ourselves that way. Training ourselves to engage in an activity that interests us, such as painting, walking through nature, or listening to music, can allow us to mentally rest because our mind is not focusing on the deadlines or other obligations we have prioritized.

When talking with high-performing students, we have found that many use these types of creative outlets to rest. They find that taking the time away from studying and focusing on something else actually helps enhance their ability to study and their motivation to learn. To do this, you can incorporate a rest day or even a chunk of a day that is dedicated to something you enjoy that is not what your daily routine consists of. Letting go of that controlled feeling we have due to deadlines or daily practices can be a hard obstacle to overcome, but once we figure out a way that works for us, we can start incorporating that into our schedules so we are performing at our best. When interviewing Justin Causey, the multi-faceted artist manager and operations manager at BlackCity recordings, he made a great point that if he cannot be 100 percent for himself [in these times], then he cannot be 100 percent for others. This is another important reason why rest is so crucial. If we want to perform at our best, we need to be well rested – mentally and physically.

Similarly, we may have a monotonous daily routine. Granted, some of us will prefer a consistent daily routine, but the grind of daily training activities can be grueling, particularly for athletes looking to reach world-class status. With this in mind, Eccles and colleagues suggest that we can break up the monotony in various ways such as switching up activities, locations, and people. Let us apply this to the domain in which we, the authors, primarily work. Academics often have the same routine Mondays through Fridays. They come to campus and are in their office, conducting research in the laboratory, or are teaching every day. Many researchers also feel pressure to be productive and extend their efforts across the weekend. The monotony of this routine could contribute to burnout at some point, sometimes before mid-semester. While in this situation, it is more difficult to switch up location and people, it is easy to switch up activities. For example, instead of using your lunch break to eat in your office, you could break up the day by going for a walk or meeting a non-work friend for lunch.

Students could take a different route to class and pay attention to their surroundings or make new friends in each class so that their social circle expands. While you are with the same people in your classes, you typically see different people from class to class. When it comes to athletes, they can easily adjust all three. For example, instead of engaging in or thinking about the sport, they can read for fun, drive a different route, take a day trip somewhere they have never been, or hang out with friends other than their teammates (Eccles et al., 2021). Each of these examples is a way to achieve some level of mental rest. Try some of them and also spend some time thinking about things you can do to break up the monotony of your routine. Tyler Tims, a doctoral student that we interviewed, discussed that self-care such as going to the gym, hanging out with friends, and being around people is how he rests and feels replenished. For him, being alone allows his mind to wander which actually makes him feel less rested. This highlights the fact that rest can look different for everyone; it is not a one-size-fits-all definition.

Remember those deadlines we mentioned earlier that potentially can subconsciously control us? Well, sometimes, being able to catch up on important tasks can be a way of mentally resting. Deadlines can cause us to feel stressed, especially if we feel as though we are not meeting them quickly enough. Stressing out in this situation is the opposite of what we want when we discuss mentally resting. If we slowly chip away at our to-do list and start completing our tasks, we are removing some of those stressors which can help remove the metaphorical weight from our shoulders. Deadlines and due dates are all too common for all of us. Moreover, our deadlines and obligations are not limited to work, school, or training. Many of us also have family obligations that can make deadlines even more complicated to navigate. It might sound counterproductive to achieving mental rest, but using any break throughout the day to tackle something on your to-do list could be helpful – sometimes 15–20 mins at a time. Your day might seem more intense at first but catching up on your tasks can lead to meeting a greater number of deadlines because you have been clearing some out of the way. Another possibility is designating a limited amount of time on an "off day" to tackle some projects. This could be a four-hour window on a Saturday once a month. I reserve this latter strategy for times when my list of tasks seems impossible to tame otherwise.

The last resting experience is being able to have a personal life outside of work, school, or sport. Not being able to have a social life outside of our job, schooling, or sport can lead to frustrations and stress – not only for ourselves but for those around us. Self-care researchers refer to the working part of our life as the *professional* self, and the *personal* self is the individual outside of the workplace (Bressi & Vaden, 2017). One aspect of self-care is ensuring that we maintain equilibrium between our professional and personal selves. Problems can arise when we are unable to keep these two selves sufficiently separate (including the state of burnout discussed in the upcoming section). Eccles and his colleagues suggest that we schedule time for personal activity. If we put it in our schedule, it is accounted for in the context of everything else going on, reducing our frustrations, which in turn, will lead to us feeling more rested.

The idea to schedule breaks was brought to Emily's attention by friends and colleagues. She never made time for her personal life and always put her job first. This led to increased stress in the home, because instead of focusing on herself and her family, she focused on the job. She knew there were deadlines to be met, she did not want to let people down, and she felt that if she stopped working, it just would not get done. For a couple of years she was burned out by the end of the first month of the semester. She was not mentally resting; she thought her frequent naps throughout the week were enough. Now, she has realized how important it is to separate her work and home life, and she tries as much as possible to not to bring work home with her or work past five o'clock so that she can keep the two separated. Emily was also not taking time to incorporate non-work activities into her day. As a reminder, these activities are individualized based on personal preferences – exercising, painting, playing or listening to music, or any other activity unrelated to work life.

All the suggestions discussed in this section will require effort to implement. You likely have excelled at something because of the time and effort you have invested. Hopefully, now that we know what needs to be done to rest mentally, we can create and implement a plan to ensure that we are getting both the physical and mental rest that we need. Once we see what works for us, we can adjust as needed. For example, Kevin Rapillo, the drummer for Rodney Atkins' band, has learned how to do just that. When it comes to rest, he stated:

> So one of the first times in a long time, I've kind of prioritized giving myself a break to say it's okay to be tired. And it's okay to need a break from running around. So that has been one of my best features – that I know when to just take a break and give it a rest.

We can assume that Kevin was suggesting the importance of prioritizing both mental and physical rest. We now consider some of the negative consequences of not prioritizing rest.

"I Hate This!" – The Impact of Burnout

We have discussed some of the psychological consequences of not getting enough rest, but perhaps the most detrimental consequence is burnout. Not getting sufficient physical and / or mental rest could lead to feeling unable, or unwilling, to handle anything else related to our pursuits – burnout. Burnout can be thought of as a cluster of symptoms due to chronic stress at school, at work, or in sports. Researchers conducted a systematic review of the literature concerning burnout and found that it can lead to detrimental effects to both our mental and physical health. Common mental health examples of burnout include emotional exhaustion, loss of energy, detachment, decreased self-efficacy, and reduced coping skills. Other problems that result from burnout can include depression, sleep problems, and increased substance use (Salvagioni et al., 2017). Frustratingly, Salvagioni and colleagues actually found that burnout led to increased rates of insomnia, thus leading to lower levels of both physical and mental rest. This literally means that not getting enough rest can lead to reaching a state of being that can make it likely that the suffering person will be less able to achieve sufficient rest.

The reputation that burnout has for being disruptive is well deserved. It can derail an aspirational performer by contributing to them giving up altogether (see Chapter 5) or sitting out for too long (see Chapter 12). Burnout also can be reasonably assumed to lower the level of effort across the board, either by choice or because the symptoms of burnout have made further effort impossible. However, a promising finding by researchers was that rest breaks as brief as ten minutes helped decrease the feelings of burnout among nurses (Stutting, 2023). These short breaks potentially could be implemented into anyone's schedule, even if they are just aimed at relaxation without focusing on any stressors or going for a walk to get away from your desk. This simple addition to our schedules could help decrease or avoid altogether the effects of burnout.

However, we must again acknowledge that the techniques described in this chapter to help ensure that you are getting sufficient rest will require your attention to implement. These efforts will include prioritizing time for rest and enforcing the time you set aside. You also will need to identify in advance some ways to rest that you believe will work for you. Once the possible restful activities have been chosen, confirm that your choices were appropriate for you – i.e., did the activity leave you feeling replenished and allow you to block intrusive thoughts about the domain from which you are seeking a break? You likely will need to make refinements to your regimen of rest similar to the adjustments you would make as you work to become a better performer. To echo Dr. Eccles once again, we need to return to making rest as much of a consideration as anything else related to attempts to enhance human performance.

Chapter Summary

In this chapter, we discussed how rest is integral to becoming a high performer but has been mostly overlooked. This is especially the case as compared to other components of becoming a high-level performer, such as deliberate practice, and there have recently been focused efforts to reemphasize its importance. It is critical to allow for both physical and mental rest, although we tend to neglect mental rest because of fears we will fall behind. Not getting enough rest can be harmful, and we should proactively seek opportunities for appropriate rest and recuperation. Finally, failure in this regard can lead to burnout and put us at risk of leaving, or failing in, a domain.

"You Look Tired"

Chapter 11: *Not Allowing for Rest/Recovery – Make Rest a PRIORITY*

This exercise will help you identify, and potentially refine, your plan for rest and recuperation. In the **first part** of the exercise, you will be asked to identify your current approach to rest and recuperation. The **second part** will ask you to identify some potential ways to improve this approach.

1. Please describe your current plan/approach to rest, recuperation, and general self-care.

2. Reflect on the approach noted in response to part 1. What are some specific ways you can go about improving it?

References

Althammer, S.E., Reis, D., Van der Beek, S., Beck, L., & Michel, A. (2021). A mindfulness intervention promoting work–life balance: How segmentation preference affects changes in detachment, well-being, and work–life balance. *Journal of Occupational and Organizational Psychology, 94*(2), 282–308. https://doi.org/10.1111/joop.12346.

Bressi, S.K., & Vaden, E.R. (2017). Reconsidering self care. *Clinical Social Work Journal, 45*, 33–38. https://doi.org/10.1007/s10615-016-0575-4.

Eccles, D.W., Balk, Y., Gretton, T.W., & Harris, N. (2022). "The forgotten session": Advancing research and practice concerning the psychology of rest in athletes. *Journal of Applied Sport Psychology, 34*(1), 3–24. DOI: 10.1080/10413200.2020.1756526.

Eccles, D.W., Caviedes, G., Balk, Y.A., Harris, N., & Gretton, T.W. (2021). How to help athletes get the mental rest needed to perform well and stay healthy. *Journal of Sport Psychology in Action, 12*(4), 259–270. https://doi.org/10.1080/21520704.2021.1873208.

Ericsson, K.A., Krampe, R.T., & Tesch-Römer, C. (1993). The role of deliberate practice in the acquisition of expert performance. *Psychological Review, 100*, 363–406. DOI:10.1037/0033-295X.100.3.363.

Kellogg, R.T. (2006). Professional writing expertise. In K.A. Ericsson, N. Charness, P.J. Feltovich, & R.R. Hoffman (Eds.), *The Cambridge Handbook of Expertise and Expert Performance* (pp. 389–402). Cambridge University Press.

Salvagioni, D.A.J., Melanda, F.N., Mesas, A.E., González, A.D., Gabani, F.L., & Andrade, S.M.D. (2017). Physical, psychological and occupational consequences of job burnout: A systematic review of prospective studies. *PloS One, 12*(10), e0185781. https://doi.org/10.1371/journal.pone.0185781.

Stutting, H.L. (2023). The relationship between rest breaks and professional burnout among nurses. *Critical Care Nurse, 43*(6), 48–56. https://doi.org/10.4037/ccn2023177.

Staying Off the Rails　12
Forgive Yourself and Regroup

I know I can look back on it and be like, "You know what? I gave it every-thing I had." I had my ups and downs, but I can look at myself in the mirror and say that I busted my butt. And I gave it everything I had. So, I can live with myself. I think at the end of the day, I think for me, I think that's what forgiveness is at the end of the day when it comes.
　　　　　　　　　　– Alec Mills, pitcher, Major League Baseball (MLB)

I do [forgive myself] now. I used to punish myself for weeks on end. Now, I have developed healthy confidence, so I don't feel the need for self-reprimanding behavior. I also realize that nothing in terms of art-istic endeavor or passion is all that important long term, as far as the world goes.
　　　　　　　– Anonymous musician from a globally-touring band who has
　　　　　　　　　　　　　　　　　　reached Gold status in sales

The crowd, if you could call it that, was small. Around a dozen or so folks were either fiddling with the label of their beer or chatting with each other as Nathaniel and his band gave it their all. None of the patrons seemed to be paying attention to the performance at all. To make matters worse, the band had just dropped their latest album to mixed reviews. While the positive ones were raving and outnumbered the negative ones, the negative ones were excoriating. They were so negative, they felt personal. These reviews combined with the luke-warm reception had Nathaniel considering whether he should just call

DOI: 10.4324/9781003377542-12

it quits. He also blamed himself for letting down not only himself, but his band, management, and producers. These thoughts plagued him for almost a year, but he stuck with it. Around the same time, a song that he had recently released took off, and the past decade or so has been successful by any metric. In this chapter, the authors discuss how easily negative experiences can send us to the sidelines, sometimes for good. The importance of regrouping and jumping back in and forgiving ourselves when necessary are also discussed.

Think of a train. When a train begins moving, it takes a while to gain momentum and get to the desired speed on the tracks. Likewise, in our pursuits, things will typically start out slowly. We likely are not going to meet our goals as quickly as we hope, because it takes time to gain and ultimately maintain momentum. Even then, we will have experiences with the potential to slow us down or even derail us. When those experiences arise, there are two things that must be differentiated: the barriers themselves and our perceptions of those obstacles. While a barrier can certainly end the pursuit of a goal, our perceptions can absolutely shape how impactful the barrier actually is – is it, indeed, an insurmountable obstacle and a cue to stop, or is it a temporary blip to consider a learning experience?

Imagine you are an aspiring singer who has been putting in the work and taking all the "right" steps to get noticed. You have worked past the pain of low attendance at your shows or the audience not paying attention. You now draw a pretty large crowd in the region – enough to generate the interest of big-time record labels. Could you withstand being told the label was no longer interested? How about going through being courted by labels five times? This is exactly the scenario that Logan Mize, a very successful performer, shared with *The Path Distilled* podcast (Harris & Tashman, 2020). If we consider each rejection Logan experienced as a derailment (remember the train metaphor), he did not stay off the rails. Logan continued pursuing his dream of becoming a successful musical artist, and it has played out in his favor.

Lainey Wilson is the Grammy-winning country singer we learned about in Chapter 7, who had been rejected seven times by the televised singing competition, *American Idol* (Norwin, 2024). To underscore Lainey's experience with American Idol – she auditioned and was rejected. Auditioned a second time – was rejected. Auditioned a third time – was rejected. Auditioned a fourth time – was rejected. Are you dejected? Auditioned a fifth time – was rejected. It will happen the next time. Auditioned a sixth time – was rejected. Auditioned a seventh, and final, time – was rejected. She revealed that she also had been rejected by *The Voice*. Despite these rejections, Lainey did not stay off the rails. She kept her train moving, and it paid off.

Are We There Yet? – Staying (Or Not Staying) the Route

It is common to have to determine whether you should stay on or off the track. While it can ultimately be costly, staying off the rails can seem very appealing at times of rejection or difficulty. Being successful is a laborious process. Alec Mills, an MLB pitcher, echoed this senti-ment in his conversation with us, "Life, in general. Sports, in general. Baseball, specifically, will beat you down. It really does." We often find ourselves in situations that require us to grind it out and push ourselves back into the mix. It can be very tempting in the midst of this process to just pull yourself out of the situation. Alec added, "it's just a men-tally exhausting thing to do every day."

Andrew Lang, founder of Leatherwood Distillery, shared the experi-ence of a fire closing down his distillery after being open for only two years. Andrew faced the decision of what to do next. He shared:

> We're shut down for about two months. I was at a decision point, because we weren't quite at the point where distribution was enough [to cover rebuilding]. People coming into the bar wasn't enough. But something in me just couldn't quit. We rebuilt; started back over almost from zero and just kept pushing along.

The decision to continue paid off. "We expanded everything; basically, [we have] quadrupled our production and our distribution," he said.

Since high school, Jonathan had wanted to earn a PhD in psych-ology. To make himself more competitive, he worked hard on his master's thesis. He developed his own study idea, created the materials, and executed the study. In order to pass his thesis, he was required to write an APA-formatted paper. He spent countless nights writing and re-writing to make it the best version possible, but he could not believe his eyes when his advising professor returned his paper after review. The feedback was that this was the worst paper he had read in a long time and needed major revisions if he wanted to move on to his defense. His train was completely derailed for the time-being. He ended up taking a semester off to decide whether it was worth staying in the program or if he should just try to get a job where he had completed his internship.

It was not until he had coffee with some friends from school that Jonathan realized he had never forgiven himself for what had happened. He blamed himself and determined that he was not at the level to write these types of papers. His friends encouraged him to re-examine the situation as an obstacle rather than an end, make the recommended revisions, and try to finish the program. At least he would have persevered after a time of adversity. Jonathan decided to go back the following semester and make a plan with his thesis adviser. Two semesters later, Jonathan graduated with his master's degree and is now in a PhD program.

Andrew and Jonathan did not want to quit, but both had been thrown off by a barrier they did not anticipate. Unfortunately, any one of us can be blindsided at any given time. When we encounter these types of challenges, it is understandable to get derailed and question whether to do what it takes to get back on the rails or change our plans and stay off the rails. One way to not go off the metaphorical track for good is to forgive ourselves, examine the situation, and then strategize about ways to meet the challenges we are facing.

"I Must Be the Worst at This" – The Critical Role of Self-forgiveness

It can be very easy to blame ourselves when things go poorly. It would have been very easy for Logan Mize and Lainey Wilson to blame themselves when they were rejected multiple times, but we can assume that was not the case, at least not in the long run. If they initially questioned whether to continue, they successfully moved past their doubts to withstand repeated rejections and ultimately earn success (see Chapter 7 for more on rejection). We are considering this to be a form of self-forgiveness.

Much of the work on self-forgiveness falls within the clinical realm and/or the type of self-forgiveness needed when we have wronged others. In both cases, self-forgiveness is needed for troubling or questionable behaviors such as excessive drinking or hostility to a loved one. Dr. Michael Wohl has studied forgiveness extensively. He and a colleague (Wohl & McLaughlin, 2014) suggest that self-forgiveness involves letting go of negative feelings and perceptions we adopt when we believe we have failed at something or that we have failed someone else. For our purposes, we can view self-forgiveness through a slightly different lens – the context of withstanding the barriers and setbacks we experience in our pursuits of success. Through this lens, self-forgiveness refers to our ability to forgive ourselves, or not blame ourselves in the first place, when things do not go as planned or for how we initially respond. To be clear, self-forgiveness should not be interpreted as not taking ownership of our mistakes. It is recognizing that mistakes and setbacks will occur despite our best efforts. Hooman Rahimi, a professional Formula DRIFT PROSPEC driver, had a very insightful response when asked whether he forgives himself when things do not go well.

> I forgive myself, but I learn from it. My slogan is 'I'm only Hooman.' I'm going to mess up. There's no chance that I don't mess up eventually. I'm going to make a mistake. But you know it's kind of something I think my dad taught me early was, you can make a million mistakes, just learn from them, you know. If you learn from every mistake, then it's, you know, it's a mistake, but it's not the end of the world. You can move on, you can grow from it and actually become better.

We discuss the self-serving attribution bias in Chapter 15, which is about not promoting yourself and your accomplishments. In a nutshell, most people take credit when things go well and assign blame to someone or something that happened when things do not go well (Allen et al., 2020). For example, Matt and Kim might both take credit for closing a huge deal with a client – each confident that the success was due in large part to the role they played in wooing the client. However, if the client ended up going with a competitor, Matt/Kim might blame the deal falling through on Kim/Matt's incompetence, upper management, or the horrible weather the day of the meeting. This bias can serve to provide a buffer to the impact of something going wrong. We presumably would be less impacted by the setback because we did not internalize it in the first place.

However, when we do place the blame on ourselves, self-forgiveness is most critical. Blaming ourselves could stem from internalizing the rejections we experience even when this would be unjustified. It is unlikely that Lainey Wilson suddenly developed her ability to perform only after auditioning for the shows that ended up rejecting her. But the blame could also come from actual mistakes on our part. This is exactly what had happened in Jonathan's case. He had made the potential mistakes of not getting feedback, proofreading, or having multiple people read his paper before submitting it to his supervisor. Before realizing this, Jonathan thought of himself as "dumb" and not cut out for graduate school. He needed to recognize that everyone will make mistakes, and he ultimately reached the point of forgiving himself. In the time since Jonathan went back to complete the requirements for his degree, he has flourished in a government position. Jonathan is now happy with his life, but he had to learn to forgive himself and not stay off the rails.

Walt Lord, a retired US Army Major General, shared his perspective on making mistakes:

> One of the things I always share with emerging leaders – and I did with the cadets yesterday – it's okay to make mistakes. We *expect* our leaders to make mistakes. In fact, with lieutenants and brand-new officers, we almost want them to make mistakes, as long as they don't get anybody hurt, if they react in the right way. So, I tell them, you know when you make a mistake, you will not cover it up. No. Don't blame somebody else. Don't try to ignore it and hope it goes away. Don't make it your boss's problem unless you also offer some solutions. What I tell them is to own your mistake. If it's a critical mistake, go to your boss and tell them you made a mistake. Tell them what you're doing to fix it, and let them know you'll be back if you need their help, if it's beyond your capability. Learn from it. But more importantly, great leaders learn from their mistakes. The greatest leaders help others learn from their mistakes. So, I tell them, be very open and honest in sharing your mistakes with leaders when you progress through the ranks. So that you can help them avoid them. And so, I think

you know, recognizing shortcomings in your own, in your own knowledge and expertise and experience, is sort of the same as reacting to a mistake.

He goes on to add, "be honest about it and ask for help." A key message here is that mistakes are to be expected as part of the growth process. There is no need to internalize the mistakes you make along the way or take them as a sign that you should stop. Feedback is critical for developing high performance and these mistakes are part of the process.

What About Grit?

Individual differences also can play a role in how well we persevere through negative experiences. We can either let the negative experience completely derail us and give up, or we can let the negative experience help us learn and grow through perseverance. Grit has been the commonly used term that encompasses perseverance and consistency of interests (Duckworth et al., 2007). Researchers have reliably found that those high in grit are more likely to have higher levels of academic achievement, career retention, physical health, and overall well-being (see Duckworth et al., 2007 for a review). Most of us will face the obstacles discussed throughout this book. Some of us will give up on a given pursuit relatively quickly. Others will stick with a pursuit at all costs.

Not everyone attains the ultimate level of success they are seeking, even when pursuing it at all costs. Their business might fail. They may be denied a promotion. They might get injured, or underperform, and fail to make the cut for an athletic team. The offer for a leading role or admission to medical school might never come. However, staying with something often increases the odds of being successful. Comedian Henry Cho shared with us his thoughts: "Stay true to who you are and what you want," and "just stick to it." This advice is applicable for anyone in the early stages of a pursuit. Henry's advice can also be applied when someone has experienced an objective level of success but then derails.

Probably one of the most well-known cases of perseverance is the acclaimed actor Robert Downey Jr. (Picotti, 2024). During his childhood, he was an actor in various films and on *Saturday Night Live*.

However, in his early 20s his life was completely derailed by substance abuse. It was not until he played a role of someone with substance abuse issues that he realized things needed to change. He reached out for help and entered a rehabilitation facility. For a while, he was back on track but was then derailed again. This time, however, in addition to the substance abuse, he found himself in legal trouble and served a year in prison. After an additional legal issue, he was fired from the well-known show *Ally McBeal* because the employers considered him a risk. He reached an agreement with his lawyers and was able to serve three-years in a treatment facility rather than prison. This could have been the moment he called it quits and stayed off the rails. Instead, he emerged from the three-year treatment sober and went back to work. It was during this time that he appeared in box office hits such as *The Avengers* franchise, starting with *Iron Man* (Favreau, 2008), and most recently *Oppenheimer* (Nolan, 2023), for which he won his first Academy Award.

Robert Downey Jr. is an excellent example of not staying off the rails after derailing. He regrouped and continued his work. Again, perseverance often pays off for the person staying the route. Removing yourself from consideration is a surefire way to not get to where you want to be. This might require adjusting how you go about getting there and what you consider success to be in your own situation. Identify how you personally define success and go for it. Katie Cole, a touring member of *The Smashing Pumpkins* and singer-songwriter, shared how her experiences with difficulties while working toward her goals led her to forge her own path:

> I've experienced a lot of failures, and I have no hesitation about calling it what it is. A lot of people are like, 'it's a learning experience; you learned so much from that' – like, in a way to kind of polish it into something shiny. It's like when I said I made all those choices that I made, and stopped following a better-known path and started sort of paving my own. It makes me responsible for the choices I made, the successes I have, and the values I have. Failures come with the successes. They're not a hindrance.

As you can see, you are not alone with feeling as though you are going off the route you set for yourself. Your ultimate goal might need to be adjusted along the way. A band with aspirations to perform in stadiums might end up making a good living playing smaller venues. The lens through which we view our progress and status can determine how we think of it. A healthy approach would be to try to stay true to ourselves and be proud of what we have accomplished. We may not achieve the final goal we set for ourselves or do so in the way we wanted. However, we remind you that growth is rarely linear. Being derailed during our pursuits can be difficult enough that we consider dropping out altogether. However, not internalizing the rejections we face, learning self-forgiveness, and/or being okay with adjusting our route when necessary can help us keep moving in the direction of our goals.

Chapter Summary

In this chapter, we discussed the importance of getting back into the swing of things after experiencing setbacks. It can be an easy choice to stay off the rails after experiencing hardship. However, we presented several examples of high performers who experienced setbacks but regrouped and kept trying. In our examples, the performers ultimately found success despite continuous setbacks and rejections. We also introduced the importance of forgiving ourselves when things do not go as planned. This strategy includes identifying where we ultimately want to be, being comfortable with alternate routes as needed, and not internalizing mistakes or setbacks. Ultimately, we can use setbacks as learning opportunities when possible.

"I Might Be Done"

Chapter 12: *Staying Off the Rails – Forgive Yourself and Regroup*

This exercise is designed to help you recognize the importance of staying the course. In the **first part** of the exercise, you will be asked to identify specific instances when you almost gave up but continued with a pursuit. The **second part** will ask you to identify some of the specific fears you had about what was going to happen if you continued versus what actually happened.

1. Please describe one or more times that you came close to giving up on a pursuit but ended up pushing through to continue.

2. Reflect on the examples provided in your answer to part 1. What are some specific fears you had about continuing and how did these fears compare to what actually occurred?

References

Allen, M.S., Robson, D.A., Martin, L.J., & Laborde, S. (2020). Systematic review and meta-analysis of self-serving attribution biases in the competitive context of organized sport. *Personality and Social Psychology Bulletin, 46*(7), 1027–1043. https://doi.org/10.1177/0146167219893995.

Duckworth, A.L., Peterson, C., Matthews, M.D., & Kelly, D.R. (2007). Grit: Perseverance and passion for long-term goals. *Journal of Personality and Social Psychology, 92*(6), 1087–1101. https://doi.org/10.1037/0022-3514.92.6.1087.

Favreau, J. (2008). *Ironman* [Film]. Marvel Studios.

Harris, K.R., & Tashman, L. (Hosts). (2020, May 24). Logan Mize [Audio podcast episode]. *The Path Distilled.* https://podcasts.apple.com/us/podcast/the-path-distilled-podcast/id1511069681?i=1000475563956.

Nolan, C. (2023). *Oppenheimer* [Film]. Syncopy Atlas Entertainment.

Norwin, N. (2024). Lainey Wilson's past 'American Idol' rejection shocks judge Luke Bryan: "Don't always get it right." *Y! Entertainment.* https://www.yahoo.com/entertainment/lainey-wilson-past-american-idol-093545138.html#:~:text="I%20tried%20out%20seven%20times,it%20past%20the%20first%20round." Accessed February 23, 2024.

Picotti, T. (2024) Robert Downey Jr. *Biography.com.* https://www.biography.com/actors/robert-downey-jr. Accessed February 23, 2024.

Wohl, M., & McLaughlin, K. (2014). Self-forgiveness: The good, the bad, and the ugly. *Social and Personality Psychology Compass, 8,* 422–435. https://doi.org/10.1111/spc3.12119.

Not Standing Out   **13**

Be Blueberry Yogurt

I can't expect everybody to want the same things, or to strive for the same type of excellence I'm going after, whether it be music or everyday life.
    – Brian Brown, hip-hop artist

The skill, the time, and the practice that it takes to get to that level is just so insane. I'll try to share that, if you really want to do that you should be drawing all the time, like these people do. It's that kind of thing. You have to let people know you can do it. I don't want to just say you can't. But if you want to be as good as these people, to get this kind of job, this is the level and amount of time you should be doing already without somebody having to tell you.
    – Thomas Estrada, feature film and video game animator

Sasha was hungry – quickly approaching hangry. She was visiting her parents and all the food that they had on-hand was yogurt – lots of it. As she scanned the containers, Sasha discovered that all but one was plain yogurt. Alas, the plain yogurt was not appealing, but she was pleasantly surprised to find a blueberry yogurt stashed behind all the plain ones. In this chapter, we discuss how Sasha's experience of finding the blueberry yogurt among the plain is akin to you standing out from the competition by amassing evidence of your accomplishments (your blueberries!). The plain yogurt will not stand a chance.

So, what was it that drew Sasha to the blueberry yogurt compared to the plain yogurt? It stuck out! It was different from all the rest. Most

DOI: 10.4324/9781003377542-13

importantly, it was the most appealing of the options. You will want to accumulate as many blueberries – your accomplishments – as possible, so you can be the blueberry yogurt and stand out in a positive way. You will have a competitive advantage when you are up against others who are applying to the same job or graduate school, competing for a spot on an athletic team, or anything else. As you will recall, in Chapter 9 we discussed how important it was to identify where you currently are in the process of completing your goals and develop a specific plan to work toward them. In this chapter, we will discuss ways in which you can stand out from your peers.

Throughout this book, we have discussed how long the road to success can be. We also discuss the multitude of potential obstacles that we might encounter and provide strategies for overcoming each of them. Accumulating as many accomplishments as possible (the blueberries!) over time will allow you to overcome the obstacle of not standing out. In previous chapters, we have discussed stages of progress toward a goal, with each having an inherent triumph as you move into the next phase. Each triumph represents an accomplishment of some kind that could help you stand out among the crowd.

The Top Candidate by Far – The Importance of Standing Out

The energized crowd was clapping enthusiastically. It was one of the best presentations by a job candidate that many had ever observed. The speaker was energetic, the topic was interesting, and the candidate's list of accomplishments was remarkable. Many were left wondering, "What else could anyone ask of a candidate?" The excitement at the possibility of bringing the candidate on board was palpable. They had stood out among even the most qualified. Unfortunately, multiple employers were equally excited, and the candidate had the luxury of multiple offers to choose between from an eager group of suitors.

We extensively discuss the importance of making our accomplishments known in Chapter 15. This includes a need to overcome the feeling that by talking about our accomplishments we are bragging. However, we first must have accomplishments to our credit in order to sell them. Then we must have an awareness that what we have done is considered an accomplishment. There likely are achievements or successes that you take for granted – ones that you might not recognize but impress everyone else. We encourage you to begin tracking your accomplishments – no matter how small – as soon as possible. Add past accomplishments to the list. As your list grows, it will help you create your own narrative (see Chapter 15). The first priority is to accumulate a list that meets the minimum requirements to gain entry to or to be taken seriously in a domain. This varies depending on the domain. In some cases, the respectable minimum will be very explicit – sometimes in writing, but in other situations, the minimum will be informal, making it difficult to evaluate at times.

We can think of our accomplishments as part of a tiered system – common/minimal accomplishments, separator accomplishments, and dominator accomplishments. This first tier, *common/minimal accomplishments*, represents the foundation from which to build, but these do nothing to help you stand out from others. They are the equivalent of the plain yogurt option in the opening vignette – the basic accomplishments that most of your competition will have. (In the yogurt example, the plain version was edible.) Examples of these accomplishments would be learning to play an instrument at a basic level, joining a research team, making an athletic team, or joining an organization. The rub is that almost everyone in the next tier will have done the exact same thing. You may stand out compared to anyone not currently in the domain but not compared to others in the domain. You will need to do more.

The second tier of accomplishments, the *separator accomplishments*, are accomplishments that demonstrate that you have begun to stand out among your peers. In these cases, they might only be recognized as successes by others within the domain. These can be objective accomplishments such as those measured by income generated, running time, or win-loss records, and they might be achieved by simultaneously doing a variety of things well. Attention to detail, doing things on time, every time, and proactively seeking opportunities for growth, all matter. The aforementioned world-class musician from the certified Gold-selling band shared a way that musicians begin to separate themselves from their peers:

They should educate themselves in musical areas and genres out-side of their primary genre. Then they will bring something to the table that their peers aren't. I have tried to do this in hopes of developing a unique style. I did this by transcribing other instruments, such as the saxophone, to get outside of the box. Often, a different perspective than everyone else is all that is needed to stand out.

The accomplishments here would be reflected as the breadth of know-ledge and the potential improvements to their playing style. While the means to separate ourselves will differ depending on the field, we can all heed this advice.

The third tier, *dominator accomplishments*, tend to be recognized by any observer. These are performances and accomplishments that sep-arate you from all but the very best in a domain. These accomplishments are readily recognized when reading the books of the best writers or watching the best athletes of all-time in competition. These performers have built upon previous accomplishments – adding blueberries until there is an undeniable difference separating them from the second tier. Continuing the advice of the anonymous successful musician, who suggests looking for ways to expand our skill set:

> For example, if I feel like I have a rock technique down really well, then I'll immerse myself in bebop, which is completely outside the old box. It's a whole other universe. This way, there will never be a ceiling. It would take you ten lifetimes to even scratch the surface of what's possible.

Since the accomplishments build upon one another in this proposed tiered system, why are we not all accumulating tons of accomplishments? The reasons likely are the same ones we have discussed throughout the book – lingering impact of traditional societal views, lack of awareness of techniques, impostor syndrome, fixed mindsets, and the like. These considerations seem to have a disproportionate impact on the accomplishments we accrue and our general success.

"You'll Never Be Able to Do That" – The Impact of Traditional Societal Views

The traditional view that there is something fundamentally different about high performers can potentially impact how we go about seeking opportunities. We must believe that we can improve before we will attempt to do so. For example, we learned in Chapter 4 that there may be achievements that we do not think are possible to accomplish until we accomplish them. This occurs at a larger societal and at an individual level. Recall from Chapter 4 the bump in worldwide competitive swimming times because of the short-lived use of a new swimsuit fabric dubbed a "supersuit" (Robinson, 2022). The bump in swimming performance originally attributed to the new fabric remained even after the fabric was banned. The mental barrier of what was possible had been removed, and a new standard was set. We often place artificial ceilings on ourselves because we believe there are limitations in place for our ultimate performance potential. This can lead us to not even attempt to move beyond our perceived limits. We also are at risk of buying into the artificial ceilings that others might place upon us. For example, a highly accomplished sibling might be held up as the standard for another sibling. The pressure of trying to live up to this standard could lead the other sibling to self-impose a ceiling because they do not believe that they are as capable as their sibling.

These perceptions of artificial ceilings might also be made explicit by others. For example, when Emily was in her undergraduate program, a professor in the program told her that she would never succeed in a graduate program – an artificial ceiling placed on her by someone else. However, if we ultimately do not participate because of these perceived limitations, how will we stand out in relation to our peers? Chances are, we will not. Standing out typically involves pushing the boundaries of what we (others) thought possible. That extra push will most likely garner attention, and related opportunities, by accumulating notable accomplishments along the way. Thankfully, Emily broke through the artificial ceiling that her professor attempted to create. More importantly, she has thrived in her role as professor – and has reached the tier of dominator accomplishments.

"I'll Never Be Able to Do That" – The Impact of Mindset and Impostor Syndrome

In some cases, we might choose to stay where we are because it is comfortable – the satisficing discussed in Chapter 2. Someone choosing not to accumulate accomplishments might be comfortable with their current status or not place much value on the accomplishments themselves. There is nothing wrong with this approach. These folks are making a choice to stay where they are. However, there are a multitude of additional factors that can impact how we approach accomplishments.

One of these is our belief about whether we are able improve – or "mindset" (Dweck, 2006). A fixed mindset adherent believes we have a limited amount of potential (the fixed part) that we will not be able to exceed regardless of what we do. A growth mindset adherent believes that we can improve our capabilities at a given task through experience and effort. There are some ongoing considerations related to how mindset manifests itself discussed elsewhere in this book. However, we can safely assume that a fixed mindset would limit domain engagement at some level. Our stance remains that we are less likely to take steps to improve if we believe our attempts to improve will ultimately be futile. This might have been a factor in the artificial ceiling one sibling placed upon themselves after being compared to a successful sibling in the earlier example.

Thus, a fixed mindset can lead to us seeking fewer opportunities than we otherwise would, leading to a decreased likelihood of standing out relative to others. This can also lead to a self-fulfilling prophecy cycle (e.g., Noskeau, Santos, & Wang, 2021), in which the lack of accomplishment and acknowledgement serves as evidence to the person with the fixed mindset. They interpret the lack of accomplishments as evidence that they are indeed incapable of improving much beyond their current status. Attempts to engage in a domain will decrease accordingly.

Impostor syndrome (Chapter 3) also can artificially decrease the number of accomplishments someone accumulates or even attempts to accumulate. Impostor syndrome can be quite limiting for anyone experiencing it. It can discourage us from moving forward or trying new things. These are precisely the things we can do to help us stand out more. Maybe we are active in a domain but feel we do not know what we are doing – that we are frauds fooling everyone else. This is limiting in many ways. We may feel that the more we are in the spotlight, the more likely we are to be detected as a fraud, so we avoid pursuing our goals and becoming the blueberry yogurt. Randall Foster, an executive in the music industry, witnessed this firsthand. He shared:

> I do feel like it's a big problem – impostor syndrome and self-doubt – in the music space. From an artistic standpoint, I feel like it causes paralysis. It sets people up where instead of making a decision to go left or right, we just stay still, because that seems to be the safest place to be. And I've seen it shut down the most talented people;s careers for a year or more.

"You Did What?" – Lack of Awareness of Opportunities and Lack of Resources

We have discussed the limitations resulting from a lack of awareness of opportunities and resources throughout the book. In some cases, we might not be achieving certain types of accomplishments because we are not aware of them or lack the resources to pursue them, so we obviously will not engage in them. Finding a trusted mentor can be tremendously helpful in this regard (see Chapter 14 for more about this). Emily inquired about an internship as an undergraduate because she originally wanted to go to graduate school to become a therapist. Emily knew these opportunities existed because they were on the list of classes students could choose from, but it was not until she talked with her mentor that she realized what they required and how important they could be.

The second issue can be even more difficult to overcome. It will not matter how many opportunities we know about if we do not have the means to pursue them. These barriers often exist because of a lack of financial means but could also be lack of time available to dedicate to a pursuit. They could also be related to gatekeeping for a specific domain. For example, someone with control over infrastructure or distribution can limit access to entry, knowledge, or resources. These limitations certainly can stall our attempts at accumulating accomplishments. These also can be particularly frustrating for someone who has the desire and confidence to pursue a goal, but finds themselves unable to progress. In these cases, how can we continue to accumulate accomplishments?

Make a Plan

One suggestion to make ourselves competitive is to develop a specific plan where we evaluate our own path and needs (see Chapter 9), and determine both our goals and a plan for meeting them. This approach will allow us to accumulate accomplishments to help us stand out. By nature of developing a specific plan, we will be setting ourselves up to accumulate accomplishments just by taking the outlined steps toward our goal.

Recall baseball pitcher Alec Mills's comment on his cycle of stacking goals:

> [A goal] needs to be attainable. A lot of times, for me, it's something that's measurable and attainable within two weeks. Okay, so then you get that go, 'Okay, let's do another one.' In two weeks, you get that goal. If you keep stacking goals, then eventually that long-term goal is going to become a lot closer and a lot more attainable than it was before.

Alec is not only moving through his cycle of goals, he is accumulating accomplishments directly by improving his skills both in practice and during games. In other words, the advances he gains in practice (the blueberry of having a better curveball) also leads to objective gameplay accomplishments (the blueberry of having a better win-loss record or earned run average).

Both authors have supervised many student research projects over the years. In most cases, the students have wanted to do what they could to stand out, and completing their own research study was a way to help achieve this. They had included this as part of their plans, and they were able to add them as blueberries to better stand out compared to other applicants who may not have engaged in similar experiences. The *Be Blueberry Yogurt!* exercise (Expert Performance International Collective [EPIC], 2023) will help you do this.

Do the Thing – Smaller to Larger Opportunities

We have all experienced a point in our lives where we feel like if we take on one more thing, we will not be able to make anything we are doing work. We have to walk the fine line between doing enough to stand out and taking on too much, which could lead to us dropping out of a domain either temporarily (Chapter 12) or permanently (Chapter 5). It is critical for you to assess what *you* will be capable of handling while incorporating rest and recuperation (Chapter 11) as part of the process.

With that being said, if you find yourself trying to decide whether to take something on – do the thing. Even though you might be tired and have what you think is a full plate, it could be this one extra role that helps you stand out. Talon Beeson, an actor and director who also teaches acting shared his thoughts on this:

> What I tell my students all the time is, you have to respect your mental health and you have to take care of yourself. But if there is any way you can feasibly say 'yes' to a project, you should say 'yes' to it.

He reiterates the need to preserve your mental health but adds, "You never know where that's going to lead."

Take Izabella, for example. Not only does she have a full course load in her last semester, she works outside of school, is completing an honors thesis, and joined another faculty member's lab to help run participants. However, she is not stopping there. She also volunteers as a mentor in a program for juvenile offenders. When writing her personal statement and getting letters of recommendation, this one extra thing made her stand out. She collected a large number of blueberries compared to the other applicants, and her efforts paid off. Izabella has been offered a position at her top choice for graduate programs and will continue working with troubled youth. She knew her end goal and what she would have to do to achieve it, so she sacrificed a bit of her social life to complete these high-impact experiences to stand out.

A secondary advantage when we "do the thing" is that such experiences can confirm that we are on the right path, or indicate that we are on the wrong track and need to consider an off ramp. Such pivots can ultimately lead to greater success in the long run. It was not until Emily did her internship at a behavioral science unit that she realized counseling was not for her. After that internship, Emily took her first psychology and law course, and realized that is where her interests lay, so she created her very own research study related to the field. This pivot resulted in her first journal article publication as an undergraduate student – a huge accomplishment that might not have happened had she not participated in the internship. Echoing Talon's earlier advice, "do the thing," if there is any possible way.

Tame Impostor Syndrome

Some of us might be cringing at the advice to "do the thing" because of our old nemesis, impostor syndrome. Maybe we feel as if we are already faking it, and doing more seems like a horrible idea. Or, we are comparing ourselves to others and feel as if we have not done enough to be considered anything but a fraud so why would we add this new thing? We often compare ourselves to others whether we realize it or not. Someone like Izabella – even with as much as she was doing – may look at themselves and feel as though they are a fraud because they have not done as much or the same things as someone else. That is just not necessarily the case. You are not a fraud just because you are not doing as much as another person. Recall from Chapter 6 how Katie Cole, a touring member of *The Smashing Pumpkins* and a singer-songwriter, caught me off guard by responding that I should not be discouraged when I mentioned that *The Path Distilled* podcast had reached 66 countries? I was initially confused by her kind words of encouragement and realized that the success she has experienced is at least triple that reach. Even though my efforts have not reached the audience size of a legendary band, I can still be proud of the reach of my podcast.

Getting Creative

We each have our own set of circumstances that will both hinder and benefit us in achieving our goals. We mentioned the impact of lack of awareness of opportunities on accomplishments. To overcome our individualized special circumstances, the advice is to "do the thing," if at all possible, and seek mentorship to help identify opportunities. However, applying some creativity might be required in some cases to pull this off. For example, doing something to put yourself in the orbit of a potential mentor or other key players can help you. However, it is not always obvious how to go about this. One way is to volunteer for something that increases the likelihood of encountering a potential mentor. Brian Bates, nationally touring stand-up comedian and cohost of the *Nateland* podcast mentioned on *The Path Distilled* podcast (Harris & Tashman, 2020) that he had felt that opportunities to perform stand-up comedy would increase if he was frequently around successful stand-up comics, and this idea paid off for Brian. In a sport, participating in a summer league, where recruits are often identified, could lead to encounters with someone who could help. Even an attempt to find opportunities of this nature could increase the likelihood that you cross paths with someone who could provide direction toward key opportunities.

Students who work outside of classes to maintain financial stability often find it difficult to engage in multiple high-impact practices, but there are other ways we can separate ourselves from others by thinking creatively about what "counts." For example, we may not be thinking of the ways our job is actually teaching us transferable skills, but if you have ever trained anyone at your job, you were in a leadership position. Look for examples of when you demonstrated critical thinking skills or handled high-stress situations. These situations illustrate transferable skills. They will be particularly important in cases for which you have limited examples that are more directly related to larger goals.

We also can be creative in finding ways to use whatever is available to work toward our end goal. There are entire exercise regimens pitched as not needing any equipment other than what is already in most houses, with the promise that we will be able to achieve results equivalent to working out with traditional exercise equipment. There is no reason to doubt these claims as lowering myself up and down from a kitchen chair taxes my muscles in a functionally similar way as using a piece of exercise equipment. There are many examples of this idea. We have mentioned some of them elsewhere – a stuffed bag serving as a soccer ball. Someone looking to improve fitness can use an array of items such as buckets or car axles. Are there ways to find similar workarounds to the particular resource limitations in question?

This is not *always* possible, but we encourage you to think of similar creative ways to ease such limitations so that you can progress anyway. *Progress anyway.*

Take Full Advantage of Training/Mentorship

Another way to potentially lessen the impact of these limitations is to lean into training and mentorship opportunities. For an athlete, this might mean taking extra reps before or after practice, or trying out the training you thought was unnecessary. If you are fortunate enough to already be receiving mentorship, do everything within your power to get as much as possible out of the opportunity. Andrew Lang, Leatherwood Distillery founder, echoed this:

> If you didn't grow up in a business setting or have a partner that actively engaged [in business], I feel like there's really no way you would know how to do it. Surrounding yourself with people that are smarter than you, better at it than you, is the only way to go. You can't have an ego in business. When you're starting out, you've got to swallow that ego and take advice.

Check your ego at the door. Communicate clearly. Ask for clarification if you did not understand something. These are themes discussed elsewhere in this book. However, it is even more important if you are facing the obstacles of lack of awareness of opportunities or lack of resources.

Willingness to be coached and receptiveness to feedback most likely will compel a mentor to invest even more into your development. This can lead to opportunities that you would not have otherwise known about. It also could provide you with an ally to help secure resources that were previously out of reach. Andrew Lang added, "Networking is huge. Any time you meet someone that's willing to help you, helping them out any way possible always leads them introducing you to someone else." Take advantage of these opportunities.

Emily recently mentored a group of five students who were hoping to stand out. The students were already willing to go the extra mile and conduct their own research studies, but they needed to learn how to take constructive criticism to improve their writing skills. Their main goal was to either present at a conference or publish a paper, neither of which would be possible without improving their papers. This required many drafts to get to their final product. Some students took the criticism and revisions better than others, but the efforts paid off. Three of them were published in a peer-reviewed journal, and four presented at conferences. All of them were accepted into graduate programs, some with multiple offers. They did what they needed to do to be blueberry yogurt. It was certainly more work and stress, but the end results were phenomenal – publications, poster presentations, and getting into graduate school. Mentorship can come in different forms, but once we match with a mentor willing to help us succeed, we should take full advantage of it.

Chapter Summary

In this chapter, we discussed the importance of accumulating as many accomplishments as possible. This list of accomplishments will then allow you to stand out among others vying for the same opportunities. Traditional societal views and impostor syndrome can hinder us in seeking opportunities out of a belief that we would not be able to successfully accomplish them. Many of us are unaware of which opportunities are available and this certainly can stymie the pursuit of accomplishments. It is important to make a plan to begin tracking our accomplishments and to take the small opportunities, which can lead to much larger ones; both small and large opportunities will add to your list of accomplishments. Finally, we proposed the importance of seeking mentorship and how this can help us accumulate accomplishments.

Be Blueberry Yogurt!

Chapter 13: *Not Standing Out: Be Blueberry Yogurt*

This exercise is designed to extend the plans developed in the Chapter 9 *I Need to Start Doing...* exercise and help you identify ways to separate yourself from competitors. In the **first part** of the exercise, you will be asked to brainstorm and/or research what sets apart the most successful performers in the domain you identified in your Chapter 9 exercise. The **second part** will ask you to identify some of the specific steps you could take to accumulate as many accomplishments as possible.

1. Some accomplishments are considered more valuable than others. Thinking about the domain of interest you identified in the Chapter 9 exercise, do some research on what the most successful performers in that domain have done to set themselves apart.

2. Reflect on the examples you provided in part 1. What are some specific steps you can take to accumulate as many high-value accomplishments as possible?

References

Dweck, C.S. (2006). *Mindset*. Random House.

Expert Performance International Collective (EPIC) (2023). *Be Blueberry Yogurt* [Exercise]. Nashville; New York City.

Harris, K.R., & Tashman, L. (Hosts) (2020, September 13). Brian Bates [Audio podcast episode]. *The Path Distilled*. https://podcasts.apple.com/us/podc ast/the-path-distilled-podcast/id1511069681?i=1000491079368.

Noskeau, R., Santos, A., & Wang, W. (2021). Connecting the dots between mindset and impostor phenomenon, via fear of failure and goal orientation, in working adults. *Frontiers in Psychology, 12*, 588438.

Robinson, M.A. (2022). Glimpsing the impossible: How artificially enhanced targets improve elite performance. *Journal of Sport and Exercise Psychology, 44*(3), 177–188.

Tough Crowd   **14**
Seek Out Feedback/Criticism

[Mentorship]'s very important. This is why I've spent so many years being a mentor and actually helping the sports psych organization develop their mentoring more. It's a role, and it's a skill. And so, therefore, people have to learn how to do that well. Just having a mentor may or may not be useful. If you have a great mentor, [they are] someone who understands mentoring; understands how to help develop others – how to help share their knowledge. Then, it's hugely important.

– Lauren Tashman, Vice President of Research and Innovation, master coach, Valor Performance; certified mental performance coach

You don't want to just constantly be twisting in the wind based on other people's feedback. So, it's finding people who you deeply trust to get to speak hard truth to you. And, this all becomes more and more important, the sort of bigger your name is, because a lot of people are around you because they think they can get something out of it. So, having a trusted group that could tell you exactly what they think, and they have enough of a track record. I would put the time into thinking about who I really am and what it is I'm trying to accomplish. Because if I don't know that, then what do I do with the feedback?

– Todd Rose, best-selling author and thought leader

A passerby might have assumed that they were walking past an intense argument. The voices were adamant and seemed highly

DOI: 10.4324/9781003377542-14

emotional. However, this was not an argument in the traditional sense. This was a meeting of high-profile researchers and their trainees, and the heated debate was the goal. The team's philosophy was that any idea brought to the group should be thoroughly vetted – a sincere belief that "an idea that cannot withstand scrutiny in our lab does not deserve to see the light of day." Importantly, this was not just lip service as the team members did not pull punches in the debate. The result was consistent adherence to a high standard in their work. In this chapter, we explore the idea of acknowledging what you are not doing well by seeking ways to obtain honest, accurate, and ongoing feedback.

We already have discussed the difficulty that we often have with acknowledging what we are not doing well in Chapter 10. Some of this difficulty can be the result of our own "blind spots" related to our performance, where we are truly unable to recognize where improvement is needed. We also generally tend to overestimate how we compare with others with regard to performance. This was the above-average effect and related Dunning-Kruger effect, also discussed in Chapter 10. We also identified two important considerations in relation to our inability to see how well we are doing. The first was to recognize that we are not good at assessing how well we are doing or where we stand in relation to others with regard to performance. The second was that we suggested that you seek out other sources of feedback in order to obtain a fuller picture of where you currently stand and help identify what potentially could be improved. These considerations, and related issues, will be the focus of this chapter.

"You sure don't take criticism very well," my thesis advisor said matter-of-factly. I shouted angrily, "What do you mean!" That last part did not actually happen. However, I was a little stunned by this comment from a respected mentor. I had always been a good student, and teachers always seemed to like my friendly, curious approach. I felt I responded well to constructive criticism throughout my undergraduate career. It was an undergraduate mentor who first nudged me to consider graduate training, so it was a little jarring to hear such an assessment so early in the process. Looking back on the experience, I fully recognize that I did not take criticism very well back then. These types of demanding interactions and receiving brutally honest feedback will be common for many of you. You might have been a member of a debate team or been in educational systems where the instructors challenged students to this degree.

Many of us need to develop the skill of accepting and integrating criticism. This is especially true when we consider the nature of moving up the ranks of a hierarchy. The demands increase – sometimes substantially – as our skill level progresses. In academic environments, these increased demands include conveying our thoughts in both speaking and writing very clearly. This means that we must truly understand what we are intending to say and be able to state it in a digestible way. Academics must also act as skeptics to fellow academics. The issue at hand in the situation with my thesis adviser was that I was conveying a defensive tone when I needed clarification for his suggestions for improvement. At the time, I had never encountered the intense demands at this level of academic training.

Immersion in an environment that required me to fully understand, and be able to articulate, my stance was the best place for me at the time. While this was one of my first experiences with this type of feedback, it was consistent for the remainder of my graduate training and beyond. Another example happened while writing my thesis. I grew frustrated with what seemed to be an endless cycle of red-ink comments and corrections from my thesis advisor. I finally asked my advisor, "When are you going to stop marking up my thesis so much?" His response? "I'm going to mark up it up for as long as you keep resubmitting." However, it was the rest of the response that reflects the tone of the message of this chapter: "It is up to you to decide *when you are ready* to defend it."

"When you are ready." Those are powerful words as they imply there will be a time when we are ready. There also are multiple layers of meanings to the phrase. The phrase could be intended/interpreted to mean: a) being sufficiently prepared to perform, b) an assessment that you are ready to perform, or c) a reflection of an eagerness to perform. Any or all of these meanings may be accurate or inaccurate. For example, you might be well prepared for something and know that you are well prepared – an athlete heading into a big event. You might be well prepared and make an assessment that you are not ready – impostor syndrome or perfectionist tendencies at work. There also will be some of us who think we are prepared but actually are not – the

Dunning-Kruger effect. The question, then, is how best to obtain accurate feedback and use it to improve performance.

We already have discussed Dr. Kevin Eva's proposal in Chapter 10 that we make feedback a systemic consideration. In particular, Dr. Eva and his colleagues brought awareness to the limitations of self-assessment, particularly as the sole measure, for assessing performance status. We agree on both points and propose a web of feedback that includes layers of coaches, mentors, computer/AI generated feedback, and other types of training tools. These sources of feedback should collectively provide enough information to help in your assessment of where you actually stand with regard to your performance.

For such feedback to be effective, you will have to make appropriate changes based on the given feedback. This means that you will have to determine which feedback is valid. In some cases, the feedback is objective, and there is no leeway for interpretation – a specific running time or returning only 35% of tennis serves. However, some feedback will come in the form of suggestions and you must decide whether to incorporate them into action – do this instead of that. Thankfully, you are able to assess the effectiveness of such advice by the impact it makes on objective measures – does your running time decrease? Arnd Krüger stated this idea well in his article exploring why Roger Bannister was able to be the first runner to run a four-minute mile. He stated:

> This is also the basis for 'coaching theory' as coaches do not care too much why somebody is running faster as long as he or she is running faster. Athletics makes testing easy because the outcome is on the track: if you are winning or setting a new record, the chances are that your theory was better than the theory your opponent was using all other things being equal" (2006, p.307).

In other words, feedback allows you to determine what is and is not working, regardless of your approach. This is a big deal! Not only can we adopt what has been successful, we also can determine whether a particular technique is actually working. We can even develop some of our own techniques if we identify something that is verifiably good based on our feedback.

"I Didn't Realize How Much I...."

I used to teach a class in which students chose a specific behavior they considered problematic and developed a plan to change it. I vividly recall how often my students stated they had not realized how much they actually engaged in the behavior. For example, some students would measure the amount of time spent on social media or track the number of sugary drinks consumed. It was not until they were in the phase of collecting baseline data that they realized the actual scope of what they were doing. Once this base-rate was identified, the students could test their plan to see if it made a difference in their behavior. It was this comparison that allowed them to determine if their strategy was effective. Did they spend less time on social media or consume fewer sugary drinks compared to when they started?

Establishing this baseline seems like a simple concept, and we naturally establish one for a variety of things in our lives. You probably know your typical interstate driving speed and whether you are adjusting your speed upwards or downwards for a particular trip. Our officemates have consistent, individual arrival times within a small window – they arrive at almost the same time every workday. It is noticeable when there is deviation from their traditional arrival time. You likely have documented your daily intake of calories or a particular exercise at some point. We use these examples to demonstrate the tendency we already have to establish our baselines and then sometimes compare whatever is happening at the time. Anyone trying to get really good at something will be engaging in a more rigorous version of this. However, we already have established the demanding nature of trying to improve performance. Because of such demands, we must also consider two additional questions – "Where should I get the feedback?" and "How will I know whether to trust the feedback?" In other words, "Is this working?"

Sources of Feedback

Feedback is proposed to be critical in the early writings about deliberate practice (e.g., Ericsson, Krampe, & Tesch-Römer, 1993). In these early proposals, the "teacher or coach" was the primary source of feedback provided to the performer. While the person overseeing the training still plays an important role, the means by which we collect feedback has expanded in a notable way. Playing chess online with opponents, from all over the world, at a skill level that once would have been difficult to match in-person locally or regionally, has long been the norm. Such matches can occur with a frequency that was also unprecedented. Surgeons can now engage in surgical simulations allowing for realistic feedback as many times as they prefer, without damaging the tissue of an actual patient. This list could continue with many more examples. It should be clear that the number of sources of feedback has grown tremendously.

The impact of this feedback on performance cannot be overstated. In one example, a group of German physicians manipulated the frequency of feedback offered to medical students learning a medical procedure with a high risk of complications when performed incorrectly (Bosse et al., 2015). Students were randomly assigned to training groups in which they would receive either low-frequency or high-frequency feedback. Promisingly, performance gains were observed in both the groups of medical students, but the best performance came from the students receiving high-frequency intermittent feedback. Thus, we can conclude that feedback played a role in improving performance and that providing more frequent feedback further enhanced performance. It also is worth noting that these medical students exhibited relatively high levels of performance from the start of training, and they still exhibited notable improvements. This would suggest that appropriate feedback can be useful across the board, regardless of current performance levels.

These types of examples are too numerous to cover in this chapter. However, we must consider that you must also know how to interpret and apply the feedback for it to be helpful. This often still requires the guidance of a teacher, coach, or other more-skilled mentor. For example, you might find that you have improved on some metric, but are clueless as to how it can be integrated into your performance and what to progressively work on as the next step. Some early simulations provided computer-generated feedback, which has evolved to the increasing use of artificial intelligence to generate feedback, but still, this feedback may require interpretation to implement. Scholars writing about this very issue suggest that there is far more information resulting from AI analyses than can be interpreted correctly (Raab, Schinke, & Maher, 2023). They provide an excellent example of this by stating that simply positioning a goalkeeper in the center of the goal for 40 percent of the shots taken by opponents would be a misguided response to data pointing out that 40 percent of shots are center shots. The opponent is often making the decision to place their shot in the position with the greatest chance of success – the spots where the goalkeeper will not be located in real time. A goalkeeper should also be familiarized via training with the other available cues indicating where a shot might be headed. As the scholars point out, this combination of cues actually leads to the goalkeepers being able to block an incoming shot.

This goalkeeper scenario is only one example, but it demonstrates the need for some form of guidance in interpreting and using feedback during training. There always has been a tendency to take new advances and broadly implement them without ensuring that the users understand the underpinnings of why it is being used (Harris et al., 2013). We might be able to get away with this when returning a tennis ball from an automated machine and still improve. However, there historically has been a surprising number of simulation centers founded without a stated curriculum (Kapadia et al., 2007; Tsuda et al., 2009; see also Harris et al., 2013). For context, simulation centers provide training environments that allow students of a domain to enter scenarios based on real situations without the risk of causing harm by their mistakes. In medical training, students are exposed to simulated clinical situations where they treat either actors posing as patients or computerized mannequins that respond to procedures, and then are evaluated on their process. Well-intentioned trainers and educators rushed to implement the promising new tools once simulators had been deemed to lead to improved performance without always realizing that it is *the way* simulation is used that makes the difference in most cases. Think about it: this is true with most things – a guitar is just a guitar and a saw is just a saw until the virtuoso plays the guitar and the skilled carpenter puts the saw to work. Neither would be effective in either of our hands. You might find yourself in a similar situation if you are unable to interpret feedback and a suitable mentor is not available. The bottom line is that AI can certainly be a useful tool, but as of writing, it is not a complete substitution for other guidance. Having said that, it very well could get there some day.

"Does This Milk Smell Funny to You?" – Being Mindful of Misguided/Erroneous Feedback

"Don't take financial advice from broke people." I have heard variations of this advice my entire life. It certainly makes intuitive sense. We should be very skeptical of advice that is provided by someone who seems to be bad at whatever they are pontificating about. There certainly are exceptions to this, such as a physically out-of-shape coach with a track record of winning. However, it rings true under most circumstances. Study tips from a low performing student? Driving tips from the worst driver you know? Thanks, but no thanks! Hopefully, our mentors will be able to assist our ongoing advancement, but we always run the risk of accepting mentorship from someone not up to par (Thomas & Lawrence, 2018). The quality of mentorship can run the gamut. We, the authors, are aware of several situations in which someone received guidance or advice for development that someone more successful than the mentor had considered ill-advised. Of course, there will be circumstances for which trailblazers are doing things that have yet to be understood. In most cases, it can just be considered poor guidance. The risk is that a mentor could end up limiting you by shaping you to do only what they have done (Thomas & Lawrence, 2018). Mentors are a necessary part of getting better and are often invaluable to your growth, so let us explore avoiding these potential pitfalls by actively seeking criticism and mentorship from multiple sources.

"Let Me Have It!" – Seeking Out Criticism/Mentorship

"Is that your best shot?!?" Like most research universities, my department at Florida State University would host speakers presenting their ideas and research. As with any field, academics commonly experience butterflies when giving these types of talks, especially when just starting out. Sound advice in the field is to prepare for tough questions from the audience (the theme of this chapter). That is exactly where the opening quote of this section came from. A new faculty member uttered a version of those words at the end of one of his research presentations – "Is that your best shot?!?" Being in attendance that day, I did not interpret his statement as a sign of arrogance; rather, it appeared to be a sign of preparedness – a declaration that he had covered all of his bases. Both our mentors created similar circumstances for us in our training programs by expecting us to be able to defend every statement, idea, plan, or action related to our work at any time. This dynamic leads one to realize that they are capable of withstanding the rigors of sharing their thoughts and to be comfortable doing so. Ongoing feedback from a capable mentor is a huge component of this process.

In contrast to the situation with my thesis adviser from earlier in this chapter, I now relish constructive feedback. I constantly seek feedback that allows me to monitor progress toward long-term goals and make decisions. I would much prefer hearing something that is at odds with what I propose than have someone not share concerns. I have noticed that many will preface such input with statements along the lines of, "I'm sorry for bringing this up," or "Sorry for being a troublemaker." In my mind, there is no need to preface with such statements as this is exactly what we should be doing. Considering as many data points as possible helps with decision making by casting the widest net possible. The same will be true with feedback as you seek to improve your own performance. We suggest actively seeking as many sources of feedback as possible.

These sources will include the measurable components that would result from tracking your performance metrics, including the afore-mentioned computer-aided feedback. Maximize the use of the feed-back sources you have found to be effective as determined by objective performance measures. You should also seek feedback from as many trusted people as possible. Granted, you might receive competing advice, but having multiple sources will allow you to account for varying points of view on your status and potential. The hope is that these viewpoints will help you construct the most accurate picture of where things stand.

One way to maximize the effectiveness of your sources is to become comfortable hearing the difficult parts. This is something that might take some work. I admittedly felt an initial burst of anger when my mentor informed me that I did not take criticism very well, but it helped me realize that it was something to improve upon. My mentor could have gone about his day without pointing it out, and nothing would have changed in his own life. However, I might have eventu-ally irritated someone with less patience, costing me in some way. The point is to seek feedback from as many sources as possible, even if it is initially hard to receive.

You also must cultivate a relationship with mentors that allows them to feel comfortable giving even tough feedback. What is the point if they provide feedback, and you respond in a way that makes them uncomfortable? This does not imply that no reaction is expected from you; however, they should be assured that you are seeking honest feedback, and that there will be no grudges resulting from it. A certain level of trust must be present on both sides. Music industry executive Randall Foster noted the importance of this type of relationship. He shared, "Having trusted confidants. Having mentors in your orbit, that you will ask for feedback, that will give you *unfiltered* feedback, that you respect is really important artistically. I think that you know everybody's got to have their tribe." Attorney Danelle Whiteside shared:

> I make myself available to hear it and try to try to take it in. Having those people to talk to, to lean on, to share, and have them pour into me. That's totally made a difference in my life, and my path and my career. I don't know what I would do without that sort of support.

This level of trust is sometimes labelled psychological safety – "a social environment within which individuals take interpersonal risks by speaking up, sharing concerns, raising questions, and offering ideas because they feel safe to do so" (Jowett et al., 2023, p.1). Functionally, it is an open communication stream. In our earlier examples, both the mentor and mentee would feel comfortable in an exchange of feedback moving in both directions. Such open exchanges can allow for ongoing feedback as to how things are progressing, allow for troubleshooting of approaches, and for any concerns to be identified. Critically, everyone can speak up without being fearful.

Psychological safety is certainly something one should strive to achieve. Very few of us, if any, would seek a situation in which we were fearful of speaking up. Not surprisingly, team "conflict" enhanced overall team performance when the team members experienced psychological safety (Bradley et al., 2012). In this case, what was being described as "conflict" meant differing opinions were provided on how to go about completing a task. When members of the five-person teams were allowed to share their thoughts freely because of a high level of psychological safety amongst the team members, the respective team's performance exceeded that of the teams experiencing a high level of conflict but a low level of psychological safety. Critically, the free exchange of ideas within the teams comfortable sharing them also led to improved performance compared to the teams with low levels of team conflict. It turns out that feeling free to speak up and exchange ideas with team members is a good thing. As expected, psychological safety has been deemed effective for increasing team cohesiveness and for enhancing a sense of wellbeing within the trainees in the few sport domain studies in which it has been researched (Jowett et al., 2023).

There are concerns that the term has become the new popular buzz-word and questions have arisen about what the concept suggests (e.g., Taylor, Collins, & Ashford, 2022). Some of these criticisms relate to the specific needs of competitive sports domains – a fear that there is an expectation that coaches be "too easy" on players or that hierarchies of skill are removed. While these concerns that the concept of psychological safety had gained widespread traction prematurely while also being misunderstood were shared in relation to sport (Taylor, Collins, & Ashford, 2022), it is likely such concerns exist in other domains making use of the premise. Thus, we ask you to once again step back from competing approaches and consider the idea of psychological safety for what it is – being able to have open communication and voice concerns and feedback without fear of retaliation or being ostracized. The training and feedback still can be as honest, sometimes harsh, as ever. Once psychological safety has been established, the feedback can be viewed for what it is – feedback intended to improve your performance. It is preferable to get such feedback from someone rooting for your success than someone who is potentially indifferent or pulling for you to be unsuccessful. Seek someone who will provide you with honest feedback and opinions from a position of mutual respect. Anyone who has put in their time will recognize where you stand and see a little bit of themselves in you.

Where Did You Come From? – Seeking and Finding Mentorship

Mentorship has been part of the process of becoming the best versions of ourselves for millennia. Socrates' mentorship led to generations of mentorship of great thinkers – Plato, Aristotle, Alexander the Great

(Ma, Mukherjee, & Uzzi, 2020) – with each mentor passing along knowledge and techniques to the next in line. While none of us will be considered in the same league as these great mentors, we can recognize the illustration of good mentorship. These relationships can vary widely, ranging from occasional, informal advice to full-blown one-on-one training as part of a formal curriculum. Moreover, informal mentorship often progresses to more formal mentorship as you become more involved in a particular domain.

Management researchers located in Italy, Silvia Bagdadli and Martina Gianecchini extensively reviewed the impact of mentorship on career success reported in 51 research studies (Bagdadli & Gianecchini, 2019). The scholars found that mentorship was consistently associated with relatively higher salaries and opportunities for promotions in about half of the mentees (51 percent). The remaining mentees either experienced no benefit of mentorship (47 percent) or experienced a negative impact (2 percent). These mixed results can be viewed positively but should remind us of the importance of *who* is providing the guidance. Dr. Lauren Tashman, Vice President of Research and Innovation and a master coach for Valor Performance, captures this sentiment regarding the variability of mentorship well in her opening quotation.

It can be incredibly frustrating to learn that roughly half of the mentees experienced no benefit or even were negatively impacted. Not only do we have to go through the process of identifying a potential mentor (or being identified) and cultivating the relationship, we ultimately might end up with ineffective mentorship. There is some comfort that the researchers found only a small percentage of mentees were actually harmed by having a particular mentor. It also is likely that you will have multiple mentors along the way. Being attuned to all sources of feedback and who is providing the most valuable advice or feedback will help you decide which mentors to give the greatest credence. You also will identify which aspects of mentorship you prefer and need the most. This allows you to further reduce or increase your personal collection of mentors as you see progress. We may have different mentors that we consult depending on the issue at hand. In longstanding and successful mentoring relationships, you will find that your mentors often will even proactively recognize your upcoming needs and act accordingly.

It is safe to say that all of us can be mostly optimistic about mentorship. Success in receiving pay raises and promotions were attributed to mentorship for over half of the employees in the review by Bagdadli and Gianecchini (2019). It also is likely that the other half of employees who were reported to have received no benefit from mentorship in the form of raises or promotions did benefit to some degree. This could be advice/feedback that made a difference in small ways or mentors simply serving as a sounding board to help navigate a tricky issue.

We propose the following ways to increase the chances of working with a quality mentor based on our experience: a) stand out, b) perform at a high level on even the small things, c) be coachable, d) network or jump in, e) cultivate relationships and ask, and f) make something easier for a mentor. Let us now consider each of these in greater detail.

We dedicated an entire chapter (Chapter 13) to the first way to increase your chances of working with a mentor, standing out. This might seem underwhelming at face value since mentorship can enhance the likelihood of standing out. It appears to be a variation of the common question, "How do I get the experience to get the jobs that require experience?" However, high-performing potential mentors are drawn to effort. They will be drawn to you if you are performing well or even if you seem to be earnestly putting in the work. Put in a more consistent effort than your cohorts, and you will likely draw the attention of someone who can help you along the way. Expect a nudge in the right direction if you handle yourself in way that exudes doing what needs to be done, when it needs to be done.

Another way to increase the chances of working with a mentor is to perform at a high level whenever possible. We assure you that even the small things are being noticed by potential mentors, and these small things collectively make you an ideal candidate for mentorship. You might even accumulate enough accomplishments to successfully stand out while you are at it.

Mike Squires, creator of the *Couch Riffs* podcast, is a long-time musician who has worked with some all-time musical greats. Mike shared on *The Path Distilled* podcast (Harris & Tashman, 2021) that his take for making yourself stand out to a mentor is to "prove it" if say you care a lot about something.

Being coachable also is important. Be prepared to hear feedback and advice, and to act upon it. It can be frustrating to offer feedback or advice only for it to be ignored. There always will be a need to discern which advice to act upon, but consistently disregarding the bulk of a mentor's advice could lead them to stop providing it or potentially ceasing to mentor you.

Networking or jumping into a domain also can increase the chances of mentorship. Andrew Lang, founder of Leatherwood Distillery, mentioned the symbiotic nature of networking: "Networking is huge. Anytime you meet someone that's willing to help you, helping them out any way possible always leads to them introducing you to someone else." Recall from Chapter 8 that Brian Bates, stand-up comedian and co-host of the *Nateland* podcast, immersed himself in the domain by hanging out with other comedians in comedy clubs (Harris & Tashman, 2020). These networking opportunities led to performing in large venues across the country. Your own benefits of networking might look different to Brian's but nevertheless can lead to greater opportunities. It could be one of these opportunities that leads to you connecting with your potential mentor.

Turning a potential mentor into an actual mentor might also come down to cultivating the relationship and asking directly. This direct ask may not be stated as, "Will you be my mentor?" It could amount to asking for advice on a common aspect of the domain or if you can get their input on something. Outside of formal pairings of mentors with mentees, the most direct request would likely be along the lines of, "Would you be willing to work with me on..." in something related to your area of need. Andrew Lang shared his experience on seeking advice, "I legitimately have this question. Can you help? And 90 percent of people are willing."

Another way of going about securing mentorship is to make something easier for the mentor – helping them with something already on their plate. Making the potential mentor's load lighter could pay off by providing them with support, creating an opportunity to cultivate a relationship, and an opportunity to gain a new accomplishment. This also could be tricky because there is a decent chance that your involvement would actually result in a greater workload for them, so be sure that you will be able to hold your own in the situation. Otherwise, this approach can be counterproductive as a means to secure a mentor by serving as a negative start to the relationship. If the mentor relationship is already established, your engagement will require an additional amount of their time and focus, but the mentor should have a good sense of the investment you require.

Chapter Summary

In this chapter, we suggested that all of us should proactively seek feedback and criticism. Many of us have a difficult time accepting feedback and criticism, even if we claim otherwise, and should work to be better in doing so. It is important to develop effective ways of measuring performance and then use these measures as a means to gauge progress. From these measures, we can then determine if adjustments are needed. Identifying potential mentors will be beneficial when seeking feedback. We provided some ways to go about seeking mentorship and cautioned about the risks of misguided mentorship. Finally, it is beneficial to have access to unfiltered feedback, and psychological safety can help create a relationship conducive to maximizing performance.

"I'm The Best"

Chapter 14: *Tough Crowd: Seek Out Feedback/Criticism*

This exercise is designed to help develop a plan to position yourself to receive feedback/constructive criticism. In the **first part** of the exercise, you will be asked to brainstorm and/or research potential sources of feedback for your pursuit/domain of interest. The **second part** will ask you to identify how many of these sources you currently use.

1. We know that feedback ideally will come from multiple sources. Do some research on some potential sources of feedback for your particular domain/activities.

2. Reflect on the examples you provided in part 1. How many of these sources of feedback do you currently incorporate? Create a specific plan for incorporating some that you do not currently use.

References

Bagdadli, S., & Gianecchini, M. (2019). Organizational career management practices and objective career success: A systematic review and framework. *Human Resource Management Review, 29*(3), 353–370. https://doi.org/10.1016/j.hrmr.2018.08.001.

Bosse, H.M., Mohr, J., Buss, B., Krautter, M., Weyrich, P., Herzog, W., Jünger, J. & Nikendei, C. (2015). The benefit of repetitive skills training and frequency of expert feedback in the early acquisition of procedural skills. *BMC Medical Education, 15*(1), 1–10. https://doi.org/10.1186/s12909-015-0286-5.

Bradley, B.H., Postlethwaite, B.E., Klotz, A.C., Hamdani, M.R., & Brown, K.G. (2012). Reaping the benefits of task conflict in teams: The critical role of team psychological safety climate. *Journal of Applied Psychology, 97*(1), 151–158. https://doi.org/10.1037/A0024200.

Ericsson, K.A., Krampe, R.T., & Tesch-Römer, C. (1993). The role of deliberate practice in the acquisition of expert performance. *Psychological Review, 100, 363–406.* DOI:10.1037/0033-295X.100.3.363.

Harris, K.R., Eccles, D.W., Ward, P., and Whyte, J. (2013). A theoretical framework for simulation in nursing: Answering Schiavento's call. *Journal of Nursing Education, 52 (1),* 6–16. https://doi.org/10.3928/01484834-20121107-02.

Harris, K.R., & Tashman, L. (Hosts). (2020, September 13). Brian Bates [Audio podcast episode]. *The Path Distilled.* https://podcasts.apple.com/us/podcast/the-path-distilled-podcast/id1511069681?i=1000491079368.

Harris, K.R., & Tashman, L. (Hosts). (2021, March 7). Mike Squires [Audio podcast episode]. *The Path Distilled.* https://podcasts.apple.com/us/podcast/the-path-distilled-podcast/id1511069681?i=1000511921710.

Jowett, S., Do Nascimento-Júnior, J.R.A., Zhao, C., & Gosai, J. (2023). Creating the conditions for psychological safety and its impact on quality coach-athlete relationships. *Psychology of Sport and Exercise, 65,* 102363. https://doi.org/10.1016/j.psychsport.2022.102363.

Kapadia, M.R., DaRosa, D.A., MacRae, H.M., & Dunnington, G.L. (2007). Current assessment and future directions of surgical skills laboratories. *Journal of Surgical Education, 64,* 260–265. https://doi.org/10.1016/j.jsurg.2007.04.009.

Krüger, A. (2006). Training theory and why Roger Bannister was the first four-minute miler. *Sport in History, 26*(2), 305–324.

Ma, Y., Mukherjee, S., & Uzzi, B. (2020). Mentorship and protégé success in STEM fields. *Proceedings of the National Academy of Sciences, 117*(25), 14077–14083. https://doi.org/10.1073/pnas.1915516117.

Raab, M., Schinke, R., & Maher, C.A. (2023). Technology meets sport psychology: How technology and artificial intelligence can shape the future of elite sport performance. *Journal of Sport Psychology in Action*, 1–7. https://doi.org/10.1080/21520704.2023.2287324.

Taylor, J., Collins, D., & Ashford, M. (2022). Psychological safety in high-performance sport: Contextually applicable? *Frontiers in Sports and Active Living, 4*, 823488. https://doi.org/10.3389/fspor.2022.823488.

Thomas, R.P., & Lawrence, A. (2018). Assessment of expert performance compared across professional domains. *Journal of Applied Research in Memory and Cognition, 7*(2), 167–176. https://doi.org/10.1016/j.jarmac.2018.03.009.

Tsuda, S., Scott, D., Doyle, J., Jones, D.B. (2009). Surgical skills training and simulation. *Current Problems in Surgery, 46*, 271–370. https://doi.org/10.1067/j.cpsurg.2008.12.003.

Not Selling Your Accomplishments

15

It's Not Bragging

The biggest thing is knowing that there's a big difference between bragging about all the little things you do and showcasing your competence trying to make a professional name for yourself.

– Tyler Tims, doctoral candidate

I always tell people whatever you're comfortable with. There's no real rule for it. I think it's important to let people know what you've done. I don't do it enough.

– Kevin Rapillo, musical director and drummer
for country music artist Rodney Atkins

I experienced an intense combination of anxiousness and excitement as my flight touched down. I was heading to a job interview at a large university, and my dissertation defense was on the horizon. I had several things going for me that would increase the likelihood of being offered a position. I had worked hard, was reasonably well published for a recent graduate, and had worked with one of the best-known scholars in the domain. While the interview seemed to go well, I got word that they were going with a different candidate. My critical mistake was that I expected my impressive curriculum vitae (CV) to speak for itself, and not further elaborating on what was on there or offering other examples of accomplishments. After some reflection, I changed my approach and pushed myself just out of my comfort zone, where

DOI: 10.4324/9781003377542-15

I actually pointed out successes leading up to these interviews. This new approach paid off. I ended up with multiple offers for consideration. In this chapter, we discuss the importance of learning to sell yourself and your accomplishments, and help the reader reach a level of comfort around sharing their own accomplishments.

John is the best dancer who ever lived. Seriously. Just ask him. He himself will tell you, "I am the best dancer who ever lived. There isn't anyone who even comes close." Stacey and her friends had the opportunity to observe John on the dance floor. Their feedback was quite different. They didn't think he was very good. Their exact words were, "Terrible dancer!" And it was not just Stacey and her friends. In fact, everyone who was asked about John's performance felt the same way – he is a horrible dancer. Why is there such a gulf between John's impression of his dancing ability and the observers' perception? John is emphasizing his own assessment of his performance without feedback or anything else to support it. There is a high likelihood that someone has, or would, provide feedback on John's dancing, but he either has not sought it out or has not listened.

We have discussed the Dunning-Kruger effect in previous chapters (Chapter 10 and Chapter 14) – the phenomenon of overestimating our own abilities relative to our peers or our actual performance measures. We also discussed the critical importance of feedback in assessing and improving performance (Chapter 14). The issue we hope to highlight for this chapter is that selling your accomplishments is very distinct from bragging. Many of us do not feel comfortable talking about what we have accomplished. It feels too much like we are bragging. We do not want to come across like John. The good news is that selling your accomplishments is quite different from bragging.

Let us envision a world in which John is actually a good dancer. Saying he is the best dancer in the world could still be considered bragging. However, he would not be bragging if he listed off the dance competitions he had won to someone looking to hire a dancer for a television show. In the second scenario, John is merely sharing his accomplishments. It is very factual.

Sharing your accomplishments in this way is applicable across domains – your batting average in baseball, amount of donations generated annually, or books you have published. The list could go on.

It is critical that we get comfortable with selling ourselves in a factual way. We all will find ourselves vying for coveted opportunities with plenty of others hoping to be selected for the same thing. Holding back your accomplishments in such a scenario is a definite way to *increase your chances of being passed over*. In the coming sections, we explore why we are uncomfortable selling our accomplishments, the consequences of not doing so, and some ways to help you feel more comfortable selling what you have done. We now consider one of the reasons that we might not be comfortable selling our accomplishments – peer comparisons

"Look at Mr. Smarty Pants"

Kiersten was identified in elementary school as academically advanced for her age and was selected for a program intended to enhance her educational experience. It was a program with an enhanced curriculum designed for students who might find a traditional curriculum boring. Kiersten was excited for the opportunity and enrolled as soon as she was able to clear it with her parents. Then came the problem – the program was being hosted at a different school. The students selected from her school had to take a bus to get there. They lined up in the hall by the door waiting for the transportation. While being selected was an honor, Kiersten hated waiting in that line, where her fellow students could see and question her. Even worse, they had to walk to the bus as it waited in the parking lot. Kiersten hated the feeling of being in the spotlight like this. Some of the other students accused her of thinking she was better/smarter than them. Kiersten's participation lasted just over a week before the unwelcomed attention caused her to withdraw. Limiting our scope was discussed in Chapter 6. This included how someone might limit themselves because of pressure from others in close proximity. This often stems from perceptions that they will be seen negatively by trying to better themselves. A root cause of this pressure to not make your goals too grand is the threat to the self of esteem of the observer (e.g., Baumeister, Smart, & Boden, 1996). The threats to self-esteem could lead to the negativity being directed toward you and your ambitious goals. Hesitation in selling your accomplishments can stem from similar concerns.

You might have experienced this negativity when asked about your own goals or specifics about your life. Attempting to become a musician, physician, or even attending a university can lead to negative reactions from others. This can be particularly surprising when we expected the person to be supportive. Despite such reactions, we should not feel ashamed about having goals and working toward achieving them. You have overcome obstacles to get where you are today! You also may have felt like giving up at some point during this process because of the negativity. These reactions and resultant insecurities can stem all the way back to elementary school as we saw with the example of Kiersten. Similarly, high-achieving student(s) garnering multiple awards during school awards days are often singled out negatively. Such reactions likely stemmed from the other students feeling left out over not getting their own awards and related self-esteem threats. The award winners who experience ridicule often eventually determine it best to keep their achievements to themselves. We have also probably felt like Kevin at some point. We might have an impressive résumé or CV, but we also may feel it is easier to show that on paper than it is to discuss it in person. Do these pressures extend to society more broadly?

"You'll Never Reach My Level of Modesty"

Society has made it hard to discuss our accomplishments with others without feeling like we are bragging. We often are taught that we are supposed to be modest and humble. We are certainly not supposed to "brag." Remember the case of John earlier in the chapter? You were likely annoyed by John based on how we depicted him. The word "bragging" has a negative connotation to it. If we feel like what we are doing is bragging, we likely will just keep quiet. Many graduate students can relate to this, especially when it comes to the number of publications they have as students. Let us say that Jenna has more publications and a richer CV than Sarah. Jenna may feel as though she is bragging if she is talking to Sarah over lunch about her productivity and everything else she has in the pipeline. Emily felt this way when she was asked to be an external examiner for a master's degree thesis defense. She had to submit her CV to show she was qualified as an "expert" in the field; the person who replied back to her made a comment about how impressive her CV was. At the defense, the CV and all of her accomplishments were discussed before the student came in. Emily felt uncomfortable because she was not sure what the CVs looked like for the remaining committee members. She did not want to talk about her CV because she did not want to appear as though she was bragging.

The unspoken societal standard that we should be modest about our accomplishments potentially has an even greater impact for certain groups. Interestingly, researchers have found that women are less likely to nominate themselves or share a successful story about themselves compared to nominating or sharing accomplishments of *other* women (Smith & Huntoon, 2014). Women who discuss their own accomplishments violate the gender norm of modesty because women are expected to be more modest than men (Rudman, 1998). However, when women discuss the accomplishments of other women, they are not seen as violating that gender norm. These gender norms can be engrained in us at such a young age that it is hard to overcome them at a later age, and they can cause a negative physiological arousal that increases anxiety.

Thus, girls and women are prone to feeling anxiety when talking about what they have accomplished. Does this mean it will cause them to promote themselves and their accomplishments less than they would otherwise? The answer seems to be a definitive "yes." Remember the study from Chapter 8 in which researchers Jessi Smith and Meghan Huntoon asked college women to write about why they deserved a scholarship (Smith & Huntoon, 2014)? This particular study was a variation of the classic misattribution of arousal studies (e.g., Schacter & Singer, 1962) in which physiological arousal is interpreted based on cues within the environment. For example, physiological arousal stemming from listening to music was interpreted as sexual attraction as measured by the increased ratings of attractiveness for faces presented to participants having listened to music compared to a silent condition (Marin et al., 2017). The women writing essays about why they deserved a scholarship engaged in greater self-promotion when they were told that a subliminal noise being piped into the room would make them uncomfortable (Smith & Huntoon, 2014). Promoting themselves led the women to experience such discomfort that they tended to hold back – unless they could attribute the discomfort to something else.

These results support the idea that, because women are typically uncomfortable promoting themselves, they are likely to undersell themselves. Women, like everyone else, must understand that when talking about their accomplishments they are not bragging or overselling. That is where the concept, discussed earlier, of accumulating a list of accomplishments helps. It allows us to share them with others without hesitation. When sharing our lists under appropriate circumstances, we would be just stating facts. Whenever we undersell ourselves, we have to realize that someone else is going to discuss their accomplishments, and they may be the one to get the scholarship, job, or award. We must promote our own accomplishments; no one else knows them as well as we do.

The traditional pressure to not promote yourself is so strong that some have resorted to something known as humblebragging (Sezer, Gino, & Norton, 2018). This is an approach taken by some to present their accomplishments in a more negative light to avoid the feeling of bragging. For example, let us say that Michelle got an on-ground interview at three different campuses for an assistant professor position. This is a pretty big feat. But instead of outright saying that, she says something to the effect of, "I have interviews at three different schools to prepare for; now, I have to do even more work to research these schools." Note that the first part of that sentence (I have interviews at three different schools) is the accomplishment, but for Michelle to make herself appear as though she is not bragging, she combines it with a complaint (…now I have to do even more work…). While the individual may feel as though they are promoting their accomplishments in a humble way, Sezar and colleagues suggest the complaint part of humblebragging may come across as insincere. Sincerity is a key determining factor in the success of self-promotion. We recommend sticking with the approach of accumulating a respectable list of accomplishments and growing comfortable with sharing the accomplishments when self-promotion is necessary – job searches, graduate school admissions interviews, securing sponsorship, making a sale, and the like.

Andrew Lang, Leatherwood Distillery founder, shared that it took time for him to become comfortable sharing his accomplishments, including serving as a Green Beret, despite the themes of the distillery being based on his military service. "Our whole brand is based around my career in special forces; our logos and the storylines behind it. And it took me two years to actually be able to tell some of those stories," he said, and went on to add that it was advice from his mentors that helped him realize he should own his accomplishments. "If you're not telling the story, what's the point of having the story behind your brand?" they asked.

"What? Was that Good?"

We have discussed impostor syndrome throughout this book and dedicated a full chapter to the topic in Chapter 3. Putting it simply, impostor syndrome is the feeling of being a fraud. This could manifest as a feeling that we do not know what we are doing, everyone will figure out that we are frauds, or that all our accomplishments were due to luck rather than ability. It can manifest in a variety of ways with regard to selling our accomplishments. One of these is the fear that, by discussing our accomplishments, we will be asked a question that we are unable to answer in the moment. This could reinforce the fear that we do not know what we are doing or that we will be discovered as a fraud. So, we find safety from those fears caused by impostor syndrome by not discussing our accomplishments with anyone. There is a kernel of truth to this fear as stakeholders often ask questions intended to test your chops. For example, a seasoned videographer might ask a newcomer what equipment they are using or about a particular function. This can be a question generated purely out of curiosity, or it can be a test to quickly gauge the newcomer's skill level. The newcomer could very easily reveal themselves as a complete novice in their response.

Another possibility is that we simply do not recognize our accomplishments due, in part, to impostor syndrome. If you are prone to seeing yourself as an impostor, it is unlikely that you will have a grasp on what you are accomplishing. Even if you do recognize the accomplishments, you might be dismissive of what they actually mean. This could be as simple as how good you are at writing prose to how advanced you are with your grasp of a particular subject; the way you play guitar or swing a golf club in textbook form. For some, they are oblivious to the ease with which they can explain things to a learner. Impostor syndrome can blind us to both the small and large accomplishments we experience along the way. What about when we recognize our accomplishments but attribute our success to luck rather than our hard work and abilities?

Think of the last time someone was rude or cut you off in traffic. You most likely had some particular thoughts and choice words for the culprit – at least in your mind. They were undoubtedly a rude person or someone with a mean streak – definitely someone you would not want to spend much time around. However, what if they were rushing a family member to the hospital or just received tragic news? The fundamental attribution error model (see Langdridge & Butt, 2004 for a thorough review and critique) distinguishes the initial explanation for their behavior, such as being a rude person, from considering something happening to the person. The recommended approach is to consider an explanation that considers what might be happening to the person – an external or situational attribution. The fundamental attribution error is commonplace and occurs mostly outside of our awareness. Our first inclination is to consider the internal attribution – the student is late "because they are disrespectful," without the knowledge that there was an unanticipated traffic backup on their route. The cashier was rude "because they are a mean person," without the knowledge that this is the last hour of a double shift and a newborn kept him awake the night before.

The self-serving attribution bias is a related concept whereby success is generally attributed to internal qualities (business savvy or athleticism), and failure is attributed to external sources (an incompetent partner or equipment failure; Allen et al., 2020). However, someone experiencing impostor syndrome might do the opposite – attribute success to an external/situational source, such as "it was luck," rather than our own disposition, such as "I was smart enough to pass this test after studying." When we do this, it is harder to discuss our accomplishments because we do not necessarily believe we deserve recognition. An obvious goal when attempting to overcome impostor syndrome is to reframe our thinking so that we attribute our successes and accomplishments to ourselves as individuals, rather than outside sources. We now consider some potential ways to make us more comfortable with selling our accomplishments.

"I'll Have Another" – The Impact of Accumulating Accomplishments

We encourage you to begin accumulating accomplishments, and keeping track of them, as soon as possible (see Chapter 13 for more on standing out). Many of you already have been doing this. For others, you can begin tracking them now and add past accomplishments into the mix retroactively. Consider a scenario where you supervised a team of 30 employees responsible for generating over $254 million in revenue during the past fiscal year, a 3.5 percent increase over the previous year. Sharing this would be stating factual information and should not be considered bragging. It might be bragging if you followed John's lead and suggested you are the best supervisor or salesperson of all time. The point is that actually accumulating a list of your accomplishments will provide you with impressive *factual* information to share. This could be the earlier $254 million sales example, that you have an article in a quality publication, or that you have won the city's tennis tournament for the past five years. These accomplishments will be very specific to you and your pursuits. Recognizing them in a way that allows you to easily and confidently discuss them is the goal. It might take practice recognizing all the things you are doing, or have done, that will show you are putting in the work. Recognizing these accomplishments might also serve to increase your self-confidence and self-efficacy.

Self-confidence is an implicit component in all the domains we have discussed in this book thus far. Self-confidence can be thought of as our perceived idea of how well we will do on a given task or in a certain situation. When considering athletic performance, self-confidence can refer to an athlete's belief of how well they will do on a specific task as opposed to a global assessment (Feltz, 2007). This is an important consideration, as accumulating a list of accomplishments should allow us to see evidence that we are actually capable of performing well – at least at the tasks related to the accomplishments. Ideally, this would increase confidence in our abilities to perform successfully within a domain, whether it be academic, athletic, professional, or something else. The legendary Albert Bandura developed a theory of self-efficacy in the 1970s that is still present today (Bandura, 1977). According to Bandura, there are four components to this theory: performance accomplishments, vicarious experiences, verbal persuasion, and physiological arousal.

Performance accomplishments are perhaps the most important of these components because they are based on our own achievements. If we do well, our self-efficacy increases; conversely, if we do not do well, our self-efficacy decreases. For example, let us consider Debbie. She has taken the time to cultivate all the leads she was provided when starting her new sales job, and she has closed three sales. Debbie's self-efficacy, at least for sales, will increase. However, if Mark spends weeks contacting his leads, specifically high-potential ones, and he has no sales to report, his self-efficacy will decrease. Who is more likely to sell their accomplishments, when appropriate, in this scenario? Debbie, because she did well with sales and her self-efficacy was increased. She can share her success at following up on leads and closing the sales when she is trying to secure a promotion or is seeking employment with a different company. Unfortunately, Mark will need to rely on other accomplishments or extend the window of his body of work to market himself as successful.

The second and third components of Bandura's model of self-efficacy, vicarious experiences and persuasion, are not as helpful as accomplishments when it comes to self-efficacy; particularly in the context of this chapter. The idea behind vicarious experiences is that we would attempt to model ourselves after others. In other words, we might determine we are doing something correctly by modeling someone who is more experienced. When we start a new job, we usually do not have all the skills necessary to complete the job daily, so we must watch what others are doing and continuously seek feedback to ensure we are doing things the right way. However, the application of this depends on numerous factors that are too lengthy to cover here. For example, it is unlikely that someone with impostor syndrome would make an accurate assessment or that we would know how to select the right person for comparison. The third component of Bandura's model, persuasion, in this context, would be telling ourselves, or others telling us, that we are doing well. As you probably have gleaned, there could be the issue of someone not believing either source. Thus, these two particular components might come into play once issues such as not recognizing our accomplishments or impostor syndrome have been addressed.

Despite securing a list of accomplishments, we often can feel uncomfortable simply stating our accomplishments to others. Our levels of physiological arousal when we are put into situations of needing to sell ourselves can reveal to us our own level of comfort with doing so. We have all been there – whether it is before a big exam, a job interview, or getting on the pitching mound, our physiological arousal increases. Some of you will already be comfortable sharing your accomplishments. Congratulations! This could feasibly stem from possessing a high level of self-efficacy and self-confidence, leading you to feeling comfortable in your own skin.

If we can find ways to increase self-confidence, we likely will feel more comfortable discussing our accomplishments. This is subtle but important, as we have earned that right! In this vein, we have mentioned recognizing accomplishments as a step toward doing this. Another way to become more comfortable sharing accomplishments is to *practice* (see the *Give Me Three!* Exercise; Expert Performance International Collective [EPIC], 2023). We interviewed Talon Beeson, a successful actor and director, and he had wonderful insight into the concept of bragging versus selling your accomplishments:

> I think there's a difference between bragging and stating a fact like, 'I booked this job.' That is a fact. 'I booked this job, and therefore I'm better than you are' is bragging. And so, I think, as long as we can recognize the line between those two things. What we're doing, it's hard to pat ourselves on the back. It goes back to that politeness idea. Oh, I don't want to stand forward. I get that. I don't like being the center of attention. I would much rather do my job and then be done. I'm not one of those actors that enjoys going out and seeing people after the show so they can pat me on the back. It's actually my least favorite thing in the world… I'm there to do my job, and my job is the thing that I enjoy. So, it's not about the accolades, and it's not about making yourself bigger. I think it's just about doing what you do. And then, taking pride in your work.

He adds, "Don't hide your light, take up space. Put your light in the world."

This is a very important point for several reasons. We should not dim our light or downplay our accomplishments because we feel as though we are bragging. We encourage you to practice sharing your accomplishments. The more we are able to share our accomplishments, the greater the likelihood of reaching our goal. This was the case with my experience described at the beginning of this chapter. I pushed myself to become comfortable talking about my accomplishments, and it resulted in gaining significant traction in my job search. No offers turned to multiple job offers. We recently have seen this general discomfort with selling accomplishments in students in our career development course. During one of our interviews for this book, I shared the rationale for asking the interviewees for their advice on selling your accomplishments:

> So, the background for the question is a lot of my students are fairly young, sometimes sophomores in college. And they've accomplished great things, and I've seen them do great things. But when you ask them to start articulating what they've done, they almost always either don't say anything or anything good. I guess they could be doing things they don't recognize, or they don't want to say it. Once you realize that they do know that they're doing those things, then you start talking to them, and they say, 'Well, I didn't want to come across, as you know, bragging.' Or, they've been taught by society, and sometimes their parents, don't oversell yourself, or don't try to stand out. And so, one of the things we wanted to do is have some gems of wisdom that we could give to them from people that have done well. [You've] already kind of pointed out what I actually tell them in class. If you do a lot, accomplish a lot of things, you're not bragging. You're just telling people. You're sharing the information about what you accomplish."

Holly Johnson, cofounder of Hobnail Trekking Company, reiterated this point of selling our accomplishments as an uncomfortable but necessary part of the process:

> One is you have to do that when you're looking for work. You just have to. It's uncomfortable, and you do it anyway. But, I think a lot of it is in the way that you tell stories, so you know, I don't think that anything that Mark said [in this interview] sounded like bragging, but he was talking about things that he's accomplished

And so, I think it's about how you say it more than what you say. You are the question [to the evaluator/observer] in the context of somebody trying to get a job, or start a business or something, or just in general.

To reiterate Holly's point, if we are tracking our accomplishments but feel uncomfortable discussing them, we can pay attention to how we phrase our points. The idea all along has been to emphasize your accomplishments as the primary focus. For example, instead of saying something to the effect of, "I am the best candidate for this position," we could share the accomplishments that would make us the best candidate. This would be something along the line of, "In my role at ABC Inc., I managed a team of five, and under my leadership, we increased project completion by at least 5 percent year over year for three years in a row. As a result, we were recognized as the company's top team." This also could be a statement about a specific amount of sales, a description of the research projects in which you were involved, or a running time – each demonstrating a concrete accomplishment. These examples are very brief; they would most likely be presented as part of an overall narrative, mentioned by Holly, that you will use to share your body of work. If we can control the narrative on how we present our accomplishments, we may feel more inclined to discuss them. The bottom line is, we need to feel comfortable in selling ourselves because it helps make us more competitive for whatever it is we are seeking.

Chapter Summary

In this chapter, we acknowledged that talking about our accomplishments can make us feel uncomfortable because we feel we are bragging. Society suggests that we not be self-centered, and many of us want to avoid coming across as the person who seems to be full of themselves. However, we proposed that it is imperative that we are able to share what we have accomplished as we are best positioned to do so. Besides, our competition will be selling their own accomplishments, and it will work in their favor. Finally, we proposed some strategies to help us become comfortable selling our accomplishments.

Give Me Three!

Chapter 15: *Not Selling Your Accomplishments: It's Not Bragging*

This two-part exercise is intended to help you become comfortable with sharing your accomplishments. In the **first part** of the exercise, you will be asked to write down three (or more) examples for each of the categories listed below. The **second part** will require you to identify three (or more) individuals with whom to share your accomplishments. We strongly encourage you to follow through with sharing these as it will help you grow accustomed to sharing accomplishments.

1. Provide three (or more) examples for the following three questions (do not forget the blueberries!). Remember that these should be specific and reflect tangible outcomes.

My accomplishments include:

I am good at:

Some reasons to hire or mentor me include:

2. Identify three individuals who you are going to share your accomplishments with.

References

Allen, M.S., Robson, D.A., Martin, L.J., & Laborde, S. (2020). Systematic review and meta-analysis of self-serving attribution biases in the competitive context of organized sport. *Personality and Social Psychology Bulletin*, *46*(7), 1027–1043. https://doi.org/10.1177/0146167219893995.

Bandura, A. (1977). Self-efficacy: Toward a unifying theory of behavioral change. *Psychological Review*, *84*(2), 191–215. https://doi.org/10.1037/0033-295X.84.2.191.

Baumeister, R.F., Smart, L., & Boden, J.M. (1996). Relation of threatened egotism to violence and aggression: The dark side of high self-esteem. *Psychological review*, *103*(1), 5–33. https://doi.org/10.1037/0033-295X.103.1.5.

Expert Performance International Collective (EPIC) (2023). *Give Me Three!* [Exercise]. Nashville; New York City.

Feltz, D.L. (2007). Self-confidence and sports performance. In D. Smith & M. Bar-Eli (Eds.), *Essential Readings in Sport and Exercise Psychology* (pp. 278–294). Human Kinetics.

Langdridge, D., & Butt, T. (2004). The fundamental attribution error: A phenomenological critique. *British Journal of Social Psychology*, *43*(3), 357–369. https://doi.org/10.1348/0144666042037962.

Marin, M.M., Schober, R., Gingras, B., & Leder, H. (2017). Misattribution of musical arousal increases sexual attraction towards opposite-sex faces in females. *PLoS One*, *12*(9), e0183531. https://doi.org/10.1371/journal.pone.0183531.

Rudman, L.A. (1998). Self-promotion as a risk factor for women: The costs and benefits of counterstereotypical impression management. Journal of Personality and Social Psychology, *74*(3), 629–645. https://psycnet.apa.org/doi/10.1037/0022-3514.74.3.629.

Schachter, S., & Singer, J. (1962). Cognitive, social, and physiological determinants of emotional state. *Psychological Review*, *69*(5), 379–399. https://psycnet.apa.org/doi/10.1037/h0046234.

Sezer, O., Gino, F., & Norton, M.I. (2018). Humblebragging: A distinct—and ineffective—self-presentation strategy. *Journal of Personality and Social Psychology*, 114(1), 52–74. https://doi.org/10.1037/pspi0000108.

Smith, J.L., & Huntoon, M. (2014). Women's bragging rights: Overcoming modesty norms to facilitate women's self-promotion. *Psychology of Women Quarterly*, *38*(4), 447–459. https://doi.org/10.1177/0361684313515840.

Advice for the Aspirational

16

We have reached the final chapter. This chapter was conceptualized later than the others. It was not until we were well into our interviews with high performers that we realized our question, "What advice would you give someone coming up through the ranks?", would produce enough content to merit a chapter. Sometimes their responses overlapped with the content covered elsewhere in the book. Sometimes their responses were related to situations or topics we had not been discussing. We even failed to ask the question on a couple of occasions. Nevertheless, we recognized the tremendous value in the advice being shared with us. This wisdom was coming from high performers with great success within their domains – bestselling authors, actors, musicians touring the world, feature film and video game animators, professional athletes, and world-renowned scholars.

This list might seem to be a class of performers who have accomplished a degree of success that seems out of reach. However, they should not be viewed this way. We discussed how much of a focus to place on high performers at their level of success because of this potential perception. The decision was to continue to highlight them. This appears to be the correct decision as we learned how much ground that most of our guests had to cover, and are still covering, to get where they are. Many of them started with modest means and worked their way up the hierarchy. These were exactly the types of stories we wanted to uncover – the idea that any of us could begin the journey with a reasonable chance of becoming successful. To be clear,

DOI: 10.4324/9781003377542-16

we are not pitching the idea that "anyone can be anything." There is a very real chance that many of us will not reach the pinnacle of our domain. The person with a great performance coming in fourth while vying for three slots will still be left out. Likewise, if 400 applicants apply for five openings at a particular graduate program, 395 applicants will need to make other plans. The circumstances you face will vary. However, it is probably safe to say that very few, if any, of you will have an easy path to reach your goals.

The strategies suggested throughout the book can provide you with tools to help you stick with your pursuits and hopefully find a way to achieve your goals. We identified some consistent themes when we reviewed the advice provided by our high performer guests: (a) be aware that it is a long road to success, (b) know what you want and what you are getting into, (c) you will need to spend time learning and putting in the work, (d) use small, measurable goals, (e) help others along the way / network, and (f) take risks / explore the small opportunities. We now present each of these in turn.

High Performer Advice 1: The Long Road to Success

We proposed in Chapter 1 that, based on what we know from decades of studying high-level performers, "you typically must work hard at the right things for some time in order to get really good at something." This first piece of advice is highlighting the "for some time" part of the quote. Recall that Chapter 1 was about how the view that high performers tend to spend time engaging in activities designed to improve performance was a relatively recent proposal. It ran counter to the view that our performance was limited by innate performance ceilings that we would never be able to exceed. The advice of our high performers mirrored the need to work at something over a period of time to find success.

Mark Williams, a world-renowned expertise researcher characterizes the pursuit as a "long, long road." Justin Causey, artist and artist manager, echoes this sentiment, "It is not overnight." He adds that it might take up to a decade before your efforts will even be noticed. And he says to think again if you expect to see quick results, "You're not going to see results of it as soon as you start." Because it almost always takes time for your efforts to pay off, human performance researcher Peter

Fadde suggests that any aspirational performer begin their journey as early as possible. He adds, "You want to work on it before you need it." By starting early and putting in the time, Fadde argues that the effects of the *training will show up when you need it*, specifically as the level of competition begins to rise. Thus, becoming a high-level performer not only takes time, it can be a grueling process.

However, as observers we often only see the end result – the high performer's payoff of performing well. Katie Cole, touring member of *The Smashing Pumpkins* and singer-songwriter, added that the hard work is the part that most people do not share and many do not want to see. Part of this process is surrounding yourself with people who are willing to work with you while you are on this long road. She adds that, "You also want people that are going to push you to get the most out of yourself." Because the road to becoming a high-level performer is so grueling, David Eccles, human performance researcher, proposes incorporating mental rest and recovery efforts into your plans if you want your efforts to be sustainable.

High Performer Advice 2: Know What You Want and What You Are Getting Into

Another theme from the high performers we spoke with was that you should have a realistic idea of what you are getting into. By all accounts, it is a long and grueling process to get to where we want to be. We shared how Katie Cole feels that this part is often not shared by the person going through it. She went on to discuss how curated what we end up seeing on social media can be. For example, completing a world tour can be grueling, but only a select version of the best and most fun parts will be seen on social media. This can lead to comments from fans or even other musicians that they would "love to be on tour." Katie shared her thoughts on this perception:

> [They tell me] 'I wish I was doing that,' not realizing that I'm performing, and my toe's fractured. Or I'm performing, and I'm horribly sick. I literally have a lozenge in my mouth while I'm singing because I'm trying not to cough into the microphone. Whatever it is. People see all this stuff on social media and go

'that's supposed to be life' or a representation of life, and it's not. It's a very small, crafted version of a part of the life.

To be clear, Katie is very appreciative of the opportunity to be on tour and live the life she has been able to live. The point was to highlight that even the best opportunities can come with a down side. This could be the daily grind of training, being away from home and loved ones, not having enough time to do much else, financial investments, and social isolation. This is nowhere close to an exhaustive list. Because of these realities, our high performers shared the importance of both knowing what you want out of your efforts and what you are getting into. Professional drifter Hooman Rahimi echoed the advice of knowing why you are pursuing a particular path. Hooman's advice was to:

> ...make sure you're in it for the reasons that you want to be in it. For some drivers, I think they go into it because they want fame or something like that, and then it doesn't work out for them. I think, if you truly enjoy the sport, and you know what you're getting into, then all the other things will be worth it.

Fellow professional drifter Taylor Hull emphasized both of the points, "you have to really love it, like really love it. And, you have to be willing to sacrifice more than you think you will." He later added:

> It takes *as much as you will give it.* The more you can invest in it, the more it's going to give you back out. So, your level of success is largely dependent on your level of sacrifice that you're willing to give up. So, just be honest with yourself of what you truly want, and what you're willing to give up to get there because there's nothing wrong with drifting for fun.

Taylor was not alone in sharing the importance of knowing what you are willing to give and what you hope to achieve on the front end. Justin Causey said this about the need to love whatever it is you pursue, "don't do it if you don't have the genuine love for it. Don't do it. Because if not, you won't have any fun in it. I have fun in it, because I generally love music." Justin goes on to mention the grind needed to be successful and that someone not loving it should "do something else because it'll drive you crazy."

Comedian Henry Cho suggested that the key is to identify what we really want and then plan from there. Hobnail Trekking co-founder Mark Johnson advised that we identify what we excel at doing and then make our plans around that. This is similar to identifying what we want and likely will be one of the underlying factors in deciding what we ultimately pursue. Musician Kandle Osborne suggests that we trust our instincts and listen to our gut feelings, "if you have a bad feeling about something, you're probably right. And it will only get worse."

The general message here is that reaching their level of success requires a great deal of hard work and sacrifice. Anyone aspiring to this level of performance should be aware of what they are getting into. This decision should be made based on more than the parts that look fun as a fan/observer. Anyone can withstand the fun parts; the question will be whether you have what it takes to make it through the difficult parts of the journey. Hooman Rahimi suggested that we ask if we could handle things not working out as planned. He said:

> My best recommendation is, don't just think about the drift aspect of it. Think about your whole life. I've seen drivers that are in their twenties spend hundreds of thousands of dollars over the years. I think of them, and I see that they live with their parents. They don't have a house, they don't have anything to their name, and it's like in 10 years' time. Is that the choice that you want to make? Because that's fine if that's your choice. If you want to sacrifice that for this dream, then accept it but also accept what happens if you don't achieve your dream. Are you willing to take that risk? And, that's probably the hardest thing for people to swallow their pride in that situation.

Hooman highlights a somewhat extreme example because most pursuits would not require that level of financial investment. Having said that, ask yourself if you can handle a situation where your plans do not work out. We hope that you never have that experience, but we agree that you should be aware of the potential investment and sacrifices that will be required during the pursuit of your goals.

High Performer Advice 3: Spend Time Learning and Putting in the Work

We saw in the first section of high performer advice that we should be prepared for a long road leading to success. Another consistent theme that emerged was the "working hard at the right things" part of our statement from Chapter 1: "you typically must work hard at the right things for some time in order to get really good at something." Much like how the difficulties and sacrifices that high performers must make can be hidden from view, so can the amount of time that high performers have spent learning and putting in the work. Actor and director Talon Beeson shared this advice:

> I would say, learn how to do the thing. Don't be that person that's just like 'that's easy; anyone can do it.' It's not easy. We spend a long time learning how to do it, and we're never done. We're always learning how to do it right. So, learn how to do it.

He underscored how common it is for the work he has put in to not be recognized with a personal experience of being approached at a party by someone wanting him to get them set up in the entertainment industry with voiceover gigs. Talon responded by asking them to get *him* set up in *their* specialty area, which required significant preparation and even specialized degrees. The person realized their request was offensive and moved on. Talon added, "Just because you love it doesn't necessarily mean that you know how to do it. If you really love it, you'll spend the time to learn about it. And, then you can do it."

So, what was the advice given on how to put the right amount of effort into the work? It reflected the suggestions provided throughout the book. The anonymous acclaimed musician suggested working on yourself daily. Major League Baseball pitcher Alec Mills advised finding a routine and sticking with it. Alec added the importance of setting measurable goals: "If you can have those little goals that okay, I hit that goal. So, that's something. That's mentally a hurdle that you can get over and say, 'okay, I got there.'" The importance of learning from the mistakes you make during these efforts is something noted by both Alec and Major General Walt Lord. Katie Cole adds that, "You also want people that are going to push you to get the most out of yourself." She shared an example of a producer pushing her, "I'll go back, and I'll rewrite it. And whatever it is. You know, if I can come up with something that's 5 percent better, it's still 5 percent better."

Thomas Estrada recommended being open to letting this process of daily improvement happen by being "pleasant, friendly, and humble." In other words, being open to feedback and not being reactive. Thomas said this:

> You're learning, you're still growing, no matter how far you go. Because you get to that point where you *just think* that you've got it down. And unfortunately, a lot of students come out of school with that already. And, it's like you haven't even worked in the industry yet, and you've got this attitude like I figured it all out. I got it all down. You're just going to fail immediately. You have to be able to put your ego aside to say, 'I don't know everything I need to learn.'

He shared a particular example of his time working on a feature film at *DreamWorks* studios:

> "You could do the perfect piece of animation. Technically it has everything that it needs to have. If it's not what the director is envisioning, or whoever's in charge, whether it's your supervisor or above them, the director or the head of the studio. I've worked with *DreamWorks* where Jeffrey Katzenberg, the head of the studio, is sitting in 'dailies' watching animation that we're doing. If your perfect piece of animation just happens not to be what he had in mind, it's wrong. It's no good. You have to do it again."

High Performer Advice 4: Use Small, Measurable Goals

We dedicated an entire chapter to goal-setting (Chapter 9) and refer to goals in several other chapters throughout the book. Thus, it is not surprising that several of the high performers shared advice related to goals. Mark Williams gave this advice on goals:

> I think the concept is the same of trying to identify, 'Okay, what do I need to do to improve in this situation or to do better?' And

then setting yourselves goals and targets, and then working on how you can achieve that goal and target.

Human performance scholar Joe Baker proposed that goals will help keep you on track during the unpredictable stretches of your journey. He stated:

> My advice for performers is to focus on the quality of the journey. And, it's almost that basic goal-setting approach that we use with sports. It's so simple but so powerful. Focus on what you can control today. And improve today. And maximize today. And then link those days of consecutively doing that into some short-term, moderate-term, and long-term goals. Sometimes things are going to get out of your control, but that doesn't mean you can't have more of those consecutive days in a row, that's going to lead you more likely into that path that you want to go.

Attorney Danelle Whiteside's advice notes the illusion of having control over the outcomes:

> There is no such thing as control. You can't control everything, and you have to really focus on what's in your power to control. And realistically speaking, although you want to control everything, there is very little that you have the power to control. You can control yourself and what you do every single day, but when it comes to others, and when it comes to your outcome, there's a lot that you cannot control.

Alec Mill's earlier quotation on setting measurable goals is also applicable here: "If you can have those little goals that... okay, I hit that goal. So, that's something. That's mentally a hurdle that you can get over and say, 'Okay, I got there.'" He added that these goals are important because success can be difficult to measure. Having these goals in place allows us to determine if we are meeting them and if tweaks are needed in our plan. Alec referred to his strategy of "stacking goals" in a previous chapter. He does this by setting incremental and measurable goals that are intended to lead him to reaching a larger goal once the sequence has been completed. Everyone mentioning goals as part of their advice has some type of professional association with sport as either a scholar or athlete. However, this tactic can be adopted by performers in most, if not all, domain areas.

High Performer Advice 5: Help Others Along the Way/ Network

Another theme that we identified was the advice to help out others along the way and that networking will be required. We have discussed gatekeeping as a means of keeping the pool smaller for some domains. Hip-hop artist Brian Brown believes that we should help others coming up through the ranks and argues against gatekeeping. He said:

> I've always hated the slogan, 'The game is to be sold, not to be told.' Because it's like, 'Why are we withholding knowledge and information, and putting the price on it?' That's not fair. That's not cool. Some people might not be able to afford whatever you feel like you're giving... It's just information. Especially information to save somebody from something, put them in a position to grow, or go down the same route that you want to take. I'm always going to tell somebody to give it back.

Major General Walter Lord echoed this approach in his advice to lead compassionately and bring others along as much as you possibly can. Rondal Richardson, philanthropist and former music-industry manager, reminds us that, for competitive fields, there often are limited opportunities available. He shared, "I think you have to remember when these great things happen to you that maybe they also didn't happen to others. Your acceptance into this [elite] group might mean someone else's rejection."

Katie Cole shared the importance of networking and knowing your own boundaries. Her advice was:

> Sometimes you do have to do little bit of this and a little bit of that to open a door. I don't mean a little bit of showing leg; I don't mean that sort of stuff. I don't mean anything that's going to be derogatory to you as a human being, or harmful to you as a human being. Sometimes there are career choices. You've got to do this interview, or you've got to meet with this person. You've

got to go out. Have drinks with this person or this festival is in town. You're going to go schmooze, or whatever it is. That comes with entertainment, because everybody wants to be special and be spoken to, and feel special. All that stuff. But you have to be the barometer of what's okay for you, and what's not. Because everyone will push your boundaries as far as they can, and you have to be the one to go, 'That's too far.' Because if you're not the one that's paying attention, before you know it, you will be here or there feeling uncomfortable with a career you're not happy with, or things that you can't undo.

Andrew Lang, Leatherwood Distillery founder, also commented on the importance of networking. He stated, "You've got to surround yourself with people that are going to help you when [you] do trip, because it's going to happen." Randall Foster echoed this need to build these relationships. Part of his advice was "always take the meeting and always build the bridge. Build the connection." Musician Kevin Rapillo suggested that for some fields, we might need to seek people with whom we want to connect. Kevin shared this advice:

So, you have to go find your people. Just go. Whatever that is. You really have to go find it. You're going to sit in your hometown and wait? You're not finding your people [there], and that was hard for me, too. Because I was in a band in high school with my great friends. And, I thought we could just go do it with these guys. Even my dad was like, 'Yeah, they're not going with you.' You know what I mean? Like that was a nice, naive thing to think, but even he knows. You have got to go do it. You can't stay in your hometown and think you're good. Do it. You've got to go find your people.

High Performer Advice 6: Take Risks/the Small Opportunities

Musician Kevin Rapillo's advice of moving out of your hometown to find your people was accompanied by his advice to not play it safe. In other words, be willing to take risks. We also have discussed how small opportunities can lead to larger opportunities throughout this book. These two pieces of advice were a reoccurring theme amongst our high performers. Rondal Richardson compared taking such risks to skydiving. He stated, "There's a feeling that you get when you're right up on the edge. You have to pull yourself out. They don't push you; you have to pull yourself." In other words, it is up to us to take the leap. Bestselling author Todd Rose gave advice on overcoming our fear of taking risks. Todd said:

> I think one of the biggest lessons is that the fear of something is almost always worse than the reality – way worse; it's paralyzing. The fear of being criticized paralyzes you so much worse than the sting of actual criticism. And so, I think that so many of us, myself included for parts of my life, end up restricting the kind of lives we live because we're afraid. We wouldn't say it that way, but it's true. There's something that's just so freeing when you get clear about the kind of life you want to live. You don't compromise on that.

Co-founder of Hobnail Trekking Company Mark Johnson gave this advice:

> It sort of circles back to what I said earlier about following paths until the end. Not having regrets. Taking chances and opportunities that are placed before you. Because either it's something for you, or it's going to teach you something about yourself. Maybe you're going to learn that's something I never want to do. But it's good to learn that, too.

Randall Foster shared similar advice about how seemingly small opportunities paid off in a big way. Randall's advice is:

> Take the damn meeting. Give everybody one meeting. If you give them one meeting, and they come, and they show you their tail feathers, don't ever be with them again. It's fine. You're out 30 minutes and a coffee. But, some of the greatest opportunities I've had come my way, from a deal-making standpoint, from career growth standpoint, from relationships, from speaking at events on panels, have come from an innocuous coffee that I didn't think was going to amount to anything that turned into something great. I think we are really the sum of our relationships.

Valor Performance vice president and certified mental performance coach Lauren Tashman adds that we sometimes do not know the magnitude of the opportunities that are available until we begin gaining experience.

Chapter Summary

In this chapter, we turned to our performers and asked them to share their advice for our readers. The goal was to give us all the best chance of finding success in each of our respected domains. The advice provided was truly outstanding. We identified some consistent themes when we reviewed the advice: (a) be aware that it is a long road to success, (b) know what you want and what you are getting into, (c) you will need to spend time learning and putting in the work, (d) use small, measurable goals, (e) help others along the way/network, and (f) take risks/explore the small opportunities.

We hope that you found this book to be helpful in your own pursuits. We believe that you are capable of reaching levels of performance that exceed what you think is possible.

Index

10-year rule 4–5, 12
10,000 hours rule 4–5, 12

"above average effect" 157–158,
  162, 164, 211; *see also* Dunning-
  Kruger effect
above-average performers 74–75,
  156
academic success: "above average
  effect" 157; accepting and
  integrating criticism 212–213;
  competing goals 82–83;
  impostor syndrome 39–40,
  46–47; rejections 112, 113, 118;
  satisficing 19–20
accommodative tendency 84
accomplishments: the
  impact of accumulating
  accomplishments 237–241;
  impostor syndrome 235–236;
  pointing out to others
  229–231; tiered system of
  196–197; *see also* selling
  yourself
Ackerman, Josh 113, 118, 120
aggression, and self-esteem 97–98
Alexander, James 35–38
ambition: advice for the
  aspirational 246–257;
  distinction from achievement

motivation 98–99; from early
  childhood 144, 149; knowing
  what you want 248–251;
  negativity around 231–232;
  stigma and misunderstandings
  96–99; "that is impossible" 53
Angelou, Maya 40
arousal, physiological 133–134,
  239
artificial ceilings 52–54; the
  advantages of not sharing
  training techniques 56–58;
  default societal beliefs 55–56;
  failing to win 62–63; impact
  of societal views on mindset
  58–60; limitations 96; not being
  afraid to try 63–66; not seeing
  possibilities 60–62; standing out
  198, 199; *see also* limiting your
  scope
aspirations: advice for the
  aspirational 246–257;
  from early childhood 144,
  149; knowing what you
  want 248–251; negativity
  around 231–232; stigma and
  misunderstandings 96–99;
  "that is impossible" 53
assimilative tendency 84
Atkins, Rodney 104

attribution bias 186–187, 236
averages 156–159; *see also*
    statistics

Baker, Joe 87, 147, 253
Bandura, Albert 237–238
Bates, Brian 137
Bay, Jason 99
Beeson, Talon 40–41, 52, 66, 251
bias: attribution 186–187, 236;
    impostor syndrome 44; racial
    44; rejections 116
blaming ourselves 187–188
blind spots 155–156, 163, 211;
    see also sugarcoating
blueberry yogurt example 194–195,
    201, 202
Bolt, Usain 2
bragging 229, 237, 239–240;
    see also selling yourself
brain activity 6
Brandstätter, Jochen 85
Brown, Brian 87–88, 254
burnout 177–178

Causey, Justin 52, 66, 174,
    247–248, 249–250
ceilings *see* artificial ceilings
chess training 11–12, 135–136
childhood aspirations 144, 149
Cho, Henry 22, 40, 105, 188, 250
Clance, Pauline Rose 34
coaching theory 213
Cole, Katie 72, 101–102, 203,
    248–249, 254–255
collective shaming 102–103
commitment 22–23
comparing yourself to others
    100–102
competence: "fake it 'til you
    make it?" 85–88; impostor
    syndrome 37–38; *see also*
    performance improvement
competitive advantage 56, 194–195
confirmation bias 55
constructive feedback 217–220
counterfactual thinking 99–103
creative writing 1–3

creativity 160
critical self-concept 42; *see also*
    impostor syndrome
criticism *see* feedback
Curran, Thomas 128
curriculum vitae (CV) 229,
    232–233
Curry, Stephen 2, 56, 163

Davison, Alan 11
deadlines: goal setting 81; and
    mental rest 173, 175
"deliberate practice" 4
derailing 189–190; *see also* giving
    up
direction of comparison 100–102
dirt therapy 173
Downey, Robert Jr. 188–189
drumming example 26
Duckworth, Angela 76–77
Dunning, David 158; *see also*
    Dunning-Kruger effect
Dunning-Kruger effect 62,
    157–158, 211, 230
Dweck, Carol 3, 9, 59–60

Eccles, David 168, 170–172, 173,
    174, 248
Ericsson, K. Anders 4, 73–74, 169
erroneous feedback 217
Estrada, Thomas 33, 65–66, 86,
    127, 155, 252
ethnic minority populations 44
Eva, Kevin 62, 161, 213
excellencism 130–131
Expert Performance Based
    Training (ExPerT) 12, 57
expertise: 10,000 hours rule 4, 12;
    value of expert trainers 11–12,
    57
expertise-based training (XBT)
    12, 57

facing rejection *see* rejection
Fadde, Peter 57
failure: failing to win 134–136;
    growth mindset 59–62;
    learning from 132; meaning of

62–63; not being afraid to try 63–65; *see also* giving up

"fake it 'til you make it?" 85–88

fatigue 169–170; *see also* rest as a priority

feedback: accepting and integrating criticism 212–213; being mindful of misguided/ erroneous feedback 217; facing rejection 119–120; honesty in 155, 162–163; making mistakes 187–188; overestimating performance 157–158; receiving praise 34, 37–38; receptiveness to 205–206; seeking out criticism 217–220; seeking out feedback 210–213; seeking out mentorship 220–224; self-awareness 160–162, 214; sources of 214–216; underestimating performance 159–160

Feenstra, Sanne 42, 44

fitness goals example 8–9

fixed mindset 9, 59, 63, 73

forgiving yourself: negative experiences 182–184; self-forgiveness 185–188

Foster, Randall 22, 33, 200, 219, 256–257

Galton, Francis 1–2, 9, 55–56

"gatekeepers" 57–58, 115–116

Gaudreau, Patrick 130–131

gender: impostor syndrome 34, 44; modesty 233; selling yourself 233–234

giving up 72–75; "fake it 'til you make it?" 85–88; goal accommodations 88–90; goal conflicts 83–85; goals - impact of competing goals 82–83; goals - impact of goal setting 80–82; impact of default societal beliefs 77–78; impact of lack of awareness of techniques 79–80; impact of lack of resources 78–79; setbacks and grit 75–77

Gladwell, Malcolm 4–5

goalkeeper scenario 216

goals/goal setting: competing goals 82–83; conflicts and changing goals 83–85; "fake it 'til you make it?" 85–88; goal accommodations 88–90; impact on not giving up 80–82; importance of 143–144; individualized nature of goals 149–150; short-term 146; small and measurable 252–254; stacking goals 146, 201, 253–254; strategies for 144; three common types 147–149; vagueness 145–146; winging it 144–146

"good enough" 19; *see also* satisficing

Goyer, Jonathan 2

Graduate Record Exam (GRE) 25–26

Grammy winners 129–130

grit 76–77, 188–190

growth mindset 9; having resources 136; parental and societal views 59–62; self-esteem 102–103; self-fulfilling prophecy cycle 199

Hawk, Tony 23, 134–135

helping others 254–255

Hill, Andrew 128

historical vs. recent views of success 12; believing that one can improve 8–9; knowing the techniques 9–12; putting in the time 3–8; starting again 1–3

Hull, Taylor 72, 127, 249–250

humblebragging 234

Hunt, Tim (Nobel prize winner) 38–39

Huntoon, Meghan 134

Imes, Suzanne 34

immersion 23–24

"impossible" achievements 53

impostor cycle 36, 43
impostor syndrome 33–35;
    common characteristics
    35–38; feeling unworthy
    38–41; identifiable signs 45–46;
    reasons for being prone to
    41–45; selling yourself 235–236;
    standing out 199–200, 203;
    working through 46–47
improvement *see* performance
    improvement
IQ test scores 156–157

Jacobi, Joe 150
Jaremka, Lisa 46–47, 117
job offers: rejection rates 113;
    selling your accomplishments
    229–230, 240
Johnson, Holly 240–241
Johnson, Mark 86–87, 89–90, 137,
    250, 256
Jordan, Michael 2, 55
Judge, Timothy A. 98–99

Kammeyer-Mueller, John D.
    98–99
King, Ronnel 136
knowing what you want 248–251;
    see also aspirations
Krüger, Arnd 213
Kruger, Justin 158; *see also*
    Dunning-Kruger effect

Lady Gaga 33–34
Lang, Andrew 136, 184, 205, 223,
    234–235, 255
language use 147
last place aversion 100–101
Latham, Gary 81
learning, taking time over
    251–252
life-satisfaction 98–99
limitations: *see also* artificial
    ceilings
limiting your scope 95–96;
    counterfactual thinking 99–103;
    self-esteem 97–99; smaller

opportunities leading to larger
    opportunities 104–105; *see also*
    goals/goal setting
Locke, Edwin 81
Loftus, Elizabeth 147
London taxi drivers 5–6
"long road" to success 247–248
long- term memory 7
'longing' for success 22, 23
Lord, Major General Walter 168,
    254

McDaniels, Darryl 133
medal winners 99–100
memory 6–8
mental barriers 53–54
mental rest 170–177
mentorship 205–206; misguided/
    erroneous feedback 217;
    seeking and finding 220–224;
    seeking out criticism 217–220
Mills, Alec 22, 41, 136, 146, 182,
    184, 201, 253–254
mindset 3; artificial ceilings 63;
    believing that one can improve
    8–9, 25–26; fixed 9, 59, 63, 73;
    impact of societal views on
    mindset 58–60; self-fulfilling
    prophecy cycle 199; standing
    out 199–200; *see also* growth
    mindset
minesweeping 10–11
misattribution of arousal 133–134
misguided feedback 217
mistakes: learning from 251–252;
    self-forgiveness 187–188;
    starting again 1–3
Mize, Logan 112, 119, 185
monotony 174
motivation: distinction from
    ambition 98–99; goal setting
    81–82; importance of mental
    rest 171, 174; impostor
    syndrome 33–34; satisficing 21

natural ability vs. training 55–56,
    74, 77–78

near-success experiences 89
negative experiences: grit 188–190; rejection rates 113; staying on-track 182–183, 184–185
nerves: impostor syndrome 36, 40–41; misattribution of arousal 133–134; selling yourself 233–234
networking 205–206, 223, 254–255
Niiya, Yu 102–103
"no" *see* rejection
Nobel prize winner example 38–39
novel writing *see* creative writing

Oates, Joyce Carol 1, 2, 130
Obsorne, Kandle 110
on-track: grit 188–190; negative experiences 182–184; perseverance 76–77, 189; self-forgiveness 185–188; staying the route 184–185
opportunities: awareness of 200–201; smaller opportunities leading to larger opportunities 104–105, 137–138, 202–203; taking risks 255–257
Orbe-Austin, Lisa 45
Osborne, Kandle 110, 118–119, 120, 250
outcome goals 147–148
overestimating performance 157–158
overpreparation 36

parental influence: growth mindset 59–62; perfectionism 128
"passion" 23–24, 76–77
pay rises 222
Payne, Brandon 155, 163
Peart, Neil 26
perfectionism 127–128; failing to win 134–136; impostor syndrome 46; never a perfect time 131–134; smaller

opportunities leading to larger opportunities 137–138; in the traditional sense 128–130; training and improving 130–131
performance accomplishments *see* accomplishments
performance goals 147, 148
performance improvement: believing that one can improve 8–9, 25–26; impact of feedback on 214–216; knowing the techniques 9–12, 27–28; lack of resources 26–27, 28–29; learning and hard work 251–252; perception of limits 63–66; perfectionism 130–131; putting in the time 3–8, 24–25; starting again 1–3; time taken to improve 73–74
performer nerves *see* nerves
perseverance 76–77, 189; *see also* on-track
physical fatigue 169–170; *see also* rest as a priority
physiological arousal 133–134, 239
practice: believing that one can improve 8–9; to improve at a skill 1–3; knowing the techniques 9–12; putting in the time 3–8
praise 34, 37–38; *see also* feedback
process goals 147, 148
procrastination 36
productivity: modesty 232–233; perfectionism 129
promotions at work 120–121, 222
psychological safety 219–220

Quayle, Stephanie 102
quitting *see* giving up

racial bias 44
Rahimi, Hooman 132, 186, 249, 250
Rapillo, Kevin 104, 176–177, 255
receptiveness, to feedback 205–206

Regehr, Glenn 161
Regula, Lauren 96, 99
rejection 110–111; as
    commonplace 111–113;
    consequences 116–117;
    physical pain of 113–114;
    possible causes 114–116;
    staying on-track 183–184; ways
    to move beyond 117–121
rejection sensitivity 121–122
resilience 76–77, 119–120
resources, lack of: as barrier to
    success 26–27; giving up 78–79;
    making good use of resources
    28–29; standing out 200–201
rest as a priority 168–171;
    considerations of mental rest
    170–177; impact of burnout
    177–178
Richardson, Rondal 105, 132, 256
risk-taking 255–257
Roll, Jelly 40
Rose, R 210
Rose, Todd 110, 256
Rubik's Cube 9–10

Sakulku, Jaruwan 35–38
Salvagioni, D. A. J. 177
satisficing: believing that one can
    improve 25–26; in different
    areas in life 19–24; vs. passion
    23–24; putting in the time
    24–25
scope see goals/goal setting;
    limiting your scope
self-assessment: awareness of
    abilities 160–162; establishing
    a baseline 214; overestimating
    performance 157–158;
    underestimating performance
    159–160
self-care 171, 175–176; see also rest
    as a priority
self-confidence: "fake it 'til
    you make it?" 85–88; selling
    yourself 239–241; theory of
    self-efficacy 237–238

self-doubt 40, 42–43, 88; see also
    impostor syndrome
self-efficacy 237–238
self-esteem: growth mindset
    102–103; limiting your scope
    97–99; negativity around
    revealing our aspirations
    231–232
self-forgiveness 185–188
selling yourself: bragging
    229, 231–232; the
    impact of accumulating
    accomplishments 237–241;
    impostor syndrome 235–236;
    modesty 232–235; pointing out
    accomplishments 229–231
sensitivity, to rejection 121–122
setbacks 75–77; see also failure;
    giving up
shaming 102–103
Simon, Herbert 4, 19–20
sincerity 234
Skaggs, Ricky 105
Smith, Clint 45
Smith, Jessi 134
society: default societal beliefs
    55–56, 77–78; impact of societal
    views on mindset 58–60;
    standing out 198
Soviet Union chess training 11–12,
    135–136
Squires, Mike 222
standard deviation 156–157, 158
standing out 115–116; competitive
    advantage 194–195; getting
    creative 203–205; importance
    of 195–197; impostor syndrome
    199–200, 203; lack of resources
    200–201; making a plan 201;
    mindset 199–200; taking
    opportunities 200–201,
    202–203; taking up training/
    mentorship 205–206;
    traditional societal views 198
Staszewski, James 11
statistics: averages and exceptions
    156–159; being rejected 112;

bias 116; high- and above-average performers 74–75, 156–157; standard deviation 156–157

staying on-track *see* on-track

stopping *see* giving up

stress: burnout 177–178; mental rest 170–177; and self-care 175–176

success criteria: ambition and self-esteem 96–99; believing that one can improve 8–9; commitment 22–23; knowing the techniques 9–12; 'longing' for 22; putting in the time 3–8; starting again 1–3

sugarcoating 155–156; averages and exceptions 156–159; awareness of abilities 160–162; honest feedback 155, 162–163; overestimating performance 157–158; underestimating performance 159–160

sunk costs fallacy 89–90

superwoman/superman 37

swimsuit example 53–54, 64–65

Tashman, Lauren 210, 221

taxi drivers 5–6

The Path Distilled podcast: audience size 101–102, 203; counterfactual thinking 101–102; goal setting 144, 150; incremental improvement 163; mentors 222; rejection 112, 119, 183; smaller opportunities leading to larger opportunities 137, 204; training techniques 130

the ten-year rule 4–5, 12

time spent learning 251–252

time taken to improve 73–74, 247–248

tiredness 169–170; *see also* rest as a priority

tough feedback 219

training: the advantages of not sharing training techniques 56–58; "deliberate practice" 4; impact of feedback on 214–216; impact of lack of awareness of techniques 79–80; knowing the techniques 9–12, 27–28; natural ability vs. training 55–56, 74, 77–78; perfectionism 130–131; taking full advantage of 205–206

Trinidad, Jose Eos 136

underestimating performance 159–160

vagueness, in goals 145–146

violence, and self-esteem 97–98

Warrell, Mardie 46

Weinberg, Robert 147

Whiteside, Danelle 253

Williams, A. Mark 19, 247

Wilson, Lainey 111, 183–184, 185

Winfrey, Oprah 96

Winslet, Kate 40

Wohl, Michael 186

work-life balance: mental rest 173; satisficing 21, 25; self-care 175–176

Young, Valerie 46

For Product Safety Concerns and Information please contact our EU
representative GPSR@taylorandfrancis.com
Taylor & Francis Verlag GmbH, Kaufingerstraße 24, 80331 München, Germany